Holy Wedlock Unholy Deadlock

simple ways to untie the knots in a husband – wife relationship

notionpress.com

Holy Wedlock Or Unholy Deadlock

simple ways to untie the knots in a husband – wife relationship

J.L.Dhar

notionpress.com

Notion Press

Old No. 38, New No. 6

McNichols Road, Chetpet

Chennai - 600 031

First Published by Notion Press 2016

ISBN 978-93-5206-929-3

Dedication

This book is dedicated to the memory of
my elder brother, Late Shri K. L. DHAR.
Atta hi Attanano Natho,
Atta Hi Attano Gatti.
One is one's own master,
and works out one's salvation with one's own efforts.
It takes one story to...
inspire a song,
create a bond,
alter a path,
heal a heart,
mend a rift,
reach a soul,
transform a relationship, reaffirm a marriage, or save a life.
One story can change the World!
The following are other published books of the author:
Essentials of Disciplinary Proceedings in Industry.
Practical Guide to Industrial Employment.
An Interview with Self—simple ways to unravel the power within.
An Understanding of Self—simple ways to harness the power within.
Comments on author's previously published books:
"I have gone through the book and I liked particularly your writing on Practice Silence."

Dr A.P.J. Abdul Kalam,

Former President of India.

"Many thanks for sending me your book. It looks most interesting and I am sure I will enjoy reading it."

Dr Karan Singh,

Member of Parliament.

"Thanks for sending me your book on Self-Help. I look forward to read it with interest."

Khuswant Singh,

Reputed Author.

"The author has made a commendable attempt to stating concisely the law relating to industrial employment. The effort made by him deserves to be appreciated and I am quite sure that this book will be well received by all concerned."

Justice G.T. Nanavati,

Former Judge, Supreme Court of India.

"I went through the book and found it very interesting."

Nandan M. Nilekani,

Former Chairman, Infosys.

"Sir John M. Templeton wishes to acknowledge your letter with the gift copy of your book, An Interview with Self—Simple Ways to Unravel the Power Within. Sir John extends his thanks and looks forward to read your book."

Marie Souder,

Secretary.

"By writing this book the author has done a commendable job of how a peaceful and creative life may be lived. The overall style of the book is simple and lucid. The book deserves to be read by all intelligent men. It is well got up and moderately priced."

D.N. Kaul,

I.G. Police (Retd.).

"Here in Bhimtal we have the solitude and right environment to take a book and enjoy reading it. I will take your book Interview with Self and read it to enrich myself."

J.N. Kaul (Padma Shri),

President,

SOS Children's Villages.

"I agree with most points in the book."

Prof K. Satchidanandan

Former Secretary, Sahitya Akademi.

"I am delighted to read your book and certainly read it word by word. It is a subject close to my heart."

Dr S. Chona,

Former Principal,

Delhi Public School.

"The book establishes that the writer is a very knowledgeable, experienced and devoted person. The book undoubtedly contains introspection and high-level thinking."

Late H. D. Shourie,

Direct, Common Cause.

"Let me first congratulate you for your new book, An Understanding of Self. I have thoroughly enjoyed reading it. An inspiring book."

Dr Rajeshwar Prasad,

President,

Indian Social Science Association.

"It is good of you to send me your new book dedicated to Swami Laxman Joo. I will read it with considerable interest."

Dr Karan Singh,

Member of Parliament.

"It was indeed very nice of you to have written to me enclosing a copy of your book. Whatever I have been able to do is only the result of team work. I look forward to read your book. May God bless you."

E. Sreedharan,

Former Managing Director,

Delhi Metro Rail Corp. Ltd.

"Many thanks for your book. I will read it with great interest and am grateful that you have sent it to me. It seems you are making a difference in the lives of many people. Congratulations."

Robin Sharma,

Author and CEO,

Sharma Leadership International.

"I have thoroughly enjoyed reading your book titled An Understanding of Self. It is insightful."

Editor,

Koshur Samachar.

"The book is insightful, intuitive and clever. The author has put into words things that you know you have experienced, however have been unable or unwilling to express. I honestly felt like applauding a few times. It is a good book and an enjoyable read."

Ingrid Hanes,

Critic, U.S.A.

"Your book. An Interview with Self became my night time reading a few weeks ago, and I enjoyed it immensely."

Connie Kellough

Publisher/President,

Namaste Publishing, U.S.A.

"This book invites you to identify, understand and control the demons within and transcend those to help yourself embrace your own inner light. Be at peace with yourself."

Hindustan Times.

"The readers are able to identify with the problems discussed in the book and the author succeeds in making one realize that one's desires are not the be all and end all of existence; human relationships have to be nurtured, and happiness is because of one's attitude and not circumstances and true freedom is the freedom to be oneself. The language is simple and the expression direct."

The Tribune.

"This book's theme is knowing oneself better first before being able to understand others. The book explains in lucid language what happens to us in different situations and how we react to them unconsciously. A book meant for persons who stand at the cross roads of life, unable to decide which road to take for a better life."

Organizer.

"This book is an outcome of learning, assimilating and probing into the deeper mysteries that make up our lives. It tries to answer fascinating questions. This book is a learning experience, both for the writer himself and for the reader."

The Eternal Solutions.

"Inviting the reader to engage with his or her own self, this book An Understanding of Self sets out to teach how one must truly know and understand oneself through practical and real life examples from which to draw inspiration."

Sunday Pioneer.

"An Interview with Self—simple ways to unravel the power within is a book to report and read."

The Hindu.

Contents

Preface

Once upon a time, many, many centuries ago, Martians and Venusians happened to meet, let me say, in the Garden of Eden. They instantly liked each other. They dated and fell in love; perhaps, it was a case of love at first sight. They married and settled on a mutually loving and satisfying relationship based on recognition and respect for their individual differences. The two together thus had a very happy and harmonious matrimonial bond.

Then they came down on this planet, called Earth, and a strange sort of amnesia set in. They conveniently forgot that they had originated from different planets—Mars and Venus. They somehow forgot that they are supposed to be different and needed to find unity in diversity. Thus, they came to find themselves at odds with each other. They started doubting and misunderstanding each other because they were speaking in different languages. They became demanding, resentful, judgmental and intolerant. And hence, their disagreements, discords and troubles started.

I have, in all humility, tried to use this metaphor in my attempt to illustrate how a *man* and a *woman* fall for each other with love in their eyes and get married. But soon enough, they conveniently tend to forget that they have come to the relationship of husband and wife as two distinct individuals from different social, cultural, educational, psychological and physical backgrounds—both having their own individual traits and temperaments. Thus in most marriages what is found is that the two spouses set on a confrontational course, which leads them on to a very rough and thorny terrain. They stumble and fall. In many cases, they even go down the cliff and are lost in the vastness and wilderness of divorce courts.

Once a source of shame and embarrassment, divorce is now being viewed by many as a new beginning rather than a dead end. Distraught couples have come to believe increasingly that when a relationship is over, it's over and there is no point clinging on to it

First, it is the proverbial *chat-mangni, pat-byaah* and then, increasingly a *pat* desperation for divorce. Such marriages are mostly conceived with just a click of the mouse. Devoid of emotional feelings, the spouses involved naturally are not inclined to give their relationship an honest try and hence don't bother to wait and go through the hurt and heartbreak of a long-distance relationship. Such crazy people, of late, are even come to throw a break-up party to celebrate the split—end of the relationship—ever keen to start a new one, soon enough.

I wonder whether you have ever cared to take a look around at your family, your extended family, your relations, your friends' circle and your neighborhood to spot a couple who are living a happy, peaceful and enjoyable marriage, in reality? Facades apart!

Just, think it over, and take a discernible look around. I am sure you would hardly find one. Why?

The fact of the matter is that, at the beginning of married life, the romantic thrills it brings are always overestimated and the uncertainties ignored altogether. The realities of marriage shock every couple at one point or another.

That exactly has put me on the path to study this complex phenomenon.

Creating a happy marriage is a mysterious process. It is, indeed, intriguing as to how two distinct individuals merge into a life partnership so that they are able to survive the inevitable crisis that will accompany them on the journey. There is no denying the fact that bonding together a man and a woman, who till now were strangers to each other, is difficult. Both have an identity of their own and marriage requires them to not only acquire the new surroundings, but also adapt according to other partner's likes and dislikes. The adjustment required post-marriage has more to do with individual compatibility than a meshing together of two ways of life.

Nobody can give to the two partners in marriage the meaning of their individual life from outside. It is within each of them. They carry it within them, like a bud that grows into a fragrant rose. But just as a rose plant needs to be cared for, manured and irrigated properly, so does a matrimonial relationship.

Each person has his or her individual personality with both positive and negative traits. The great epic *Mahabharata,* in a subtle way, is everyone's story.

If one strips this great epic bear of all characters and reads only the emotions, then, it is a universal story that plays out every day—hot temper, rage, greed, jealousy, revenge, lust and so on and so forth. But it is within the capacity of each individual person to add positive dimensions as against negative to one's personality and move on empowered. It is important to give each other room to grow and to accept one another for who he or she is. The two spouses need to respect each other's individuality. It is impossible to find two leaves identical or even two identical stones. Similarly, it is not possible to find two identical human beings. No person exists like another, nor shall they ever be. Each person is unique. God has endowed a human being with so much reverence that every individual is a unique entity…no person is a repetition. From this insight, the two spouses have to understand that in any sphere of one's life activity, one is the performer—the person who acts—and that his or her any action has to be done in a state of full awareness, like a good and versatile singer, dancer or lover.

Living in a consciously meaningful way in matrimony means each spouse has to love and respect each other's individuality with all its strong and weak points. Both should be focused to see in each other's personality not what is wrong or negative, but what is right and positive. Then only they can use their individual potential in the best possible way.

Many couples seeking to heal their acrimonious tiffs and rifts in their relationships could well find this story related to themselves and their own journey through conjugal life. It could thus help them to reinforce their matrimonial bonds. There are many things about getting married and making a marriage last that all couples should know. This book could, hopefully, provide leads to a happy married life and act as a humble guide of insight, inspiration and enlightenment. It could help put distraught couples on the road to conjugal love, peace and stability—together—by promoting a greater understanding between the two partners.

I do not directly address the question as to *why* men and women are different, and why conflict is almost in built in their relationship. This is a very complex issue to which there can be many answers, ranging from biological differences, heredity, parental influence, education and birth order to social and cultural conditioning by society, the media and historically. However, we need to understand that every process in the universe needs energy, including conflict. Most often, two people get into a conflict when their ideology, mindset, value systems, habits, behavior and belief systems differ. If all of us were same, there would be no conflict. Like electricity, there is a need for a positive and negative pole for the current to flow. Similarly, it is the differences between us that lead to sparks and conflict in a married couple. Behind every conflict lies differences—a different point of view, opinion, standpoint, belief, a different perception, emotional response or a different habit—these differences cause irritation, anger and frustration and make us want to explode with anger and rage and hate each other. We are then labeled *intolerant.* The opposite of intolerance is tolerance. One man or woman or one group or a sect, goes about charging the other as *I'm tolerating you: tolerating your nonsense.* This leads to counter charges and so on and so forth. Why not replace the word *tolerance* with *acceptance?*

Lord, grant me the strength to accept the things I cannot change, the courage to change things I can, and the wisdom to know the difference.

St Francis of Assisi.

Of late, there is a lot of ruckus in our country on intolerance and one section of people or the other add fuel to the fire that makes the citizens feel, in general, insecure. We have some known personalities returning their awards in protest against intolerance. But, in doing so ,are they helping any cause or are they creating more confusion by behaving like any illiterate, intolerant person on the street? We, as responsible citizens, need to learn tolerance in order to coexist peacefully—be it with one's wife/husband, neighbor, relative, colleague or anybody in the community. Tolerance quiets the inner critic that chatters in one's mind. By cultivating a mind of acceptance, we can automatically be tolerant, which can then generate and promote goodness as against meanness. When we cultivate such an attitude, we will become filled with God's grace. That grace is the foundation for peace and success in life—be it an individual's life or a nation's life. Acceptance looks like a passive state, but in reality, it brings something entirely new into the world. That peace, a subtle energy vibration, is consciousness. It means living life consciously.

Although the benefits of applying the insights offered in this book are obvious and fundamental, this book, however, does not claim to replace the inherent and perennial need for both partners in a matrimonial bond to understand, first of all, their individual personality traits, their weaknesses and strengths and then recognize those aspects and accept each other *as is where is!* No partner should attempt to force the other to change.

Change can only take place when the individual in question himself or herself honestly feels the need for it. I have attempted to explain how this mechanism could be worked out without any resentment to move forward in a relationship with an open, trusting mind to resolve the conflicts, which ultimately would lead to a mutually satisfying, fulfilling and loving relationship, and usher in bloom and fragrance in one's wilted garden of marriage.

It is not a story about blames or faults but about trying to perceive where one has erred and then trying to discover where one's proactive power lies, which is within each one of us—but generally lying dormant.

The story could be painful and shocking, but at the same time, encouraging and inspirational. It could make you laugh, cry or simply understand life a bit better. This book is much about *what's in the mind.* I pray this story touches the readers in a deep way so that they feel rejuvenated and thus stop living miserable lives.

Let me, however, say that I am not sitting saintly or expertly on some high *wisdom* pedestal. I am nobody to preach. Neither do I intend to do so. This book intends to try and show some of the easy (*or is it difficult*) ways and means to chip off the rough edges and smoothen the bumps in one's marriage. Though at seventy-eight and having remained married to a single woman for over fifty years now, I honestly feel, I still haven't received all the answers to the puzzle that a marriage literally is. My wife still remains an enigma to me, or so I sometimes feel. Indeed, marriage is constant work in progress. The road to this destination ever remains under construction. Hence, one has to look out for pitfalls, to be able to tread on the right track. Let it be marked that with all its problems, this institution of marriage is nowhere near extinction.

I love quotes, anecdotes, comic gags and little stories with a discernible moral. Examples and stories that fit in with what is being said or discussed, including the inspiring quotes, add life and reality to any writing or conversation. A writing that is carried on entirely on abstract philosophical level can be boring. Stories, as such, do not prove anything in the sense that statistics can prove anything. But these illustrate a possibility, apart from the liveliness and *actuality. Stories* hope to find or create significant connections between things, people or spaces. They help us to see how choices and events are tied together; why things or situations are as they are and how we would like them to be. Thus, to properly dress and add meat and flavor to the text, I have most appropriately tried to sprinkle stories, here and there, on the pages. I relate to these stories as part of my daily vitamin routine that are required to strength the inner self. Good, right quotes or simple stories are the *cream* of our learning.

I cannot decide whether writing this book was sheer pleasure or cathartic. But, I feel, the plot or canvas of this book gave me an opportunity to try and study the many facets of a husband–wife relationship, and probe the reasons why it seems, of late, that the institution of marriage is crumbling in the face of stresses and strains that a present-day married couple come to face almost immediately on getting married. What does a couple want—a happy married life or a miserable one? Obviously, nobody wants misery. So, in the final analysis, it turns out to be a lot easier to do it *right* than to do it *wrong.* That is one simple *mantra* for both spouses to meditate on so as to live a happy, harmonious married life. Much of this book, as you will come to mark, has focused on getting more out of your marriage by being proactive instead of reactive and thereby learning to recognize and understand the things you are prone to having been doing *wrong* instead of *right,* and to effect the necessary changes in your thoughts and actions so as to readjust, redirect and re-accommodate with your wonderful and amazing partner called *husband* or *wife.* There is a lovable quality to their repartee. You won't mind their love–hate relationship because you relate to them, you feel for them. The story line may well be about you and your journey through life. While you turn on the pages, you may quite possibly find yourself faced up with similar problems and, therefore, try and seek answers to your own predicaments. Thus, this could be the book that possibly can speak to most of you directly.

It would seem to be an easy thing, really—the reading of a book. You pick up a book, open it, fix your gaze on a page and begin reading. Well, maybe so, may be not! In reality, though there is a mystical bond between the writer, the book and the reader, the author may actually be trying to figure out his own life on the pages; not the reader's. As the Irish poet, W. B. Yeats once told an admirer of his book:

"If what I say resonates in you, it's merely because we are both branches on the same tree."

So is my wish with this book.

The making of this book required the talents, participation and efforts of so many people. My deep gratitude to all of them. In particular, I sincerely wish to express my gratitude to Mr Naveen Valsakumar, Mr Jana and Mr Barath Janakiraman of Notion Press and their entire Project Management Team. Needless to say, I want to say a big thank you to my wife, Krishna, for being there, besides me in my life, to support and sustain me.

Thank you, and may God bless you all.

J.L.DHAR

Email ID: jldhar@rediffmail.com
Mobile: 9873488737

Acknowledgement

I Would like to thank the entire **Notion Press** Team for this support in bringing out this book successfully.

The Prince and The Princess

Not very long ago, there lived a prince and a princess.

The prince's name was Raghav. Of course, he was no real prince for he had no such pedigree. But, the way he dressed, spoke, walked and conducted himself through his body language, he looked every bit royal. Naturally, his friends thought he, indeed, was a person who could be called a prince.

He had a face that one would normally notice even in a crowd—high cheek bones, graceful eyes that were inquisitive and talkative, an aquiline nose with a large forehead that creased heavily when in irritation and a head taller than any of the boys around. He spoke in a soft and cultured language, which his buddies cherished for its diversity and delivery.

Raghav got friendly with a girl in college, named Rosy. She was a gorgeous woman with a bagful of attitude—with deep blue eyes and a captivating smile worn on her face, always. Both liked to be in each other's company, and kept meeting regularly until Rosy's father, an Army Officer, got transferred out of Kashmir. Raghav missed her company for a long time. He, however, had a dream of finding and meeting his own princess charming some day and then living happily ever after.

And soon, he ventured out to find his beautiful princess. Her name was Ragini. She wasn't a real princess, either. But her face was fresh, regal and soulful, with a tall figure and striking personality, and she addressed everyone gracefully—exuding a glamorous vibe of her own with aplomb, and a glint in her eyes. She looked every inch like a princess. It happened later that both went on to meet often, focusing on each other alone and promising to never fall out of love. Although she appeared simple, and didn't have any hang ups or put on airs, yet sometimes she behaved and wanted to be treated like a princess. She also had the cherished dream of finding and meeting her own prince charming some day and then living happily ever after.

And, indeed, such a day arrived in the lives of both of them. Prince Raghav and Princess Ragini stumbled and came face-to-face at the reception counter of their college. As if straight from a Bollywood movie scene, two of Ragini's books fell on the floor, and Raghav hurriedly bent down to pick them. He did so and said, "I'm so sorry." "That's alright," Ragini replied. Their eyes met involuntarily. Both felt excited, a bit confused and even nervous. To him, she appeared as fresh and pure as a newly bloomed rose.

Both looked at each other furtively, and then let their eyes do the talking. A small invisible bridge was being perhaps erected instantly. Sometimes, eyes speak more eloquently than words. She smiled a small enchanting smile that in a way conveyed untold secrets of her heart, as eyes skittered away. And soon, he was dazzled by her smiling gaze that revealed a kind of unalloyed blissful solace to his pounding heart against his chest. A woman's smile is fascinating to a man at all times, as he now realized. In fact, winks and naughty carefree smiles share a special place among the sexes in the dating game. That perhaps she knew, Raghav mulled.

He continued adoring her luscious face and found himself drawn to her. But beyond the trespassing of eyes for those fleeting moments, there was no talk between them, much less any love talk. But what struck him on seeing her was something unlooked for; it was the expression of her eyes—soft, serene and truthful, and above all, her smile, which transported him to an enhanced sublime world.

Later, whenever he thought of her, he could call up a vivid picture of her to himself, and would lie in bed to conjure up the shine and sheen, complete with innocence, on her pretty face. She seemed to have lodged herself in his thoughts. He found himself dreaming—she by his side, who, half out of coquettishness, tries to evade him, and he chasing her, catching her in his arms and crumpling her on the bed; she glances at him, and he naughtily smiles; in a moment, his arms get around her, and he feels his lips on her cheeks as he murmurs, "*I love you.*"

But, it was only his soft pillow that he found himself murmuring to.

As providence would have it, they again came face-to-face at a common friend's wedding. Oh! That meeting. Shyness had disappeared from their faces.

To Ragini, all the impulses of her youth seemed to have flared up into distinct emotions on her face, the lusciousness of which he kept adoring. He thought to himself, "She's exactly the girl I've been waiting and praying for." The two seemed to connect instantly, for their appeared to be on the same page.

Love me for a second, and I will make the second last for a lifetime.

Unknown.

They talked, and talked a lot for a long time. Their love for each-other was flowering. Falling in love is such an incredible feeling—there is flutter in the lovers' hearts, twinkle in their eyes, a smile on their faces and bounces in their steps, with dreamy scenes of romance and what not…? Ooh! If only it could last for a lifetime!

Anyway, Raghav proposed and soon they got set to get married, with the consent of their families It was jubilation time, bordering euphoria.

The Marriage Solemnized!

On the day of marriage, the groom, properly attired with a colorful headgear, rode a well-bred mare of snow-white color to head the marriage procession proceeding to the bride's place, while the women, led by the most elderly among them, who wore indifferently tailored loose garments—short *pheran* embroidered all around the neck and whose otherwise sagging heavy breasts jiggled pendulously like two jellies that heaved rhythmically—up and down—as she took dancing steps, leading the group in typical Kashmiri chorus singing called *Wanwun* merrily, which is special to auspicious occasions like a marriage. This was a sort of a typical folk singing, without any accompanying musical instruments, and was believed to usher in religious sanctity and holiness to the proceedings.

At the head of the wedding procession was the fifteen-piece band players dressed in dark magenta coats with yellow cross-straps, black trousers, golden caps and blue wide belts, who were playing popular film tunes on their saxophone, clarinet and drums. Raghav's maternal uncle Amit started dancing bawdily, jerking his hips, while some of the guests reached out to keep company feverishly, doubling over the laughter at his coquettish twitching. Soon, many boys and girls together thronged around the dancers, clapping and keeping to the beat—intoxicated with the heightened eroticism of the wedding night. And then, suddenly, Amit spotted the bride's elder sister, a svelte figure, and accosted her to join in the celebrations, which she willingly did with calibrated dancing steps in great gusto. She perhaps outwitted him by her superb dancing steps, with her eyes to the floor and pulling and jerking her limbs spasmodically with matching languid grace and charm, to the amazement of everyone around who repeatedly applauded her amid their doubled up laughter.

Then gradually, almost imperceptibly, the tempo of the drum beat quickened to reach its crescendo, amid *Wanwun* and burning of wedding incense called *Isabund* (*handful of seeds that are thrown on live coals, a Persian habit with a Persian name*), to ward off evil spirits, to dispel the evil eye and to create an ambience of celebration. The smoke and special type of perfumed aroma and the sound given off when the seeds sputtered and burned on red-hot coals is a quintessential part of wedding nostalgia. The feverish air in the surrounding environs resounded with the clamor of the celebrations.

The two erudite *Gurujis* (priests), one each representing the bride's and groom's side, arrived in the *mandap* and sat on a slightly raised cushioned platform where they, after generously sprinkling rose petals all around, proceeded to lay out their paraphernalia—the *hawan-samigrihe*—on the large green banyan leaves, with the burning sticks of holy incense and *dhoop*, the colorful strings of *naada-chadi*, the pellets of camphor, the trays of cut-flowers, the garlands, the rose petals in a heap, the vermilion with sacred threads and the half-torn, dismembered, pale-colored booklets containing holy *mantras* (verses).

And there amid the playing of *Shehnaaye* and blowing of conch shells, that filled the air, the groom, attired in rich embroidered creamy *bundgalla* suit that looked elegant with a flower-bedecked saffron-colored headgear, flanked by his stunningly looking demure bride who looked all poise in a *zaree* wide-bordered crimson red sparkling *lehenga* (designer dress) resplendent with sandalwood paste, heavy gold jewelry and bold vermilion *tilak* that sprawled across her forehead, was led slowly but gracefully into the *mandap*, smiling and raving at the gaggle of photographers and video cameras, while the *Gurujis* kept reciting sacred *shlokas* (holy verses) from scriptures to usher in the divine blessings.

As the two priests now started chanting *Vedic Shlokas*, which resonated through the cool and crisp ambience in the flower-bedecked lawns, the blessed couple got to listen to the proclamation made by the ancient sages that a human has four duties in life—*Dharma, Artha, Kaama* and *Moksha*—made possible only through a passage into *Grihastha-ashram* (matrimonial life).

Vivaha (marriage, meaning responsibility) or *Shaadi* (derived from the Persian word *shaad*, meaning happiness) symbolizes more than just a consummation—it is meditation or *yog* that prepares two individuals to embrace a new life.

The presiding priest, who was scholarly and erudite, told the groom and his bride that they were set to start their divine journey of marriage together, amid joy, gaiety and celebration while, as per belief, God joined them and their families in showering divine blessings, as the couple comes to take their first step together, out of the total of seven—the *Saptpadi*. Walking those seven steps together around the sacred fire, it is believed, even strangers become friends and lovers, as the two souls merge into one, the bridegroom leading the way to signify the following:

First step: May Lord Vishnu give you food to cross over this first step;

Second step: May Lord Vishnu give you strength to cross over this second step;

Third step: May Lord Vishnu make you the increaser of wealth to cross over this step;

Fourth step: May Lord Vishnu bestow happiness upon you to make our home full of joy to cross over this fourth step;

(And now the bride is leading)

Fifth step: May Lord Vishnu give you wealth in the form of animals to cross over this fifth step with prosperity…

Sixth step: May Lord Vishnu keep you pleasant in all six seasons to cross over this sixth step;

Seventh step: May you be my friend, supporter, good guard and nourisher to cross over this seventh step.

So with both their hands placed in a firm yet gentle handshake, the groom and the bride took those vows amid Vedic chants, in the presence of the omnipresent God, and thus the twosome entered into their new future together—*Kutumbha* (family)—with the promise of togetherness till eternity.

And as the *Khaana* (dinner) was served, the guests forgot minor things like decency, good manners and etiquette and abandoned their good behaviors—even if they were in the middle of greeting the bride and groom, exchanging pleasantries with their relations and friends or were engrossed in some animated talk or discussion—to make an almost desperate dash towards the buffet dinner tables and grab a dinner plate on which they piled up almost every item of food laid out in one go, as if they had been hungry for days on end or that the food would vanish soon enough.

"*Waah*, there are nonvegetarian dishes as well, yummy, great!" some people squealed excitedly while a few women commented disapprovingly, "But there's no fish item. Strange!" while loading their plates with a second helping. "*Lekin Khaana bahut* spicy *hai*," (the food is spicy) complained another." *Tabee to tasty hai*," (that's why it is tasty) commented the next.

There was a foreigner guest from London, who wore a white fedora and had a hoop earring in his right ear. Actually, he was a friend of the bride's family who had specially flown in for the event. He found most items hot and spicy.

"Why don't you have a *Raj-kachori*?" he was offered.

"But, what is that?" he asked, in his Oxford accent.

"It is a large, crunchy *kachori* lined with soft spices and stuffed to the brim with lentils, *papdi*, sweetened curd and *chutneys*—take one, have it—and it is a meal in itself," he was explained elaborately, live.

He tasted and liked it. "I am full," he said.

"*Chaat-pakodi ya gol-guppe nahi hai kya*?" enquired a woman to the waiter.

"*Hai naa, Ji*," (Oh, yes) who showed by the gesture of his face turned the right, which meant, "There in that stall."

The guest from London catching the word *gol-guppe*, said, "Love nothing more than South hall's *gol-guppas* where my Indian friends often take me."

Said a guest, "That is wonderful. Come on, now taste that authentic Indian stuff."

Guruji sat cross-legged on his seat of folded cloth. His long sleek hair with salt and pepper streaks was oiled and brushed back to cascade over his neck in a graceful curl. His well-groomed greying beard and moustaches set off the soft curve of his sensuous lip, with large black eyes, made larger with a generous measure of *surma*.

He looked what he was, a *Guruji*, the high priest of *chaat*.

He was serving four customers at a time, moving his long bare arm from tray to tray at once—picking up with the perforated *gol-guppa* (or what is also called as *pani puri, puchka* or *batasha*) in his hand, a single pea, two grains of savory *chana*, a soupcon of spiced potato mush, dipping his hand into a huge earthen jar of *sounth* (water made sour with ingredients) and placing the complete *gol-guppa* in the *dauna* (container) held out by the customer to feel the burst of taste in his mouth. *Guruji* did all this with so much elasticity, grace and ease that his arms hardly seemed to move, and yet each crisp, dripping morsel, coming forth in turns, was ready to be received so willingly and so eagerly, while the recipient was still smacking his lips with the tip of the tongue to savor the lingering taste of the previous one.

"This tangy dish is something that no one can do without because a true blue foodie knows that it is an appetizer, a precursor to all the scrumptious food on the menu," the foreign guest was told.

"Oh, *gol-guppas*! I need to taste them every time I see them. Simply just not to be missed," said a young woman to her companion, and both had a blast consuming the dish.

For dessert, among various types of sweets and ice-creams, there was a stall offering piping hot *kulad* (earthen pint-sized container containing sugar-free boiling milk laced with freshly made syrupy *jalebis.*) The vendor, sitting cross-legged on his designated seat, would measure the right quantity of milk, as ordered for, from the iron *kadaee* (huge container), in which milk was kept boiling on the hearth. The milk would then be poured into a wide-mouthed brass container only to get laced with hot *jalebis*. Holding the container in his right hand, he would then take it right above his head level to pour the contents into another equally wide-mouthed container held in his left hand at ground level to create a sharp fall, as if a little milky stream was going down the hill to its base. And then, he would raise his left-hand container above his shoulder level and simultaneously lower his right-hand container to ground level to create another fall. This synchronization of action with skillful precision—from right to left and back to right—would continue quite a few times till the milk had got lukewarm.

It was a spectacle to be seen. And while pouring the milk, thoroughly mixed up with *jalebis*, into a *kulad*, he would blur out the age-old maxim "Nothing cures a cold, cough or sore throat better than this drink taken at bed time."

And if a guest had the time and interest to listen to him, he would regale in saying, "And let me tell you about the origin of *jalebi*—this very popular sweet made by deep frying batter in a pretzel shape and then soaked in sugar syrup for a couple of minutes—crisp on the outside, soft and chewy on the inside—that can be traced to Iran and Persia, where it is called *Zulbiya*. *Jalebi* was brought to India by Mogul emperor Jahangir."

Acerbic Mom-in-law and Acidic Daughter-in-law

Singing wedding songs and showering rose petals and dry fruits on the bride, she was welcomed into her husband's household.

Raghav's mother who had entertained, even nursed some definite expectations of her daughter-in-law (*Bahu*) for bringing in a huge dowry, felt sad and dejected when she found that *maetmur* (a piece of gold jewelry) that traditionally a mother-in-law (*Saas*) gets as the first present from her new *bahu* while she enters into her husband's household so as to symbolically gain entry into her new abode, had turned out to be a damp squib. It was much below her expectations. Additionally, the bride was neither found suitably bedecked in jewelry nor had she brought in any worthy dowry. Now the mother-in-law considered this as some sort of a loss of face amid the relatives assembled for the wedding, particularly the womenfolk, who, in any case, were in the habit of instantly taking stock of jewelry items worn by the bride on her body, and simultaneously doing the valuation.

The facial expression of Raghav's mother turned out, in a sense, to be so acute, such that any person would be capable of distinguishing the glutinous vapor of hypocrisy with which the *saas* had greeted the *bahu.* Her face was a sight of total frustration. One could read volumes of disgust from her facial expression—a face that would have seemed more appropriate at a mourning than at a marriage gathering.

Raghav watched her mother helplessly. He recollected how immensely enthusiastic she had been to see her son married. At times, when a particular proposal from a prospective family did not mature, she would suffer bouts of depression and go despairing, and at times, even went hysterical. She, perhaps in her own mind, had nursed the hope that having a *bahu,* was to expect her to pay obeisance to the implied authority of that redoubtable person called *saas.* But nothing of the sort came her way. Her hopes were belied.

A son's marriage has a deep, soulful mystique for any mother; it is the deepest urge of her starved psyche. Most commonly, she is more anxious to put it to effect than the young man himself. In fact, she is the mother-bride of the boy, and experiences an inverted spiritual orgasm.

In the fuss and flurry of things, when, like the queen bee, she presides over the preparations for the wedding, and all drones must go homing to her, she is perhaps reenacting her own nuptials with song and story, with myth and fantasy and with ritual and ceremony. She whips herself up into a state of bridal fever, till, in the end, she is literally hoarse, reduced to a pantomime.

True, when the shy, half-veiled, trembling bride crosses the threshold of the new house—with a ceremony of oil and anointment—she is virtually brought in as a kind of the Queen Mother's trophy, a vassal to do any duty unquestioningly and unsleepingly till the end of her days. Her *saas* will thus order and determine the disposition of the bridal bed, see it festooned and fixed, caress the white vaginal sheets lovingly till the *zero* hour strikes at the dead of night, and the little *dove* is left fluttering there amid chuckles and smiles. Short of jumping into the bed herself, she does everything possible to make it her own affair.

This could be understood both as a psychological and a metaphysical necessity of the mother, as Raghav came to realize. This inverted triumph was perhaps the only authentic moment of his mother's life spent in drudgery and chores, in repression and silence. No wonder, therefore, any Indian mother longs eternally for her son's marriage before her death, for death too is a bride that comes veiled and wooed.

Quite naturally, Raghav's mother too had expected that it was time for her to enjoy her mother-in-law-hood, in full measure. Perhaps, traditionally, she had heard or seen all that happening in her own time and space, when daughters-in-law would remain at the beck and call of their respective mothers-in-law. A daughter-in-law would be called to order by the mere look of her mother-in-law's eyes, and without the possibility of any real conversation, she was expected to follow her dictates. Her own *saas* generally sat at her cushioned seat where her *bahu* would serve her tea and meals, particularly the hot-boiled milk in the afternoon, laced with a generous sprinkle of blanched almonds, cardamom and sugar to taste that was served in *kenze-khos*—goblet-shaped brass cup with a fixed pedestal or base stand to hold with—(most males and almost all women then in Kashmir didn't touch porcelain or chinaware as it was thought sacrilegious to use anything made of crushed cow bones). That *khos* was specially earmarked for *Sasuji's* use only. She would hold its base stand with one end of the short towel and with the other end, the accompaniment, namely freshly made *parantha* (home-made bread) in *desi ghee* or butter—along with the aroma of cardamom laced, steamed, sweetened milk would assail the server's nostrils and invariably make her mouth watery but she could dare not keep aside a portion of it for herself or even just taste it. Initially, it appeared that her *Sasuji* was sipping or sucking hot milk with a calibrated short sip, and that created a vacuuming noise from the *khos,* but soon she realized that it was to ensure that she didn't scald her lips. She did it deftly. But occasionally, she would almost swallow it in gulp, and if it was too hot she would tilt back the head with her mouth open, to blow the burning sensation away. She savored every bit of that sipping and chewing business. Watching her, alternately take a careful sip of milk and then a bite on the bread was a perfect sight for the hapless *bahu.*

Raghav's mother had, hence, known what it meant to be a dutiful daughter-in-law, in attendance, always and ever. Unfortunately, nothing of that came to pass in her case vis-à-vis her own daughter-in-law, which overtime led to strained relations.

Her world of fantasy could not endure this—the poetry drained out of it even before the drama. As goes the popular saying, once the varnish and the paint was off, the buntings and the bands dispatched, the fat was much sooner in the fire than one could have imagined. When the bills start arriving—there is hardly a wedding in India that is not a financial disaster on either side—the bride's dowry is the obvious pecking point. And the intriguing relatives, and there is no dearth of them, intentionally read between the lines and make stories to sow seeds of animosity, mistrust and discontent between the two women, who then are forced to take warring positions.

Raghav's mother came to believe that her gullible son had been entrapped by a clever, scheming manipulative lass, without bringing in any worth-the-name dowry. The girl must have done some black magic to ensnare her otherwise obedient son. She held the view that marriages need to be arranged with great care, the bride had to bring a suitable dowry befitting the status of the family, should come from similar or higher social background, and must understand the family values of loving, caring, sharing, serving and obeying her in-laws.

Whatever the bride's folks might have done and given in dowry, there always has been a distant, decrepit aunt of the groom, or an uncle thrice removed, who has not had her or his share of the loot, which leaves them grumbling. And the mother-in-law makes this a matter of her *Izat* (prestige). It is sad that most people instead of bridging the bridges, create chasms.

It's better to lose your pride with someone you love, rather than lose that someone you love with your useless pride.

Chinese Proverb.

It usually has been witnessed that when two young people get married, both their lives go through tremendous change, even bordering turmoil of sorts, and they are expected to learn to live together and build their relationship as husband and wife.

The only thing more complicated than a one-on-one love relationship is the complex web of interactions with family members. Each individual manifests his or her own personality, preferences, standards, attitudes, values and philosophical outlook.

Nature and nurture conspire to create an overlapping effect among family members in many of these areas, but it is never a perfect fit. That is where the strife begins. The *saas–bahu* relationship starts off on the wrong foot, thanks to stereotypes. Then even small things can make the daughter-in-law feel that she is being judged on the wrong side and hence unduly rubbed and pressured. Indeed, the conflict between a mother-in-law and a daughter-in-law is perhaps universal.

The Chasm!

Family relationships need careful thought and maintenance, just as love relationships do. Perhaps, they have an even greater need, because many family relationships are inherently imbalanced and because family relationships are for the most part dictated, not chosen. One might choose one's mate; but can't choose one's mother, father or other relatives. Thus, the newly married couple, besides adjusting with each other, have also to learn to live with their respective families. For the bride, in particular, to adjust and get along with her mom-in-law is certainly a daunting task because history bears testimony that between two of them the relationship somehow or the other invariably gets embroiled into knots, differences, misunderstandings and deep personality problems. Often they get sick of each other. They can't stand the presence of one another. They stop talking, and if at all they do, it is dripping sarcasm, even highly toxic.

Sample this conversation between a mother-in-law and her daughter-in-law: (Ever heard about the acerbic mom-in-law and her equally acidic daughter-in-law?)

Saas: "*Bhagwan ne tumhe do aankhe di, chawal mein se do–chaar pathar nahi nikal sakti*?"

Bahu: "*Bhagwan ne tumhe baintees daant diye hai, do–chaar pathar nahi chaba sakti kya*?"

(Translated, it would mean mother-in-law asking her daughter-in-law that when God has given her two eyes, why can't she separate little pebbles out of rice? And she, in retort, asks that when God has given her thirty-two teeth, why can't she as well chew those few pebbles?)

It is an old Indian saying that when two steel vessels come into contact, there shall be noise. This is a case of a woman bashing another woman. But when it becomes deafening, which it does with time, leading to very toxic relationships, the helpless *son* of his wishful mother or the harassed *husband* of his demanding wife is sought after—and he is expected to take sides. If he sides with his mother, he is labeled "*Mummy's boy,*" and if he supports his wife he is called "*hen-pecked husband.*" Poor fellow! Either way he is bound to suffer ignominy. He, in a way, gets torn in two parts, to start with. He gets into a dilemma where he is stuck between his mother and wife. But eventually, as a husband, since he has much to gain from his wife, he gradually slips away from the hold of his distraught mother, and gets under the clutches of his nagging wife. Human beings can never be separated from sex. There is an essential synergy between the two. One is born out of it.

The first chasm got created when Raghav's mother threw that petty *maetmur* at the face of her *Bahu.* "Give it back to your father, and tell him not to belittle my prestige, not to insult me like this," she said scornfully. It appeared obvious from the frown she brought to her forehead that it wasn't a chasm, but a deep, dense cleft that was bound to get widened.

Unfortunately, between themselves the two women could never be in peace and harmony, anytime thereafter. Yes, as has generally been witnessed, it starts, of course, with lighter banter, becomes a little barbed with the passage of time, and eventually settles down to an undeclared war of nerves. They initially avoided each other as a rat avoids a cat or a cat avoids a dog, and with time they perhaps felt like tigresses on an uncertain turf. They even felt asphyxiated in each other's noxious presence.

By and large these two creatures anywhere, in any frame or in any age, have had some sort of traditional animosity, and that is how they have been and continue to be portrayed or projected in cinema and television also—the indomitable duo.

However, with the arrival of the westernized, educated daughter-in-law, things have been changing. While cinema and prime time TV serials continue projecting the *saas* as a personified dragon breathing fire into her daughter-in-law's life, the real scenario has of late a different take. The slow erosion of the authority of *saas* has undoubtedly put the eternal scheming mother-in-law with poison-laced tongue on the defensive. The twenty-first century mom-in-law has generally become more tolerant, even a bit on her guard because the new-age brides are less tolerant and don't really like to be told what to do and what not to do. They like to take charge rather than take instructions. Financial independence has heralded intolerance and the young daughter-in-law is out to find ways and means to pressurize and push her hubby to move out at the slightest hint of discord. She is ready to fight for her rights. The age-old battle between two women to win the affection of and control over this one man (the son of the mother and husband of the wife) is also thus altering. Hence, slowly, mothers-in-law are being pushed into a situation where they have started liberating their sons and loosen their apron strings.

The *withering away* of mom-in-law's state is seldom contemplated as a *historical necessity.* More often than not, it is taken as an irrational wave or wind that has, for the moment, thrown her metaphysical apparatus out of gear. But, by and large, she has no doubt at all, that a mere Master's degree, or a Ph.D, which has got the modern *bahu* her financial independence, cannot match the massed erudition of her *saas's* mentors who have invested her, from eternity to eternity, with authority that *passeth understanding*... And no doubt, she is right, for no modern *bahu,* with all her Freudian, Marxist or existentialist claptrap, has yet found an answer to it. The old cow still, in most cases, remains sacred even when one may starve her to death. One may put a whole ocean between her and the hateful *bahu,* but she still remains a force and a presence.

It's the age-old power struggle that blights millions of marriages. And now, the reason behind the feuding between the two warring forces has been answered—wives are programmed to dislike their husband's mom. Even if a wife or girlfriend wanted to like her in-laws, she already had an expectation that they wouldn't get along. It can be a source of great conflict and part of the problem, which sometimes stems from issues between the mother and son. The (*issues*) have not been resolved when he starts a new husband–wife relationship. Almost two-thirds of married women complain they have suffered long-term stress because of friction with their husband's mother. Sadly enough, both women assume that each was undermining the other deliberately. This mutual unease may have less to do with actual attitudes and far more to do with persistent female stereotypes that few of them manage to shake off completely. They don't seem to understand that both the mother and wife are struggling to achieve the same position in the family—primary woman. So the woman bashing woman continues unabated, generally.

Nuptials with Song and Story!

It took Raghav time to understand the fact that his mother and wife, in their own time and space, had no hesitation in making judgments—because both perhaps held that there were whole domains of conduct within which they would not admit the possibility of any argument, and there was no denying the fact that both defended their respective stands. Their spite towards each other turned more insidious. Unfortunately, in the process, Raghav suffered the most—a case of wick burning at both ends.

The intensity of the animosity between Raghav's mother and his wife became evident on the nuptial night itself when he and his bride came face-to-face to meet physically for the first time, while young women sang the epithalamium, or song for the wedding chamber. He was desperate to meet her in flesh and blood, after all the agonizing wait—to touch her, to feel her, to live with her and to enjoy the warmth of her supple body.

She sat there on the flower-bedecked nuptial bed. He came and sat closer to her with an intense look on his face, and put his arm around her stiffly. He smelt of sweat and something else, and she tried to move away. She was not in a proper frame of mind; she was upset because of the nasty treatment meted out to her at the hands of her husband's mother, right from day one. She wanted to give vent to her hurt feelings. She wore a strange look.

The trouble with most women is that they get all excited about nothing, and then they marry him.

Cher.

"Why are you sounding cold?" Raghav asked. "This is our nuptial night. I want to spend time with you to discover every facet of you, to explore the intricacies of your whole persona, to study you, to understand you, to touch you, to smell you, to enjoy your company—taking you in fully, completely. But your obstinate attitude leaves me with nothing exciting about you."

She wanted to respond. But could say nothing, for she thought, even if she did, he wouldn't listen. She had got the definite, incipient realization that just then he was all charged up with frenzied passions—raw and hungry—and hence keyed up for a different sort of experience, with sex coiled inside him like a tight spring that demanded release. For him, all other things would come later, she understood.

"After all, what is the matter with you, really?" he now asked a bit calmly, and said, "You must know to get on track the situation that has gone wrong. I will talk to my mother and sort out the misunderstanding.

You must not lose patience so soon," he urged, rather impatiently.

She didn't respond. Not that she meant to spoil her first night with her husband, but surely expected him to be gentle, graceful, and wanted him to ease her concerns, instead of rushing through the business that she thought he had uppermost on his mind.

"What's this? Why don't you respond? Why are you behaving like this?" Raghav now asked with a furious look on his face. His voice was nearly hysterical, with a tempestuous expression on his face.

Ragini continued to remain silent. Something at the back of her mind ached deeply because of the very first indecent treatment that she was subjected to at the hands of her *Saas*, and more so because her husband didn't have the guts to rise in support of his newlywed wife. She had felt her feathers ruffled. She was annoyed and angry, therefore. She wanted to speak her heart out to her husband, whom she expected to listen to her, to understand her hurt emotions, and to sympathize with her. But he was not in a proper frame of mind so as to be receptive, she thought. Seized by a sudden fist of anger because of his wife's indifferent posture, Raghav's face turned like stone, but beneath its unmoving exterior he felt the heavy pulsing of his blood as he stared down at her parted lips and her determined expression, and yelled, "Why the hell you don't understand that you are married now and you better behave like a good, dutiful wife. To make success of a marriage, you need to change, adjust and accommodate?"

If there is such a thing at all as instructions in philosophy, it can only be instructions in doing one's own thinking.

Leonard Nelson.

"In the exact manner, creating a happy marriage is a mysterious process. It is, indeed, intriguing as to how two distinct individuals merge into a life partnership so that they are able to survive the inevitable crisis that will accompany them on the journey. There is no denying the fact that bonding together a man and a woman, who till now were strangers to each other, is difficult. Both have an identity of their own and marriage requires them to, not only acquire the new surroundings, but also adapt according to other partner's likes and dislikes. It's exactly for this that I said I want time to understand you and your folks," his wife retorted…and continued in abated breath, "Unfortunately expectations from the woman on getting married are far too many, particularly in the Indian traditional society. It is a paradox that while the *maang* is of the wife, the *sindoor* is of the husband; while the *throat* is of the wife, the *mangalsutra* is of the husband; while the *wrist* is of the wife, the *bangles* are *worn* in the name of her husband; while the *womb* is of the mother, the *infant* is known by the name of the father. Isn't it an irony of sorts? The misery of any daughter-in-law is all too familiar theme to be missed. Our folk-songs, folk-tales and, indeed, our mythological texts are full of passionate expressions of grief and torture suffered by young brides. What is completely missed out is the fact that she not only loses the hitherto safe and comfortable environs of her parental home, but also total identity. She adopts a new name, a new address, a new identity and is given a new name, as if it was her second birth. Coming from a different family background, she may be respectful towards her in-laws in her own way, unaware of the fact that they are judging her from their own perceptions or predetermined notions, and may at times term her as unmannered, arrogant and insolent. While a new bride may adapt to her new family values over a period of time, expecting her to change overnight is illogical. Therefore, she deserves understanding and compassion. She certainly would like to spend quality time with her husband and his folks, and carry the happiness and peace from there to all spheres of her life. She cannot just be a beloved, a wife; she is a daughter, a sister, a friend, a professional and a woman of dignity with her own pursuits too. She cannot and should not be expected to give up all that for her husband. But that doesn't mean that he would not still be the most important focus of her life."

Following such an eloquent presentation, there was hushed silence. Raghav gazed at her all through with a bated breath, and when their eyes met in a long moment, he saw the cat-like dilation of her black eyes.

But Raghav thought it prudent to keep his cool, and just asked, "What do you want?"

"All I would want is that before getting into the clutches of *husband-wife* expectations let us try and understand each other in a better way so as to be good friends and partners in matrimony. I mean I want to be myself with you, in your company. Let us recognize each other's feelings, emotions and respect one another's individuality," she replied.

Thinking her statement to be a very odd one, which his countenance expressed, he asked, "What do you mean by being yourself? Ask yourself, just ask! If your partner is thirsty, you don't refuse and scare him away. You need to give him water. If he is tired, let him rest peacefully. But that sense comes from genuine, unconditional understanding, from listening and putting your own needs and desires aside. And why raise all these issues now—right at this moment, at this hour—when it is our nuptial night?" he asked in a strangled voice.

And he got up and stood in front of her, waiting for an answer.

"We...we scarcely know each other," she stammered.

"Know each other?

What...?

Are you getting crazy? You appear to be constipated with lot of nonsense, humbug. Haven't we been in love before marriage," he retorted—anger glinting in his eyes. Aren't we married now, Ragini?" he asked with a brusque aggression in his voice. "And tell me, is one's nuptial night meant to raise all those petty issues, right here and now? How can you be so grim, defensive and obstinate? How can you be so emotionless?" he demanded.

"Emotions don't come machine made, you must know. It is a matter of chemistry," she retorted with the swiveling of her head, as if she was wanting to go through massive withdrawals due to pangs of anger.

And...and how do I say it?... I mean how am I supposed to understand your that chemistry or whatever? How well we can get to know each other if you put on this *touch-me-nottish* air? And, in any case, you're supposed not to bring up a topic that would create uncomfortable silence," he now blurted in a tone that betrayed his short fuse.

In that moment of anger, she took him to be an utterly selfish person. But she kept mute, sinking into a tongue-tied silence.

"I feel like you are consuming me, unnecessarily, without any reason. Waking up to you appears to have become a chore, an ordeal, an obligation. It is stifling. This way we shall go stagnant, and fall into a rut. Before the honeymoon, it could be the end of the relationship. I sometimes wonder how we got here?" he charged disdainfully and continued to spew out words in a manner that immediately deprived them of meaning as far as Ragini was concerned.

"Have people near you spent their whole lives agreeing with you," demanded she in a most painful perplexity, "Or is it just that you can't bear to think someone else might have a different opinion, a reasoned point of view, which might just be the right one?" She looked down as she said this, taking only a side glance at him so as to observe the effect of her words on him.

"May be," he responded, and met the question in her eyes.

"But, why raise all these nonissues, now? This is how it has been all through, and why did you...?" Raghav retorted sharply, cutting his sentence halfway.

"Impossible," she whispered quietly to herself with the toss of her head. Going into a typical contemplative mood, because his intemperate, dubious, hostile expression, and the uncertainty in saying something, which he thought in his head, but didn't, was so irksome to her. But she kept her cool.

"Why are you doing this? You're getting no joy from it, are you?" he asked her infuriated.

The sharp look in his eyes died as she remained unemollient and moved out a bit, which consequently made him turn away from her in a huff, violently flanging himself on one side of the double bed to lay still, although he felt heat flaring from her to him. As she quietly laid herself on the other side of it, trying to sleep, Raghav said, "I wish you could keep your mind aside in the moment and feel with your heart rather than think with your head."

She saw the fierce desire leap into his eyes, but once again didn't respond as she felt she was just then incapable of making love. She was feeling exhausted and deflated. Shock ran through Raghav—and something else. Desire, a burning one, at that! His eyes were flashing black fire, and Ragini could detect the raw scent of, what she thought, animal passion. He was foaming at the mouth as if he had a snake bite, with eyes vapid.

Taking a look at him, Ragini turned vigilant first, jittery next and defensive later, and in doing so drifted off into sleep. She did not wake up all at once, but lay for some time, drifting between sleep and waking, struggling out of confused dream that she was lying there, on the beach where she had so longed to go, and that the waves were pounding her body.

And then she woke up to realize that she was on the bed, not on the beach. And it was not the sea waves pounding her body, but he, her husband, who was forcing his body on her, his lips clung to hers. She felt a quick panic. A shock like lightening quivering through a birch tree ran through her. She drew slowly away, reached for her hand and held her limp fingers. Her voice was strangled in her throat. She tried to resist, but couldn't. She just put her hands on his chest to push him away, but it was like pushing a rock. She could do nothing except turning her face away. She felt her body like a rag, as she felt aroused and horrified—all at the same time—swimming around in one big mess on the bed, needing to come up for air.

"Don't you act so bloody *virginal*!" he screamed at her, in a thrall of passion.

A shudder went to her heart, and a tremor shook her body.

Continued he, "Can't you be generous, just once? Bloody, bloody-minded woman!" lowering the dome of his head into the cup made out of his palms. He didn't raise his head for quite some time, as if he was trying to find a way out of the impasse, while she looked towards him insolently, her black eyes wide and opaque with shock. She felt tired, stifled a yawn and thought it prudent to make no answer lest it might provoke him to an undesirable level of acrimony.

Her silence irked him all the more and a frown creased his forehead and the mouth tightened into a thin line due to rage. She felt like a spineless creature in search of a burrow to hide herself. Her husband looked at her with bleared eyes for a moment, and then a horror sprang up in them that convulsed his whole features, the sight of which left her terribly shaken and unnerved because of the ferocity in her husband's stare—the spite that traveled through it as clearly as a prey getting gulped down in the long jaws of a crocodile. She staggered back with a livid face, with perspiration breaking upon her brow, holding her teeth clinched. Now, all hell broke loose as he raised his right hand, drew it back to inject force into it and slapped her hard and firm, first on her left cheek and then on the right with a reverse swing.

Hot heads and cold hearts, never solved anything.

Billy Graham.

Her countenance got sunk in woes and shrieks, which revealed the tremors she had felt. And the cries she gave out were not for the physical pain, but for the violation of her right to herself, an affront to her individuality, as a woman. She felt mental weariness overtaking her—the hopelessness that assailed her, which came upon her like an obsession. She couldn't get any sleep and continued thinking for a long time—adding thought to thought. A lot of it she couldn't handle at the spur of the moment. "I never expected that this would be my first night with him. Perhaps, I have been too naïve or gullible, foolishly incredulous. Possibly, I remained too weak and meek," she told herself, while experiencing both desire as well as agony—desire to avoid any ruckus in her relationship with her husband and agony to think, "How could he take his wife for granted like this...like a piece of personal furniture—a fiefdom?"

And next moment, from her facial expressions, she appeared feeling repulsive about the general assertion about woman's *natural* inferiority—need for male support rather dominance, and the beliefs or traditions that enforce the assumption that the key in a marriage is the ability of a woman to endure patiently for survival.

Ragini allowed her tears to flow copiously, while Raghav then slept a languorous sleep.

Dealing with the Failure!

Raghav later brooded, quietly feeling sorry for his most unbecoming conduct. "Give and take isn't necessarily a bad word. However, it is certainly something that can be elevated to a lofty status or be relegated to something demeaning and insulting, depending on intentions," he thought in his swirling head. And then questioned himself internally, "Were my intentions bad, demeaning?" Not being sure, he felt gloomy.

He decided to approach his wife, feeling sorry for what all happened at the spur of that moment.

"Ragini, I'm sorry. I shouldn't have treated you like that."

She looked at him, and he could see tears welling up in her eyes. That again unnerved him. "Please forget about it, please!" he now urged.

Though her husband's pleadings threw her into some little relief, nevertheless, the uneasy sense of odd feeling continued to spiral inside her for quite some time, vividly carrying its hateful memory. It kept biting her. She perhaps had not been able to place the incident out of her mind.

Troubles are like babies,
they only go bigger by nursing them.

Anonymous.

However, she decided to calm down, and soon the rough sea of her mind got smoothed as high rising waves, that were bashing her, were suddenly ironed out. She wiped her tears and pocketed the insults, and silenced her indignation.

Raghav kept on cajoling her, persuading her to forgive him. So, she now felt inclined to respond to the appeasement of her husband, who had been caressing her emotions. "Was he acting sincere or just resorting to deceitful cajolery," she thought to herself. She had been told men act selfish.

Nevertheless, she didn't feel comfortable with the turn of events, and she kept mulling on the thought that perhaps traditionally it had been ingrained in her mind since her birth that she is inherently weak and expected to go by the wishes of her husband or else suffer.

"Women may be attracted to the idea of equality and freedom, but men continue to look upon a woman as the weaker sex and continue to expect her to be protected as fragile and vulnerable. Her father guides her in childhood, her brothers zealously guard her in youthful years, her husband guides her after marriage, and her sons take care of her in her old age. That is how in our traditional societies, Indian women mostly have been looked at or treated," she kept musing on such thoughts.

"I want to go to see my parents," Ragini now told Raghav. That made him a wee bit nervous. In a bid to smoothen her ruffled feelings and emotions, he said, "No. I suggest let us go out for an outing. She declined, timidly though. He didn't insist.

And she made preparations to go there. He didn't stop her. But next day morning, he managed to have a word sent to her, asking her to meet him at a certain market place. She again wanted to refuse but her mother (for whom, like anyone else in her position, the son-in-law, whatever the merits or demerits, is invariably the cynosure of eyes) prevailed upon her, and she had to agree to accept her husband's invitation.

It was getting close to 2 p.m., and Raghav was awaiting her arrival. Instead of using a car, he had booked two horse-driven carriages, so as to give a regal treatment to his heartthrob in every sense.

And why not? After all it was their first outing together!

He spotted her coming from a distance, and noticed a new sense of elation in her gait—her body swaying like a flower-laden branch in a gentle breeze. As if to make a prudent statement of her elegance and uniqueness, she came draped in a georgette sari with border of miniature purple peacocks and *pallu* drawn over her head, a sign of sartorial grace, standing in calm splendor—her wide, delicate eyes resolute in expression, and a smile aching to erupt on her otherwise blushing face.

She greeted him with felicity as she pulled up her sari's delicate gold tasseled hem so as to ensure that it didn't cover her full shinning face, whose cheeks were gleaming like the high polish of a Kashmiri apple in full ripeness.

As Raghav's eyes were filming over her, he extended his hand to help her get into her seat. She sat in the corner, away from him. His hand crawled across like some secretive crab to grasp her hand. She felt the heat and obliged by inching closer.

Love is not measured by how you feel,
but how you make the other person feel.

Julie Andrews.

So here he was riding regally, having her by his side, sitting on the rear seat in an elaborate sprawl placing in style his one leg half-bent over the other, close to feel the sweet warmth of his honey-trap's thighs. He felt a shock of exclamation at her body touch. To him, she looked a woman who shimmered with beauty. He came further closer to her as if drawn by a magnetic pull that in a way made him resemble a macaw in heat squawking out mating cries across vast, dense and deep valleys of Kashmir.

Seeing Raghav's ecstatic face, she smiled a small laugh, giving a wink stealthily, who then took her slender hands into his and cupped them, as if under an obvious secret pact—*one,* that he loved his ladylove passionately and, *two,* that he wants her to get reassured about it.

He couldn't take off his slanted eyes from her blushing face, which emitted a shine, while her eyeballs kept moving, side to side, like an astute Bharathnatyam dancer. Light tendrils of joy crisscrossed their faces that brought out tinkling peals of merriment.

As the carriage reached the Residency Road, Raghav wanted to stop at the *Mir Paan* Shop, the iconic point for any youthful person to stop and buy *paan* and a pack of cigarettes. However, Ragini noticed that most young people there were throwing lecherous glances at young women passing by while it appeared as if nothing moved in the world except people's jaws, with a stubborn grinding motion that defied logic, with a subtle rhythm, taking utmost pleasure in chewing and holding red spittle in bowl-shaped mouths, which soon began to drip out from the corners, forcing the man to let loose a streaming jet of *paan-ki-peek* (masticated betel juice) splashing the road in red diagonals, and all around in the corners of the rainwater drains. Sensing Ragini was feeling uncomfortable, Raghav decided to move on forthwith and the horse carriage trotted down the snaking drive on the boulevard by the side of famous Dal Lake as the wind picked up pace, and in that misty ambience that obscured view, he could record nothing but the regality of his wife as consoling as a paragraph from one's favorite novel or as uplifting as a stanza from one's prized poem, or even as soothing as listening to some soulful *gazal*. He felt invigorated as a sensible and manly husband to make his wife feel womanly, indeed, desirable in full measure.

The couple later hired a *shikara* (boat) from Nehru Park to have a ride on the Dal Lake, that had the Shankra-Chariya hill temple, on one side and Hazratbal Mausoleum shrine on the other end, and stretches of water—deep and vast—touching the banks of Mughal Gardens, in the far end.

Raghav instantly remembered having always felt smitten by the total grandeur of Kashmir valley, his birthplace. "I was born in paradise," he whispered in his own ears, as if reminding himself of Kashmir's opera *Bombur te Yamberzal* or the *Narcissus and the Bumble Bee*. He had enjoyed hearing farmers sing that popular folk song, in chorus, while cultivating their lands—*yamberzal* extolling and inviting *bombur* to visit her, who circles it with a loud hum—as if it was a beloved seeking out the lover.

That was exactly how he felt about his birthplace where he was born and had grown up—Srinagar, a city set like a jewel in the lap of Kashmir valley—so breathtakingly beautiful that it was impossible not to see the hand of God in her dense forests, mist shrouded mountains, sloping hills, deep lush green valleys and Mughal Gardens, whose grass was clean with lawn laundry that wipes away the mud, the insects, the nettle and thistle that start from hill tops, descending down into terraces, having blooming flowerbeds and rising fountains, to the ground touching the banks of the huge Dal Lake, spread over miles, and other sparkling lakes, dotted with that majestic tree called *buuen* (Chinar) providing shade to tired limbs in summer and adding glitter of gold to the locale in autumn when its leaves fade and fall—turning the entire landscape golden yellow, which then people collect in heaps here and there and burn to convert it into fuel for their *kangris* (*fire pot made of terracotta around which an outer casing of white, red and green colored wicker is woven, providing a handle bar to make it portable for use by all people—one for each—old or young—in Kashmir to keep warm in the biting cold of the place, most part of the year*).

Truly, nature's bounty has made the valley a paradise on earth. That is why the great Persian poet *Firdous* had rightly penned that if there was a paradise on earth, it was here, it was here!, he remembered having read so.

While being engrossed in such self-talk, his imagination showered a rain of his childhood and adolescent memories. He became deeply engrossed in those memories of the past. "Memories are truly like relics from a golden period," he mused. As those memories flooded his mind, several scenes came flashing back rapidly like flashes of strobe light in a discotheque.

It used to be spring time—the air laden with coolness of icy mountains; the breeze carrying the fragrance of green valleys; the ice melting; the freed piss flowing in the streams around with gush; the birds chirping, making musical notes; the flower buds turning to bloom; the narcissus disappearing almost overnight, as if in obeisance, to flower into almond, cherry and peach blossoms.

It was the spring time, and used to often rain alongside sunshine. He got to remember writer F.H. Burnett's famous quote:

"Is the spring coming?... What is it like?" he asked.

"It is the sun shining on the rain and the rain falling on the sunshine..."

After finishing his annual examination each academic year, he would come to reside with his maternal uncle in the vast premises of Nishat Water works. This place, situated at the foothills of Pirpanjal mountain ranges, offered visual feast to one's eyes—luxuriant forests, mist-covered lofty peaks, gurgling streams, pastoral flowerbeds and terraced valleys of paddy fields down below that rejuvenated the onlooker's mind, body and soul. Attached to its periphery there was a huge orchard, which had variety of fruit trees. This was the time when cherries would ripen and were seen dangling on the branches in the early morning breeze like a pair of earrings on a damsel's moving head.

The orchard used to be contracted out to the highest bidder by the Government.

So it was prohibited to even touch the fruit, not to talk of eating it. What Raghav would, however, do was to get up very early in the morning at around 5 a.m., when the orchestra of birdsong used to be in full swing with the soft call of the cuckoo and sharp whistling of the birds that he couldn't identify. He would hurry to go up the cherry trees, one after the other, and eat that delicious fruit to his heart's content each morning. About an hour later, the muezzin's soulful azaan used to urge devotees to get ready for namaz. Soon the contractor's men, who kept watch, used to attend to their job of warding off any intruders, be it humans or birds. Birds, however, usually would heartily feast on the many types of fruit that had periodically ripened. To ensure that there were no intruders or birds spoiling the ripened fruit by pecking into it, the watchers had in place all sorts of arrangements to create huge scaring notes, including very strange oral sounds like long loud doleful howls through stretching of their vocal chords or through blowing of long coarse whistles from time-to-time to scare away and ward off the enemy of their haul.

But Raghav would invariably give them a slip by being out there very early in the mornings, with deep blue starry sky above, their depth unnerving, and soon enough early morning sunrays were falling on heavy dew drops on the green velvety grass and blossoms on peach and apple trees. He would thus eat ripened cherries to his heart's fill stealthily while the watch and ward laborers were still asleep, and would then hurry to return to his bed before anyone noticed.

Those watchers, however, suspected something amiss when they would find broken twigs, scattered leaves and seeds of eaten fruit strewn all around the trees that had been invaded while they slept unmindfully. However, unable to solve the puzzle, they would huddle together most of the time, particularly in the afternoons, to play cards, as the sun carved out their shadows on the mud wall of the hut used as store.

Once, the stepbrother of Raghav's maternal grandfather—a tall, thin, wiry old man with bones poking out into his skin and sagging jowls, sunken thin face, and a bit large startled eyes, which looked prominent from the thinness of his face, having snow-white bushy eyebrows and grey tufts of hair on his ears that altogether gave him a look of age and severity happened to be visiting his nephew and his wife for a few days.

Raghav had met him earlier also but that day he found the old man having gone thin as air, and thought that if he was on a seashore, wading in knee high water and a wave happened to crash across, it could wash him away like a wafer.

Raghav had a small laugh within himself, as the old man otherwise appeared mentally alert. However, because of his age, the sleep had almost left his eyes.

"Down to the last day, even the last hour now, I'm an old man, lonely and unloved, sick and hurting, tired and exhausted of living. I'm ready for the hereafter; it has to be better than this," he would often murmur, in a breath that wheezed through his paper-thin chest, while sniffing that brownish powder or something held by his thumb and index finger into his nostrils, that would then send him into a bout of sneezing, following which he would fall flat almost breathless—holding his head so tight as if it was going to burst open.

Most of the time, the fidgety old man coughed—a wheezy cough—ground the phlegm in his throat, and spat out the weight of age into the narrow-necked steel container kept for the purpose by his bedside or straight in the direction of the open window, by the side of which he had his bed laid. Thick viscous substance was secreted by the mucous membranes of the respiratory passages, and having been off- loaded, for a while calmness would envelop him. "Give me a glass of lukewarm water," he said to Raghav that day, in his gruff voice, raising his head on his long neck and screwing up his eyes.

Raghav got him the water which he drank in sips as if to moisten or lubricate his dried-up throat veins. The container into which he spat from time-to-time had got filled up to the brim, and now asked, "Raghav, go and throw off the phlegm and put the container in place, duly washed." For Raghav, that was too much to put up with, and he refused. The crocheted old man uttered foul words.

He spoke in carefully modulated tones, supporting his words with gesticulations in which his lips, eyes, hands and even fingers, his monocle and spring glasses actively and effectively participated. He was at his worst or best when he spoke explosively, arrogantly, defiantly or abusively, particularly if someone refused his dictates or questioned him about his peeves and infuriating habits, like violently coughing and gargling before the break of dawn while others were fast asleep, flooding the bathroom, spitting all around in the washbasin or converting the windows into a make-shift clothesline, particularly for drying up his half-wornout undergarments.

One would often notice him counting his money, mostly made up of coins of all Denominations, which he would stack in neat rows for easy counting. This he would do many times a day routinely, compulsively. If any kid asked some, "No," he would say feebly but firmly—speaking the way he always spoke by making strange faces—perhaps to make his words seem larger, fuller and stronger than himself, as if the amplitude of their meaning was directly related to the thinness of himself.

It was not easy to make peace with him. He was a bachelor who had treasured his privacy as a miser guards his gold. Whether he held any gold or not is a moot point, but he certainly guarded his money which he would discreetly hide from any penetrating glance of anyone going into his room to serve him tea, which he drank almost endlessly.

One day, having somehow come to know of Raghav's early morning exploits into the orchard, he held out a threat to him, as if he was nursing a grudge, "I am going to tell the contractor about your escapades in the fruit gardens."

"But why? what have I done to offend you?" asked Raghav. "You never do what I ask you," he replied, and it scared Raghav, who begged him not to do so, for Raghav knew that the old man wanted to blackmail him.

"I promise to do whatever you ask for," he assured, which made the concealed knot of grouse that the old man had carried inside him loosen and melt away, a bit.

He then quickly laid himself down on his stomach and ordered, "Come, get on to my back." He carried his backache for how long, no one knew, but whenever Raghav ran into him earlier also, he would invariably stretch himself on the floor and ask him to get on to his back, which had to a certain degree arched, perhaps under the weight of his age, and he wanted to press it hard to get relief from pain. Raghav would invariably excuse himself on one pretext or the other and run away. But cut to that day, he found himself pinned down, and had to do his bidding.

He sheepishly obeyed and put palms of his both hands gently on his vertebrae.

He called out to tell him, "Mount yourself on my back and get up on your feet."

Raghav knew the old man perhaps still wished to see his semiarched or loose bow-like back straightened under wait, and become hard and firm. Keeping his fists clinched as if to exert full pressure of his weight, and so he did as was directed.

The old man yelled, asking for lighter pressure at a particular point. Raghav

Followed his directions. "Aaha…aahaa…" he muttered; a noise like wind blowing through an aperture, as if to convey, at once, his pain and relief from it, though momentarily.

"A little above," he said, showing with his pointed finger as well, as if navigating Raghav's feet.

Raghav moved his feet a little farther.

"A little—a fraction more—to the left," he now pointed with the reverse flick of his left index finger, as if to put him on the right track.

Raghav followed his instructions.

"Another friction left," he now demanded by a small suppressed word of mouth that almost got half-stuck in his throat because of the pressure of cough.

Raghav obeyed dutifully, if only grudgingly, to ensure that he didn't spill the beans.

"Yes, yes! There only, right at that point, there only, hold on to it, don't let it go, and now press hard to kill the pain," he feebly exclaimed with a sense of intense relief, almost drowning his choking voice.

Raghav laughed quietly with a hint of maligned pleasure, and stood still lest that cesspool of pain in old man's back was missed, and was lost. And when the load turned out to be unbearable for the old man's aching back after a while, he with a slight shrug of his shoulders asked him to get off. "Get off, get off," he shouted. Raghav hastily jumped off to give him immense relief, and saw his eyeballs bulged out, and the tendons in his neck stood out in high relief.

Several seconds, perhaps even a full minute had passed, when he turned to get-up lazily, and Raghav saw his naked belly, the frayed crumpled skin having distinct brownish marks obviously left by overheating of skin exposed directly against the heat of kangri, to brave the knifing cold of Kashmir's winter months, and which had overtime gone crisscrossed due to age into creases of wrinkles that ran to and fro as if forming rivulets. And just as he crawled away slowly to his bed, his half-tattered underwear got torn and beneath it a creeper of outgrown thick hair of salt and pepper hue became visible from his pubic zone that gave out an obnoxious stench. Raghav clamped his nostrils. The sight was repulsive and he felt like spitting, right in that direction, even on him, perhaps. Old as his eighty-nine winters or more, he sounded terribly depressed by that aging body that he was living in. Raghav jabbed his fingers at his mouth by sensing that every part of his body seemed to be calling out for his ultimate resting place. The old man was in the December of his life, Raghav came to visualize.

Why did people grow so old? Only to wither in pain and then die! he kept musing…couldn't then understand, that it's what life is all about!

That day on, he strode in the orchard, unfettered.

But, that was then.

Right now, the boatman slowly and steadily released his small craft, out of the ghat (shore) by untying its string from the peg it remained tied to, into the deep lake waters with the help of a long bamboo-like pole called humtul, by pushing the ground of the shallow waters near the bank with it, and then the boat was oared away with the help of an oar—a wooden heart-shaped blade nailed into a wooden thick handle—the oarsman sitting stooped over at the rear of the boat to propel it by leveraging his oar against the water.

During the course of the ride, they were approached at places by young girls hailing from the floating lands nearby—ridding very tiny boats the edges of which almost touched the water level and on the unstable tip of which they appeared to be precariously sitting on their haunches like a monkey perched on a shaky branch—selling fruits, flowers or even fish, held out on khelvather (lotus leaves) of the size of a full dinner plate on the emerald green impermeable surface on which water droplets rolled over like mercury.

For the couple the boatride turned out to be a cozy, cushy and gay affair with heavily cushioned sort of laid-out bed, and matching pillows and curtains all around to unwind and make love. In the breeze whiffing through the vast lake, the decorative canopy flags and flower-patterned curtains, in deep and garish colors, fluttered, as if moving about carefree. The ride was royal and invigorating.

All in all, it was a great day of fun and enjoyment for the two exclusively, which saw them in each other's intimate physical and emotional company, particularly in the dark, secure and secretive ambience of that cinema hall where the unbuttoned, half-clad movie glamor of the gorgeous, curvaceous and genial heroin did not as much matter to Raghav as the physical proximity of his own honey-dove—two of them sitting huddled in the far end corner of that cinema hall, making their own love, till the movie came to an end.

Raghav mindfully behaved incognizant of the previous night's brush that his wife had with his hot and intemperate temper. On her part, she also quite naturally did not rack up the issue.

Both wanted to leave that bad patch behind and move forward.

You have power over your mind—not on outside events.
Realize this and you will find strength.

Marcus Aurelius.

The Ugly Turn, Yet Again!

On reaching home, Ragini had to face the wrath of her Saas, whose permission had not been sought for the outing. She had taken it as an affront to her authority.

"Am I your maidservant to cook for you while your highness goes out romancing your husband, and serve you hot on your return?" she shouted at the pitch of her vocal chords.

Poor Ragini, sort of contracted into a wrinkled or dried-up state, while Raghav kept quiet, and gestured to her to keep mum. All the same, his mother's eagle eyes noted variations in her son's behavior. "Truly, you don't have any idea what colors your son is going to show after you show him his bride," she got reminded of what one elderly lady in the neighborhood had forewarned her.

Her son, nevertheless, didn't have the guts to tell his mother that it was at his insistence that Ragini had agreed to go out with him. Therefore, she took it upon herself to somehow summon the courage to tell her Saas all that needed to be told to square up the matter. But it didn't work. Her Saas continued to create far greater ruckus on that otherwise simple issue. She even started crying and wailing that she had created a wedge between maa–beta (mother and son).

"I know from day one you have not liked me. In fact, you hate me from the core of your heart," Ragini now mumbled.

"How could you have the cheeks to confront me, to charge me like that?" she demanded, enraged. "You better stop it here, you brazen faced woman or I'll pull your tongue out."

Sensing the matter getting volatile beyond proportion, Raghav asked his wife to keep quiet, raising his voice.

"But why?," she demanded.

"Can't you just keep quiet? Don't aggravate the matter," he persuasively said.

"But tell me what is my fault?" she insisted.

"Just, stop. Or else…!" he shouted.

"Or else what?" she asked in a raised voice.

The agony of such like acrimonious situation, which had overpowered them earlier, got renewed, when in a fit of intense rage, Raghav used abusive language against her and her parents.

The situation got escalated.

The poison of his words having entered her veins, Ragini shouted, "What?"…the shout created a resonance in Raghav's mind, as if it was a fat coin or something akin to that, which had got dropped on a smooth, hard marble floor, and it resonated for a while. He could see the terror in her eyes, but remained impervious, perhaps because he remembered Shakespeare having said that a woman when in anger, speaks in two languages—first, one gets the bare words and second, one gets the meaning of those words.

"What did you say?" Ragini asked again, her lips quivering and then kept biting her lower lip and squeezing her eyebrows, as if she was now intending to convey the meaning of the word What?

"Just what you have heard," Raghav, putting up a brave front, curtly replied, uninhibited by her body posture. "Shall I mouth it again?" he asked, as if to instigate her or perhaps to browbeat her. The altercation was getting loud and nasty.

She felt the gathering of blood and pain. There was stunned pause and silence till she got further infuriated and shouted, "I warn you, don't you abuse my parents or else…!"

He came forward and clapped his hand over her mouth. "Shut up, you stupid. Or else…?" he charged angrily, in return.

She resisted and he then grabbed her neck. She pushed him back in self-defense. He lost his balance and fell to the floor with a thud, his forehead hitting the floor and bled. Rubbing his palm on the spreading pain, he could only think of hate for her.

He got up, ran to the kitchen, opened the drawer there, picked up a big knife, and turned on her.

She experienced a sort of bristling state of her skin produced by fright, and ran back to shut the door. She could reproach him only by the tears, which streamed from her eyes with passionate violence—a reproach, however, that was wholly ignored by her husband, as he started banging the door hard, which she held down with all her might. Frustrated, he then started stabbing the door with the knife.

She was terrified.

There was a lull moment.

Momentarily, it stopped.

And then she heard a loud breaking of glass. He had smashed a side window and was trying to climb inside. In his desperate rage, he tried to kick it down, screaming and shouting mouthfuls of abuses. She quickly ran out of the room, and down the stairs, all the way shouting for help. Her eyes were red and swollen and full of tears. A neighborhood woman passing by just then took her in her arms, and she felt like weeping anew. He chased her like a dog down the stairs but finally stopped his pursuit, fearing public outrage against him.

This tussle saw the couple stranded at distances to each other that had got created between them, again. They didn't feel like talking. Though together in a room, it was a venomous loneliness for both of them. They sat apart speechless—the quietness sitting between them like some enormous rock or rough tormenting sea. She had bolted herself into the dark cave of vast stillness of that of a graveyard. Perhaps, she had learned to turn her anger towards herself and box it away.

She showed no reaction or emotion and simply batted her eyelids quite a few times as if some foreign particle was aching her inside, and then rolled down the shutters on her eyes to avoid his gaze. She appeared drifting and turned indifferent because talking to her husband became stressful for her, while he cold shouldered her.

There was no much talk between the two, for a long time.

Much later, they did talk, not to each other but at each other. And, indeed, very loudly and violently, both being in a very bad temper. He grew rude, and became insolent, while she seemed to have resolved never to take another step backwards. He could see plainly that she was not herself, which she so far had assumed like a garment with which to appear before the world. He let her alone, and walked away.

It was a great agony to be in that volatile situation, very painful. Although he could not weep, she did, cupping her face, sobbing, weeping and crying so intensely that patches of dark skin under her eyes, shaped like garlic cloves, appeared, and her eyeballs were rheumy from chronic weeping, worry and sleeplessness.

Next morning, he looked ardently into her face. She looked back at him. He paused, but made no response. But when she moved away and turned her head off, she gave him so scornfully a piercing gaze, as if she meant to convey that she wanted the distance between them to grow. She was precisely what she appeared, a woman full of disgustful resentment.

Taking Up A Job!

Ragini came to find that it was getting intolerable to face the intrusiveness of her mother-in-law while her husband was away at work. So for reasons of finding a way out to evade her as also with a view to gain financial independence, she decided to take up a job, although she knew her husband never wanted her to do so. Once earlier when she had casually touched upon the subject with him, he had very much sounded like a fossilized mindset with old and traditional viewpoints, who believed that it was for the head of the family alone to go out to work and earn the bread and butter for the family. The wife needed to stay at home to look after the household chores. The elders felt safe under her care. He bought all the essentials for the home, and she managed and used them painstakingly, cleaned and maintained the household, prepared meals for the family, cared for the elderly and mothered children to bring them up with care, concern and warmth. Between them, they were the two forces to run their household efficiently—committed to create a sweet home out of a house—father as the head of the house and mother as the heart of the home. While he was Shiv, she was Shakti—as believed traditionally.

Raghav had come to have these notions ever since he had watched his father saying and believing in his own lifetime that a seed has two forces (contents) in it—Shiva and Shakti. When the seed is sown into the earth, Shakti sprouts out of it and takes roots underneath, while Shiva sprouts out and takes the form of branches and leaves. The one part is invisible (being underground), and the other is visible (being above the ground). Similarly, in every household, husband and wife are the two forces—Shiva and Shakti. Man is the force of Shiva, who goes out to work hard and earn a living and is seen, while the woman is the force of Shakti, who looks after the home and hearth with warmth, compassion and serenity, and remains unseen. She is like a fountain for a good, happy and sound household; he is the edifice resting on the soundness of the foundation. The two together make a home happy and healthy. A mystical union of yin (receptive) and yang (dynamic) or Shiv–Shakti energies, that brings a couple to the alchemy of fusion. There is an integration of diverse energies which crystallize into self-creation—new life and unity.

But that was then.

The scene has drastically changed since the times of Raghav's father.

Ragini ignored the hostile attitude of her husband as far as her taking up a job was concerned. She applied and got one, much to the consternation of her husband and his mother.

Ragini was struggling for individual identity. She had thought that a job would give her that. She was naturally enthusiastic about taking up a job, even if it meant annoying her husband. Her taking up a job created further animosity between the two. But for the time being, her happiness lay only in being away from her intrusive mother-in-law during the daytime and at the same time gain economic independence.

But this decision put everyone concerned into serious mental turmoil.

If we are incapable of finding peace in ourselves, it is pointless to search elsewhere.

Francois de la Rochefoncauld.

The couple started drifting. And as days and months passed, both felt hard pressed for time. So both had little time to be in each other's company. They got into a situation where both the spouses would come home tired at the end of a hard day's work in office. But the husband expected all the comforts on returning home, while his wife expected him to help her in the household chores. He feels entitled, being male–head–to rest and relax, and expects his wife to get into the kitchen to serve him a hot cup of coffee or tea, depending on his mood. She starts cribbing for she expects him to wash the cups and saucers in the absence of a maidservant. But the husband keeps ignoring her expectations, and instead takes up the day's newspaper or some old magazine to read or switches on the television to his favorite TV channel or simply sinks into a couch in a stupor regardless of any concern for the pleas that his wife is making.

Raghav and Ragini had with time got into such a distraught situation, a situation that saw them get into a shriveled state. As the couple got more frazzled, each started cutting each other out of the loop. Just talking to one another became stressful. Each tried to ignore the things said or actions did that annoyed the other for as long as one could. But then, at some point, he or she would blow up at each other, due to which they often got embroiled in nasty arguments and shouting.

The Family Way!

So Raghav and Ragini kept bouncing back and forth between fights and too much distance, with a rare sprinkle of occasional bliss.

Marriage is a war in which you go to sleep with your enemy.

Anonymous.

Time is the greatest healer, they say. So the couple moved on with the passage of time, leaving behind those rough patches, and when young Raghav was aflame with desire, when the moon had descended into his bride's eyes and kisses fell on her lips like moths or rose buds, when her slender neck pined for the warmth of her husband's breath, when she couldn't any longer stand to bear any indifference to her husband's advances, the cupid played its game, and the two young throbbing hearts met to cohabitate.

And it soon became known that Ragini was in an advanced stage of her first pregnancy. Raghav's parents, particularly his mother, felt joyous on the prospect of having their son's child in their lap. She felt grand. And now the cold and indifferent Saas started caring, looking after, and nursing her Bahu. The ice between the two hostile women started melting. Both acted positively and decided to retrieve the relationship of Saas–Bahu, which had started off on a wrong footing.

With time, when the catty moments between the two erstwhile warring women got over, and they became friendly, somebody asked them as to what had they learned from the bad experiences they had, they unanimously replied, "What not to do in the relationship of Saas–Bahu."

The bonhomie between his mother and wife made Raghav happy, and he got drawn to his wife who now looked to him much more young, charming, and captivating.

Love not only gives, it also forgives.

Spanish Proverb.

After sometime, Ragini's parents, true to the tradition, wanted to have the first delivery of their daughter at their own place. And so, when she was carrying for around eight months, she went to her parental house.

Meantime, Raghav changed his job and had to shift his base to a place called Bhatinda.

He took up the new job there, but felt lonely. He had to eat out—both mornings and evenings.

He didn't like it, and craved for company.

Meeting the Old Classmate!

One day, he happened to be eating in a high-end restaurant. After a while, like a fizzy drink, an effervescent gorgeous lady breezed into the dining area in a flurry—spring in her steps, a twinkle in her eyes and oodles of glamor and style. Silence filled the restaurant as everyone instantly watched her entering as if she was a stream on a hill, wriggling its way through rocks and boulders. Raghav's sharp gaze also got drawn towards her, and he saw her luminous visage that was more than glowing. He couldn't believe his eyes when he recognized her as his collegemate, and called out, joyously, "Hi, Rosy…here, It's me."

All others now craned their necks to look at Raghav, jealously though!

Rosy turned around a bit and giving him an equally wondrous look, responded, with a wave of her right hand, showing her ring finger wearing an oversized diamond that flashed imperiously on her immaculately manicured finger. Raghav, leaving his food, got on his feet to rush to her seat, who exclaimed, "Oh! It's you, Prince. Just amazing to catch up with you here."

He responded, "Wonderful meeting you after almost ages. You still remember to call me as Prince! But how are you here, Rosy?"—stretching and rolling the syllable sy around his tongue as if wanting to make her name sound unbelievably syrupy, sweet, sexy and all that. Meeting her was, to him, like reaching home, and finding his old beloved there on the bed.

Rosy looked at him and loved the look in his eyes. Then she met the formidable glint in his black eyes and suddenly some of her composure left her, as he caught her fair slim fingers within his grasp to shake her hand, allowing his thumb discreetly to slide over her smooth, flexible wrist where he could feel the pulsating beats of her pulse.

"Yeah, yeah, me too feeling fascinated to meet you," she responded.

Raghav loved her voice, and felt her touch as soft and slim as a young sapling—probably just as supple—he now said with gusto, "Oh my God, you look fabulous; you smell great. What are you eating; what are you wearing?" arching his thick black brows in surprise he enquired.

She shyly smiled a thank you.

"What do you mean?" she then asked.

"Meaning often takes the charm out of words," he merely said, with a small smile on his face.

"Calm down, Raghav. Don't you sound philosophical. You have released posers as an archer does arrows…(pause) Well, I have a very healthy lifestyle. I don't smoke or drink. I stick to a mix of cardio and yoga and go for healthy food—so all that shows on my face. I don't believe in the concept of size zero, but one should be fit enough to wear anything," she replied, smilingly. "But how come you are here in my town," she now looked at him askance, sidelining any further curios and pompous compliments.

As he retraced his old association with her, Raghav set out to seek clarification, "Your town, what do you mean? For sure I know you're from Lucknow," he blurted out an expletive.

"I got married and this is my husband's hometown," she informed, fastening her loose hair with hairpins on the nape of her neck.

"Well, well, let us sit, and talk our hearts out," Raghav urged.

"Tell me all about you; when did you get married? What is your husband doing?" he now asked.

"He is an industrialist, runs a manufacturing unit here with which he is mostly busy," she revealed and asked, "But what about you, your family?"

And Raghav told her about his marriage, his wife and his job.

"Come on, when are you going to introduce me to your wife?" she showed her keenness.

"My wife is in an advanced stage of pregnancy and is now at her parents' place in Srinagar for her delivery," he informed.

"Okay, fine. Why don't you come over to my place to meet my husband," she invited. "Come this evening."

He responded at once by presenting himself at her home that evening, with all his disarming naiveté. But her husband was still away on work. She was alone at home.

And then there was scarcely a day which followed that he did not see her or was not reminded of her. He tended to live every instant of the time he had been with her during college days. He didn't seem to want to go to his own home and alone to bed for he felt his body on fire. He saw pictures of her in his mind, of she doing with him what he wanted to do with her. He kept fantasizing.

If you can't keep her into your arms, keep her in your heart.

Katherine Hepbum.

"I have taken so many cold showers that my skin has started to wrinkle like the thumb and finger tips of a dhobi, washing clothes on a cold riverbed, and I know my balls have shriveled. She just doesn't go out of my mind," Raghav kept telling himself to justify what all he was up to. But there was a nagging thought that his mind was alerting him about. All the same, he kept brushing it aside thinking there was nothing wrong with married men to have a girlfriend—ensuring that left hand doesn't know what the right is doing and vice-versa. He thus became prolific in designing pretexts so as to be in her company. His attitude became one of good-humored subservience and tacit adoration for her old classmate, whose beauty and charm still looked fresh to him.

"Why don't you come over for dinner tomorrow? My husband has promised he would be home early and happy to meet you," Rosy told him one day. He saw enough in her face to impel him to take her hand and hold it, while he said his lingering goodbye.

"Goodbye," she responded, with a smile that to Raghav appeared flirtatious. "Yes, there is sex appeal dripping through her," he mentally told himself, and bade goodbye in return, his eyes shifting to her fulsome but taut breasts that seemed to stretch her T-shirt tight to let two upper buttons get unbuttoned, the sight of which made him to linger his departure with a lascivious look on his face.

"Now what are you waiting for?" pushing him with her left hand, she said, "See you tomorrow evening."

The Intimate Dinner!

Raghav reached her place on time, the next day.

Rosy shook hands and introduced him to her husband, "Meet my old collegemate, Raghav," she said holding his left hand.

"Hello, I'm Dinesh. Nice meeting you," he responded and the two shook hands, warmly.

She still reveres elegance and panache, Raghav told himself mentally. There was nothing subtle or hidden about her charms; her beauty was all there, flaming and apparent—the spun-gold hair that was combed with a confining pin to hold securely; the deep blue eyes that were like nothing but sapphires; two lips that were so lively that one could think of some delicious crimson fruit. The lines of her body were clean, clear and symmetrical; it was a body which occasionally fell into splendid poses. She had put on a little, just a bit flesh on her thighs, but it did not seem to detract an iota from the grace of every step, pose, gesture or utterance, he kept on telling himself quietly in his mind, while his eyes kept roving all over her.

And then, they sat for dinner.

"Rosy and I have been happily married for the last ten years," Dinesh told him. "I am lucky to have her as my wife. See what a lovely meal she has prepared and even brought out the candles for the event," he continued.

"Oh! thank you darling," Rosy responded.

Raghav kept listening.

"You don't speak much. Between we two, we talk a lot," Dinesh said, looking towards Raghav's face..." You know what, when on the dining table if husband and wife have nothing to talk, know it there are problems in their relationship."

"And!" Rosy joined in, looking at her husband sideways, "I mean the other part."

"And, what," he asked,... "Oh! I got it now. The second part I seemed to have overlooked," he recalled while looking towards his wife, and then turning to Raghav, "When you hear only the sound of fork and knife hitting the dining plates, know it there is a serious problem."

Everybody laughed aloud.

"So we make it a point to talk as much as possible at the dining table only, while eating with our hands to ensure the forks and knives don't hit the plate, and we get the feel and say that *all izz well* (a la Bollywood actor Aamir Khan in the movie *Three Idiots*). Sometimes we even end up feeding each other, allowing our fingers to linger on in each other's mouth," Dinesh said good-humoredly, as if to make sure that the laughter kept coming back.

And they laughed a renewed laugh, Dinesh uproariously, nonstop, as he went about making a drink for himself and another one for Raghav.

When they sat down to eat, Raghav, however, did not seem to care much about the décor or the delicious food laid out on the dining table. As he pushed his food around on the plate, he talked to Dinesh about the college days and the nice time spent there with Rosy, after gulping down two large glasses of scotch.

Rosy felt a bit uneasy. Her husband appeared eager to know more, while he had vodka with a lot of fizzy water and a huge squeeze of lime, said, "You know, what...? I have switched to vodka. Initially, it was like medicine but I've got used to it."

"Dinesh, enough of that booze," Rosy wanted her husband to stop.

"Oh, dear! It's good company today. Let me enjoy. And then it helps me to have my appetite whetted," he replied, coolly, offering another glass to Raghav and making one large glass for himself."

"You were telling me about your college days"... Raghav interrupted to ask him, "I didn't find either of you on FB. How come?"

"If you want longevity to your marital relationship, just delete your partner from your Facebook friends' list," Dinesh responded. And added, "Even better, couples who are in love with each other, should delete their Facebook accounts entirely to have more time to spend with each other. If anything, I want less information about my wife. I want more mystery and unpredictability."

"Oh! I see," Raghav could just say this.

Continuing, Dinesh now said what he wanted to say earlier on, "However, since you were talking of your college days and the nice time you both had spent there. Rosy, I believe, was your girlfriend. Isn't it?" Dinesh said without any inhibition because all inhibitions get lowered once tongues get loosened by alcohol and when taste of good starters overtake one "What do you talk, darling? Raghav and me were classmates—just good friends," Rosy intervened.

Raghav, feeling a bit odd about Dinesh's extra inquisitiveness, wanted to change the topic, but could merely think of saying, "You said you have shifted to vodka, how come now this...scotch whisky?"

"Oh! I don't miss having a glass of it because I've switched to vodka," he replied, adding, "On busy days, when Rosy and I crave to have company, but have no desire to move out to our favorite restaurant or invite some friend at home, we always settle for drinks (for her only soft drinks or juices) and nibble evenings." And he kept talking. "Truly, alcohol fuels conversation, may be even one-sided conversations," Raghav thought to himself. But with that sort of cocktail, Dinesh soon felt heavy in his head and had a quick bite as he wanted to retire to his bed early.

"Raghav, I am sorry. I am feeling giddy. I want to lie down. Excuse me," he said and placed a soft peck on Rosy's right cheek, while asking her, "Take care of your friend, please."

"Goodnight, darling," she responded.

"There are two kinds of people in every party, be it at home or outside," Raghav thought in his head, "Those who want to leave and those who want to stay on and enjoy. The trouble mostly is that they are married to each other."

"You seem to be contemplating on something subtle," Rosy inquired.

"Nothing serious actually," he replied, "Just this...what to do if you and your husband reside on opposite poles when it comes to socializing?"

"Oh, no not that way. He is a great party animal, but today he must really be feeling unwell," Rosy said in defense of her husband, but from her facial expression, it appeared she was feeling awkward because her husband didn't stay on to give company.

It was shortly before midnight that Rosy and Raghav found themselves alone.

Just then the lights went off. Rosy got up to light a candle, but stumbled. Raghav held her in his arms to save her from a nasty fall. In the process, the strap of her dress gave way and Raghav's hand came to touch her bare right shoulder. His fingers just lingered on in the area around the nap, as if he discreetly meant to foreplay. She felt the heat of his hand, gasped and pulled back.

"What are you up to?" she squealed, as if protesting—her voice low and whispery.

Raghav perhaps was trying to woo her as no other man had, with the innocent affection of an old batchmate. But before he could think of an answer, the lights came on, and he withdrew. And then, he took her hand to his lips as if wanting to feel and decipher the softness and suppleness of her smooth velvety skin. He kept entertaining this thought that brought a sort of a mischievous smile to his face, as if the excited romanticism of college days had come back upon him like a remittent fever.

"What is that smile all about?" Rosy asked, gazing at his face.

"Nothing particular. Just got reminded of our college days together," he responded.

And then, he made a remark about her vivacious personality and charm, to say, "Oh, my God! you still look ravishingly beautiful—just enigmatic, an epitome of dignity and style. Gregarious could be a synonym for you except that it is hard to pin you down to any one adjective or label."

Rosy liked it. She felt flattered by the attention, even though it perhaps discreetly revealed to her the guy's slippery morality to further his own cause just then. The two old friends, however, talked more about the wonderful time spent together. Lulled by the steady sound of falling water from the water fountain kept in the far corner of the huge dining room, which invoked a sort of romance in the ambience, conversations between the two then turned to the long duration of their wonderful friendship. Raghav for a brief while imagined her as a woman full of precise pleasures.

"I know what you want to hear" (laughs), she said. Brushing aside her inhibitions, she seemed to like his romantic talk, and felt pampered leading to a surge of old emotions for him. People with a natural eye for beauty, one may often find that an appreciation transforms into attraction, she thought and felt like telling him that no one has ever talked like that to her. They didn't say *God* unless they were uttering a prayer.

"Was Raghav making a prayer?" she mulled.

Raghav sat by her side, so close that his warm scent penetrated her pores. She felt the heat in his stare and the warmth in his expression. He moved closer, and his heartbeat, under his chest, took up speed like a bullet train, as if to reach somewhere fast—the body catching up much before the head could grasp,

She looked at him in a way as if she could see inside of him. They looked into each other's eyes for a long moment, as if they were oblivious of the fact that it was almost getting past midnight. "Eyes make a fine art of emotional manipulation," she thought.

Raghav, meanwhile, let his hand casually slip off his leg to touch her left thigh, sending a wonderful warmth tingle through her skin. Flutters took up residence in her stomach, and she felt dampness below. Her body felt fragile, like a gentle wisp of breeze. It seemed both alien to her and yet utterly acceptable. It shimmered from his skin in a hot, almost tangible radiance—so that despite knowing she should be distancing herself from him, she found herself curiously debilitated, unable to move or think, or to… And her body responded to it, despite her brain's warnings to ignore the man's advances. Her mind was telling her one thing and her heart another. No matter how much she tried to tell her heart to stop feeling so exuberant, it went right on feeling the way it wanted, it liked.

Rosy caught his eyes, and found a smile, an impish smile. He met her gaze and the connection he couldn't deny seemed to spark to life. She had no idea what to do?

Nor had she any clue how she was supposed to respond. She drew a startled breath, perhaps an admission that the growing nearness between them was not for him alone. He moved further closer, because he felt beyond thought, beyond reason and beyond stopping.

She felt the heat of his hand still on her left thigh and enjoyed it. She responded warmly. The two felt their bodies emotionally hot. It was a sort of a blackout. He caressingly ran the palm of his right hand and the five fingers tenderly up over her cheeks and right into her curly hair that covered half of her right cheek. This caused a wild sensation into her limbs and her teeth felt like tucking into his fingers. His caresses, tracing a line, slowly took her to the edge of ecstasy and back again. A quick impulse that was somewhat spasmodic impelled her fingers to close in a sort of clutch upon his hand. He felt the pressure of her pointed nails in the flesh of his palm.

She felt gradually drawing towards him even though everything in her head knew it was wrong, undesirable and unacceptable—all that and much, much more. But, as if it was beyond her control, she released herself unwittingly, and gradually moved over on the couch and willingly accepted Raghav's tight, warm hug, and their lips and cheeks brushed against each other—lips light as the touch of a butterfly's wings although far more sensual—sending a honey-thick flush through their bodies…

But…! before they could slip into the nakedness of pure and simple sexual pleasure bordering lust, Rosy suddenly yelled: "*Stop, just stop it…right there. What happened to us*? *Gone mad*!" having gained awareness as to what they both were up to, through a hasty mental calculation.

A voice inside had shouted a discreet warning, and she instantly wrenched herself away from him. Her sanity had flooded back, and she felt the tiptoe of awareness shivering its way down her spine. She stared at him nonplused. Suddenly, her expression changed to consternation. Something had just occurred to her—a fall out of implosion. "*Oh, God! What happened to me*? *I have not been like that. How did I lose control of myself*?" she remorsefully shuddered. Her body tightened at the thought.

Sniffing with moist eyes, and then breathing deeply, she sermonized, "*We shouldn't be doing this.*" The panic in her voice called out to her to take charge of herself instantly and she stood up.

The look she gave him—ice-blue eyes narrowed, cynicism tightened her mouth, even the angle of her head as she turned it away from Raghav—reflected her disbelief, dismay, dejection and all that.

Raghav recoiled as though he had been slapped, and his hand flew to his mouth. He felt shaken but collected himself, his blood beating hotly in his temples. Observing her with grim remorseful eyes, he rose noiselessly to his feet with drooping shoulders beneath the heaped up guilt and left, saying to himself, "*I would better leave.*" "*Goodnight,*" he almost whispered sheepishly more to himself than to her, and fled out of the door—all the while reminding himself that no one knows when *mausum* (weather), *mizaaj* (mood) and *mukadar* (luck) can change.

A hopelessly awkward ending to the rendezvous!

A very agonizing thought kept passing through his mind. He felt restless, and all the while the drumbeat of restlessness got louder.

"*What must she be thinking of me? Oh, my God!*"

He felt bad, unpleasant, awful, selfish, uncaring, ungrateful, mean, illogical and irresponsible—perhaps all of them put together. Panic and guilt invaded him, all around. He was full of nausea, which overpowered him as if he had suffered a bout of food poisoning. He found himself sweating, and took out a snow-white handkerchief to rub his face. But he didn't do it as people do when they wipe sweat. Instead, he went to dry his tears stealthily for he was at the verge of crying.

Indeed, he was nauseated with himself.

While returning to his house, it started drizzling. He stopped and wished that it rained heavily so that he could possibly wash down his sins. He felt desperate.

The Remorse and Confession!

After Raghav had left, common sense splashed over Rosy like an ice-cold shower. She searched frantically in her mind as to how did this terrible lapse happen. The pang of pain mingled with guilt squeezed her heart. She sounded near to tears and recoiled in disgust and buried her head in her arms, and cried. "Oh hell, how did I get into this? How am I to get out?" she moaned in her wet sleeves. At once, she wanted to hit herself. Her heart almost froze. She perhaps wanted the floor to open up and swallow her, as if she was Sita of epic Ramayana.

But then she persuaded herself to think that here perhaps was a person who seemed to her responsible for a large part of that sordid affair. She realized that emotional involvement with a friend is bound to create undefined boundaries, where expectations have no set models and could vary crazily, thus setting the ground for misunderstandings—a situation that could be rife for disaster.

"Could he be a predator? A sexual predator!" she thought over, but didn't think him to be so. "Did I use my sensuality to lure him," she asked herself mentally, and thought that most of the men as well as women, just do their own selfish things. "But, I certainly am not to do anything to use my sensuality as a bait and consider sexual allure as synonymous with women empowerment," she told herself resolutely.

However, she couldn't stop cursing herself for having given in to those besotted passions that were outright stupefied. Her face burned hotly with guilt as she recognized the path along which her thoughts had trespassed. With calibrated gestures her dismay was apparent on her face. She felt wiped and whispered, "I wish I could curl up and die! I wish I could vaporize and blow out of the window."

There was a cold, narrow crooked look in her eyes as if it was a warning to her. "I shouldn't have done this, I know," she repeated in her mind, many times over. She saw her thoughts recast her eyes, as a giant movie reel seemed to be playing in her head from beginning to the end and back again, as if she was the third party watching the whole episode in slow motion. She shut her eyes, as if she shouldn't watch, like a bad part in a blue movie that one knows one's husband doesn't want you to see, but one looks anyway. And then when it is all over, one feels guilty and it hits like a stab wound, and one is left with an overwhelming feeling of guilt and shame.

There was, naturally, a dull pang of regret—deep regret for having betrayed the trust of her husband by allowing her passions to overpower her, though momentarily. The pang of pain mingled with guilt squeezed her heart. She didn't blame Raghav, so much, as her own self now.

For her it was a slow, dreary realization, creeping over her like an insect from the rubbish dump. "I can't live with such nasty, nagging thoughts anymore," she told herself, as she laid herself on the bed, breathed a big, genuine sigh of relief—a feeling that was unfamiliar but very reassuring.

She felt as if a mist had been lifted from her eyes, enabling her to look up and comprehend the significance and sanctity of marriage—a marriage she was determined to enjoy and celebrate with her husband, and never to let it fall apart.

And she decided to unburden herself of that guilty feeling.

Lying on her bedside, she drew her knees to her chest to press hard against her bosom, and held herself, as if trying with all her might to keep any part of herself from slipping away. She was not dwelling on any particular train of thought now for she had done all the thinking that was necessary after Raghav had gone away. She understood her mental state because, "I spent many hours dismayed, angry and disappointed at myself. I want to tear away all pretense and come clean before Dinesh, my dear husband," she told herself.

Among the conflicting sensations which assailed her, there, however, was neither shame nor remorse for she now had feverishly decided in favor of coming clean before her husband by confessing everything to him, and not to get bogged down by guilt pangs.

That night Rosy slept fitfully.

Indeed, she couldn't get any sleep.

She was in restless state of mind and body pain, and moved from one posture to another till she grew hysterical. After all, she was carrying a guilt on her conscience. It was hard on her mind, too much taxing. The guilt that had sunk by now into her skin, took on a startling thickness, making it almost difficult for her to even breathe.

Her regret was deep, so deep that, she thought, it would take a shovel to dug it up.

A feverish anxiety attended her every thought in the mind and she, indeed, was in turmoil.

She honestly wanted to confess and make it clean, whatever the consequences. She knew that truth will not make her rich but it certainly will make her free from the remorse. "There would be no repeat of what had just happened. No, never," she resolved in her mind, determinedly.

In the morning, after lying awake for a long time penitently, she felt a piercing ache to go to her husband just then to talk it over to him candidly and honestly about the episode and make an honest confession. "Even if truth can be humiliating and sad, "I knew I could justify my answers," Rosy told herself, definitely.

"But any incautious words could make her husband clench his fists and could lead to ill-disguised fury that could be reckless," she cautioned herself.

So she walked over to him, who was still in bed. She sat on the edge, leaning her head down on the pillow by his side. She initially said nothing and couldn't answer her husband who wished her, "Honey, a very good morning to you."

Instead of responding to his greetings, she avoided looking at him and didn't meet his eyes. She was afraid lest he might view it as an act of breach of trust, bordering infidelity. She torched herself with such obnoxious visualizations. But she never wanted to lead herself into any concealment or deceit, and began to cry a little, wiping her eyes on the sleeve of her gown.

"What's the matter, dear?" her husband asked.

Turning, she thrust her face, steaming and wet, into the bend of her arms and sobbed.

It unnerved Dinesh. “Is there anything I can do?” he asked, the rasp of desperation creeping into his voice, as he saw a new unfamiliar weariness on her face.

She found it not easy to tell him why she was crying, but certainly wanted to have a good cry all by herself.

He panicked, “What’s the matter with you, after all? Why do you look insipid, distressed and disconsolate?” he now asked, anxiously.

She couldn’t reply.

“Please, for heaven’s sake, let me know what is it that is bothering you,” he implored.

Her eyes slithered away, and she looked disconcerted. “Don’t lie to him,” her mind seemed to scream from within, silently but persistently. And she said, “I have to make a confession,” she said in almost a whisper.

“What confession? What have you done? What exactly do you mean?” he asked in quick succession.

She found him watching the movement of her lips intently, and tried not to squirm in embarrassment.

“It’s something very important and personal that I need to tell you, right here, just now.”

He now looked askance and felt obfuscate, bewildered. “You appear tense. What is it all about?” he urged and let his gaze drift all over her body, while she kept revealing to him what all had happened the previous night. She explained that Raghav and she had both been tipsy and emotional, and that she had lost her cool, right conduct or common sense, for a few brief fleeting moments.

Dinesh’s response was atypical. He was discernibly upset; he even felt a cringe fawning but didn’t behave obsequiously.

“What did you say—lost your cool!” inquired he, in a pretentiously smooth and dexterous tone, “But I thought perhaps you and he had…,” his voice dropped with innuendo, and he shrugged and let his voice trail off—the pause giving rise to a hundred silent questions in the mind of his wife, Rosy—making her feel as if her husband said, "I want to see it all with *your* eyes. Tell me more. All that you both did… I mean wanted to."

Perhaps, it was a clever way to elicit more information from her, she thought, and clinched her fingers to keep them from trembling. "It was a sort of a mad impulse, at the spur of a frenzied moment. It just happened momentarily and I snapped it in time," she tried to explain her position, while attempting to construct and wear a flicker of a composure on her face, in an attempt to give credence to her statement, but it came out as a grimace.

Dinesh's eyes gazed her skeptically.

Then she saw him rise to his feet, his face as unmoving as if it had been carved from a piece of granite, his mouth hard and his eyes cold. While she was mentally working hard to stave off her own trepidation, she somehow felt that his heart went to her, despite his forbidding look.

After all, she remembered that they had once made a vow to be honest and truthful to each other. And here, she had come before him with all the revelation, plainly, honestly and truthfully.

It wasn't easy for her, she knew, but for the honesty of purpose to which she stood committed. One thing blazingly clear in her confession was that she was awfully ashamed of her unbecoming conduct and that she had decided to undergo a period of atonement in an attempt to wash off her sins.

Dinesh looked around the room with a mixture of anger, fear and even compassion, all put together.

He, in a way, felt a bit guilty too.

"Why did I leave my wife alone with him, particularly when he was drunk," he thoughtfully sort of kept cursing himself.

"And here she is herself revealing to me all that had happened," he kept adding thought to thought. She could have said nothing about the episode. If she meant to be an adulteress, she would have hid it in the bottom of her heart; could have buried it somewhere deep within herself. And I probably would never have come to know of it," he realized.

He felt relieved and could breathe easy.

Love is learning to Stay Married!

And then Dinesh felt very secure about Rosy's honesty of purpose and her love for him, and he realized that she was protecting him in a subtle way by telling him about the dirty incident. He could see that she was both heartbroken on account of Raghav's predicament of having run into that sort of a dirty situation at her home, unintentionally though, and also being extremely worried whether or not her husband would forgive her. Embroiled in such thoughts, he told his wife, "There is no right or wrong but just a case of one's perception."

She looked at him with relief in her eyes.

Although Dinesh's first feeling was anger, he realized that making a scene would not make him feel any better, or solve the problem. In fact, he would probably make a minor issue into a deep rift, putting their marriage itself on rocks, he realized, and thought one could create a bad guy by looking within, and the best way to find dark motivation was to admit one's own darkness.

He then realized, Rosy perhaps had been feeling insecure about her looks and charm because of the lack of care and attention from her own husband who mostly kept busy with his business till late hours, and thus never spent any quality time with her, which perhaps in a subtle way made her vulnerable to Raghav's romantic attention.

He remembered what his father had told him way back about the family code: "Dinesh, my worthy son, based on my own life experience I want to give you a piece of wisdom, which I have learned at great personal agony and peril—*whenever there is any problem between you and your wife, both of you should sort it out between yourselves because nobody else can.*"

He appeared contemplative, almost philosophical and rather calm. He sounded almost spiritual that moment—in a strange reflective, rather. Than meditative mood. Hence, rather than exploding with anger or being overcome by mistrust, he thus tried to understand Rosy's actions from her point of view. He decided to be empathetic. "It has gone terribly wrong. Never imagined

I could ever get into such an awful situation. Please, forgive me," his wife implored, while shedding huge tears.

"Such emotional gestures takes on meaning. It is only in those heightened moments that the significance of everything became clear. Is it too much to live with so much meaning?" Dinesh contemplated and he then told his wife of his anger and jealousy and how after having spoken to himself dispassionately, he was able to overcome those hurt feelings. "It is said nothing is right or wrong, thinking makes it so," he now told her. "Two questions were uppermost in my mind when I decided to think and understand the whole issue: One, do relationships matter when it comes to choosing *right* over *wrong*? And two, who's to decide what's *right* or what's *wrong*?

After all, every person is a victim of circumstances that he or she lands into at any given point of time. Relationship between the couple, especially, the positive ones, should grow and become deeper and more genuine as time goes by. But unfortunately, most spouses put their focus on relationships in the wrong places—dwelling on the misunderstandings and forgetting all the things they have in common and what they love about each other." Dinesh said to reassure her of his unflinching love for her while taking her into his arms. And then hugged her warmly, reassuringly and said, "Rosy, my dear, you know what…? Charles Dickens wrote, '*Never break four things in your life—trust, relation, promise, and heart because when they break, they don't make noise but lots of pain.*'"

Rosy looked into his eyes, soulfully, into which her husband's esteem now rose phenomenally.

And said he, "Life is some smiles and some tears, but I don't want to see anybody crying. I can't put up with that. I believe, crying is such a marvelously personal thing that I don't recommend it, ever. And if you must cry in public, then cry out of joy because any other type of crying is a sheer waste of time—weeping you are alone, laughing you are in company."

And then he took her into embrace, and whispered, "Don't you worry, my sweetheart! I have nothing against you," and she clutched his hand, warm and mellow—a source of infinite reassurance, as he whispered again, "Rosy, it's just fine with me. You don't bother. I have full trust on you."

She responded, "You continue to amaze me with your innate capacity to turn life around even when it's crunch time."

"You know what?" he responded, "Trust is the foundation upon which all relationships are built, and mutual respect is the mortgage with which each partner pays for that relationship. And that is a two-way street. Then after explaining intentions, Dinesh drove across the town to Raghav's apartment. There he, without waiting to have his request of admittance answered, opened the door, but then apologized for his intrusion by relating the cause, in a manner, so graceful, so frank, so forthright that his person, which was undoubtedly handsome, received additional grace and charm from his soft voice and expression, in spite of the gravity of the situation.

"Rosy told me what all happened. I know she has been always sincere to me, and I trust her," Dinesh said as he sat down on the couch in Raghav's living room, who somehow felt Dinesh's eyes laser into him, which left him red-faced and at a loss for words. He felt so restless that he could barely stand to stay in his skin. Beads of perspiration assailed his forehead, and in a frank admission said, "Let me at the outset plead guilty. I feel awfully sorry for my undesirable conduct."

"I certainly didn't like you to have conducted yourself that way. You attempted to escalate physical intimacy with my wife Rosy. In case she had not been in deep love with me and valued her marriage to me, it could have resulted in disastrous consequences for both of our families. She acted bold and with sanity, and that is how an awfully dirty, demeaning situation had been averted. She has been honest in her confession, and that brought dignity to my relationship with her. However, I can persuade myself to understand it just happened at the spur of an emotional moment. I am not angry. I assume this was a mistake and won't happen again, right?" Dinesh said, matter-of-factly.

"Oh God! No, never. It has been a horrible thing," Raghav assured him.

"Let me call it a mistake, and you know, what…? The word that I refer most often to (*in my work which is also interconnected to my personal life*), for being a vehicle for moving forward towards an ideal perfection, would be *mistake.* Mistake is often regarded as something negative but to me it is only the beginning of discovering something positively fundamental. Being in love doesn't bring the rest of life to a standstill. What you look for is an inland of peace where you can plug in to recharge before returning to the chaotic world. Love cannot and must not be allowed to create a terror zone of its own. The role of love and people you love in life should be to provide you happiness. And where it's a matter of *heart,* there should be no role of *mind,*" Dinesh explained.

"I am so sorry, awfully sorry. My conduct has been disastrous," Raghav said again.

"Now that requires a different sort of courage and determination, to make amends once you make a mistake. You know, what…the most critical thing to remember in the midst of grief is that time heals all. Soon enough the tears dry up, the heartache stops and what remains is, of course, a regret," Dinesh counseled, injecting a positive note.

"Please forgive me," Raghav urged, once again.

"Don't be daft," he replied with dignity. "It's alright. *Raat ghae, baat ghae*" (by-gone is by-gone) and continued, "You know my father used to say that nobody can give a person the meaning of life from outside; it's within him or her. A person carries it within like a bud that is going to flower. The blossom vanishes on its own as the fruit grows. So does one's lower self-vanishes as the *Divine* self grows. Living life in a meaningful way involves flowering your potential in the best possible way—living in the *present,* living *today.* My father used to tell me that there are two days in a week one should not worry—two days which should be free from fear, tension and apprehension."

"Can you guess which could be those two days?" Dinesh asked Raghav, who came up blank faced.

"Saturday and Sunday, most would reply to my father," Dinesh informed.

"No, you are wrong," he would tell them and then would proceed to reply himself.

"I'll tell you. One of these days is *Yesterday* with all its mistakes and worries; its faults and blunders; its aches and pains. Yesterday has passed forever and is beyond our control. We can't recall it. All the money and resources at our command can't bring back yesterday. We can't undo a single act that we performed yesterday, we can't erase a single word we said yesterday. Yesterday is gone forever."

"And which is the other day?" he would be asked impatiently.

"The other day we shouldn't worry about is *Tomorrow*—with all its possible adversities, its burdens, its large hopes and promises. Tomorrow is also beyond our immediate control. Tomorrow's sun will rise, either in splendor or behind a mask of clouds, but it'll rise. And until it does, we have no stake in *Tomorrow,* for it is yet to be born. This leaves only one day, and that is *Today.* Any person can fight the battle of just one day. It is when you and I add the burdens of those two awful eternities—*Yesterday* and *Tomorrow*—that we break down," he would say matter-of-factly, and continued, "It's not the experience of *Today* that drives a person mad; it's the remorse or bitterness of something which happened *Yesterday* and the dread of what *Tomorrow* may bring in. Let us, therefore, *Live,* but one *day* at a time," he would sermonize, and go on to conclude, "The fruits of the actions one takes now are yet to come. In a distinct way, one needs to firmly believe, *I'm tomorrow, or some future day, what I establish today. I'm today what I established yesterday or some previous day.*"

"That is a hugely inspiring thought, pregnant with lots of meaning for living life in today," Raghav now said with wonderstruck eyes.

So let us leave everything behind and move forward in friendship. Indeed, I can easily believe that it must have been a great relief to you to acknowledge your situation to me, and I feel assured that you shall never, never have any passionate reason to repeat such a conduct anywhere," Dinesh advocated, and then narrated a short story to him:

"The story is told about a formerly notorious thief in Tibet, Ben Gungyal, who went to become a great teacher. After renouncing thieving and cheating and after spending long hours in solitude doing meditation, he evolved himself and became a respected yogi.

Once he was invited by a family to their house for a day-long recitation of scriptures. At a point when the family members stepped out of the house for some work, the yogi, who was a tea lover, found that the tea he was served was a bit too weak. Looking around, when he found no one nearby, he walked directly into the kitchen and located the tea container in which dried tea leaves were kept. He decided to take some tea leaves without telling the householder. The act was a result of the instinct left behind as residue of his previous deeds. As soon as he put his hand into the container, his awareness came to rescue him. He became aware of this unmindful act of his and found himself shouting, 'Thief! Thief!'

When people around heard him shouting like this loudly, they came running to him in response to his call. When they saw him, they got surprised to find him holding his own right wrist with his left hand. He told them, 'I have caught the culprit.'

This story is often cited as an example of self-restraint, awareness and guarding the door of senses. That is why saints and seers recommend continuous practice of living life in awareness and mindfulness. You see, if an evolved soul in the story above could lose focus and falter, what to talk of ordinary people like us?"

"You have an amazing capacity to act in positivity—to understand and be considerate, indeed, magnanimous to such an extent. You are, indeed, a great human being, with a very big forgiving heart, I must say," Raghav responded enthusiastically. His facial gestures and the obliged look in his eyes also endorsed his such expressions, which sounded natural, without any alloy or varnish.

"And finally, we need to understand that relationships, particularly that of husband and wife, are like birds—if you hold them tightly, they die; if you hold them loosely, they fly out—but if you hold them with care and concern, they remain with you forever. Broadly speaking, managing relationships and our ability to empathize with others are the two skills that make us a better *person.* Between every stimuli we receive and our response to it, there is a gap—this is our freedom of choice or the time needed to determine what our response should be. Those attuned to the skills of emotional intelligence, are better equipped to make this crucial choice. Emotional illiteracy is basically at the root of all the problems in the society—theft, rapes, depression, separation, divorce, suicides, etc.

Between a stimulus and response, a person has the freedom to choose. There is that fleeting moment—the thin, narrow space. In this, one can possibly check one's self to respond violently based on one's instinct or otherwise. Look at the word *responsibility—response-ability*—the ability to choose one's response to a given stimuli. Highly proactive and positive thinking people can recognize that *responsibility*. Such people can carry their own weather with them. Whether it rains or shines, it makes no difference to them. They are value driven.

If we want to make relatively minor changes in our lives, we can perhaps appropriately focus on our attitude and behavior. But if we want to make a significant quantum change, we need to work on our basic paradigms. It is said: "*For every thousand hacking at the leaves of evil, there is one striking at the root.*" We can achieve quantum improvements in our lives only as we quit hacking at the leaves of attitude and behavior and instead get to work at the very root—the paradigms from which our attitude and behavior flow. Indeed, there is nothing wrong with people except their attitudes. Since there is no *delete* or *reboot* button in life, the only method known to us to reduce tension, is to say sorry—to apologize and ask for forgiveness."

Dinesh's such thoughts of wisdom left Raghav mute, bereft of any speech, even numbed. Everything Dinesh did and uttered was just right; everything he said was wisdom, he thought to himself, and ardently felt like listening to more of what Dinesh was saying.

And Dinesh continued, "I have read that there are three central values in life—the *experiential* or that which has happened to us, the *creative* or that which we bring into existence, and the *attitudinal* or our response in different circumstances or situations. The highest of these three values is *attitudinal.* In other words, what matters most is how we *respond* to what we experience in life. Anytime we think the problem is *out there,* that thought or mindset is in itself the problem. The problem is how we see the problem. If I really want to improve my position or situation, I can work on one thing over which I have control—*myself.* That is all I felt like talking about. Okay, bye. Take care," said Dinesh, offering a warm handshake and left.

His gentleness was not confined to words and gestures alone, for within an hour after he had left, he arranged to have a basket of fruit, fresh from his own orchard, delivered at Raghav's apartment, who felt humbled, humbled beyond measure.

"It had started with a bang—this controversy—but it ended in a whimper," he told himself and thanked Dinesh from the core of his heart about whom he kept on thinking for a long time, as to how graceful and broadminded he has been—a great human being with tremendous vision, accommodation and sincerity.

Alongside, he immensely appreciated the boldness, straight-forwardness, nay honesty of purpose that Rosy had exhibited in coming clean before her husband, who in turn received it in the right spirit, with a huge heart. He felt enormous respect and admiration for this amazing couple, while fully understanding that stories like these otherwise generally end up in nasty break-ups. Not everybody remains unscathed after a secret, and those kept away hidden from prying eyes for a long time get uncovered, Raghav realized, with an undernote of discreet fright within as far as his own wife was concerned.

"An event that had begun innocently enough as a simple dinner party of old friends had rapidly escalated into a potentially awkward sexual encounter. Handled badly, it could have led to the most ugly sort of incident that people come to read about so frequently in the newspapers," Raghav visualized and shuddered, which, for a long moment, led him to think that some secrets are best kept hidden. "But if they ever tumble out of the closet, what will happen?" He didn't know, but what he did know was that usually emotional mistakes of this sort, when come to light, are sure to undermine all the relationships involved, which could lead to festering emotional wounds that often result in separation and even divorce."

The Good and The Horrible News

It is the rare person, like Dinesh, who stops and thinks before deciding how to *act* and does not *react* in such an emotionally surcharged situation. It is a person with far sight and clear conscience like Rosy who acts honestly with awareness and has the courage to speak the truth. It is a couple like the two who know how to give vent to their pent-up or suppressed feelings so as to sort out the misunderstandings or messed-up things in a positive, productive manner, and move forward. All such thoughts slowly but surely came to be assimilated by Raghav, and he also felt encouraged and decided to come clean before his own wife, Ragini.

He connected the phone to talk to her instantly, but was told that she had developed labor pains and had got admitted to a nursing home. He felt concerned.

Next day, however, he got the good news that she had given birth to a male child, through a caesarean section. He felt awash with happiness. It was a moment of great rejoicing for him and his mother.

"Bringing life on earth is the most beautiful gift of God to you. Thank you so much for creating that life, giving me a son, making me a proud father," Raghav told his wife on phone a day after.

"Giving birth to our son has been the most intense and life changing experience of my life. I never felt so vulnerable, but so strong at the same time. When the infant finally came into my lap, I felt unconditional love. I felt a huge sense of accomplishment. I have never felt so complete and empowered in my life. It has made me so much more a woman," she almost spoke in one long breath and he could then hear her gasping for breath. Such were her emotions, simply overflowing, adding flesh and bone and song along the way.

Soon Raghav joined her in Srinagar. The infant was named Rohan, whom he would fondle each morning by touching his cheeks left and right as if in rhythm and calling out to him, in jubilation, and the infant kept responding by vigorously stretching and jerking his tiny limbs and gradually bursting into a giggle and chuckle with his wide open toothless mouth, giving out that faint milky smell, on his gleeful face that was as smooth and as pleasing as a well-orchestrated symphony. The infant gave everyone around unalloyed pleasure.

After a couple of days, Raghav with his wife and child returned to Bhatinda. He thanked Ragini so much for bringing his son to life, for bringing him up to him *nay* for giving him to them—making them as proud father and mother.

Ever since, Raghav kept feeling that if there was anyone other than God who could create, it is the mother. It is rightfully said that of all rights of women, the greatest is to be a mother, he thought. Quite naturally then, kid Rohan, with his seamlessly soft brown body, uncreased shins and smooth pink soles had always been his mother's night's rest, and that rare luscious laughter of the afternoon. She secretly rejoiced in the arc of his eyes, the scroll of his lips and the pendant of his earlobes, as he would tumble asleep in her embrace and in doing so he would tend to broaden the geography of his mother's heart and extend its vocabulary.

Notwithstanding the bliss, both of them were now experiencing in the company of their son. Raghav was desperate to reveal to his wife what all had happened while she was away. He was tossing with the idea—*Should I*? *Or shouldn't I*? He was fearful and was consumed by fright, lest she comes to know of it from any discreet source. "The revelation could mean infidelity charge being slapped on me," he feared.

But he wavered and was irresolute for he wasn't sure how she would take it. Hence, he felt the tendency to push the affair under the carpet. But, all the same, he didn't want to carry the heavy burden on his mind. He was feeling as if worms were crawling around in his whole body that made him ache and be under mental restlessness. The secret he was carrying around was in a subtle way eating him up, alive. His face wore the pale color of an old newspaper lying in a store room, somewhere. Tears bubbled up in his eyes. But he no longer wanted to cheat on her. He felt emboldened by the exemplary conduct exhibited by Dinesh and his wife. "If Rosy, as a woman, can do it before her husband, why can't I, as a man, before my wife?" he mentally went through the exercise, and decided to come clean before his wife. So, he kept rehearsing in his mind what all he needed to say.

And that evening after returning from office he said, "Ragini, I have to tell you something that is like a rock on my chest. I want to take it off. I can't hold it any longer."

"What? What is it?" she asked. The way she looked at him, it appeared as if her eyes were sneaking out questions.

"I trust you will listen to me calmly," he urged with pleading eyes.

In the suspense, she felt a gnawing sensation, as if some animal was prowling around inside her gut. Just then, the telephone bell rang. Raghav picked the receiver and it in a moment fell down from his hand. He felt stunned to get the message that his father had died because of a massive heart attack.

Ragini desperately wanted to know what all her husband had to tell her, but sensing that it was inappropriate moment, kept quiet and joined Raghav in packing some clothes and a feed for her son Rohan and all left to catch the first available flight to Srinagar. Unfortunately, the flight while trying to land at Srinagar airport got suddenly caught up in a very rough and turbulent weather. It started raining incessantly. The aircraft hovered over the city for about fifteen minutes in a desperate attempt to find an opening to land till the pilot felt constrained to flash a caution sign on the signboard. It read: "*There is an emergency. Fasten your seatbelts and pray to God for safety.*"

That triggered extreme panic among the passengers who felt violent jerks, as if the plane was shivering. Children started weeping bitterly, which unnerved their mothers beyond measure. It came to be whispered that the plane was running out of fuel. The shrieks of most of the passengers, particularly of women and children, got agonizingly louder. Elders kept ardently praying.

But immediately then, as if to answer the frantic prayers, the sky opened up a bit and the pilot could land the craft safely. The passengers felt relieved and heaved a sigh of relief.

Reaching home, Raghav came to know that the funeral had already taken place and the mortal remains of his dear father had since been consigned to flames, who had died due to brain hemorrhage. His end was characteristically calm. He had slipped from life into death painlessly, almost imperceptibly. The entire family was shell shocked and were thrown in a state of great grief and agony. Initially, disbelief overtook them. They were oscillating between dazed anguish and hopeful disbelief. Raghav hugged his mother, sobbed and cried without sound—the deepest wail of all. She sat in a corner, blank faced, bereft. In the troubled straits of her mind, it was for her a tragedy of unimaginable magnitude. She had lost her life's companion, whom in his lifetime, she perhaps held him both in revere and contempt, but now it was all wailing time. She sat composite but remote, immersed in the pond of unspeakable tragedy, till a periodic unsettling moan, joined in by other visiting women in mourning, in somewhat a theatrical mode, which shattered the mournful calmness of the house. Soon, she would get breathless and people around would console her that everyone who is born had to die some day or the other. It is an act of God—the irrevocable truth, the only truth of life.

During the period of mourning, Raghav remembered the letter—*A tale to tell*—that his father had sent to him some years back in response to his own note to him in which he had in a subtle way shown his utmost helpless concern for having been asking for money from his father off and on to support his postgraduate studies and who in spite of his own tight financial position, fulfilled every need of his son gladly.

Indeed, Raghav treasures that letter to this date, and often times had been reading it ever since, to put himself on course, generally. Today, he remembered his dear father very intensely and felt like taking out that document to share it.

A tale to tell

There was a huge apple tree. A little boy loved to play around it every day. He would go around and pick up any ripe apple that might fall off the tree and eat it. He later learned to climb up its branches and eat the apples and even took a nap under its shade.

He loved the tree and the tree loved to play with him. Time went by. The little boy grew up and he no longer played around the tree every day.

One day the boy came back to the tree and he looked sad. "Come and play with me," the tree asked the boy. "I am no longer a kid. I don't play around trees anymore," the boy replied. "I want toys and I need money to buy them," he continued.

"Sorry, I don't have money, but you can pluck all my apples and sell them. Then you will have money to buy your toys," the tree showed him the way.

The boy was excited at this offer. He grabbed all the apples on the tree and left happily. The boy never came back then. The tree was sad!

One day, however, the boy returned and the tree was so excited. "Come, come and play with me," the tree welcomed.

"I don't have time to play. I have to work for my own family. We need a house for shelter. Can you help me?" inquired the boy.

"Sorry, I don't have a house. But you can chop off my branches to build your house," the tree assured the boy.

So the boy cut all the branches of the tree and left happily with the wood.

The tree felt glad to see the boy very happy.

But the boy never came back since then.

The tree was again lonely and sad.

One hot summer day, the boy did return and the tree was delighted.

"Come, come, come fast and play with me," the tree implored.

"I am sad and getting old. I want to go sailing to relax myself. Can you arrange a boat for me?" asked the boy.

"Use my trunk to build your boat. You can then sail far away and be Happy," said the tree.

So the boy cut the trunk to make a boat, and went sailing and never showed up for a long time.

Finally, the boy returned, once again.

Sensing that he had come once again in search of something else, the tree said, "Sorry, my boy, I don't have anything for you any more—not even the apples, which once were there in plenty."

"But, I don't have the teeth to bite," the boy replied.

"No more trunk for you to climb on," lamented the tree.

"I am too old for that now," the boy said.

"I really can't give you anything; the only thing left is my dying roots," the tree said with tears.

"I don't need much now. Just a place to rest. I am tired after all these years of great toiling," the boy replied pathetically.

"Good! Your old roots, I believe, is the best place to lean on and rest," replied the boy.

"Come, come, sit down here and rest," the tree urged.

The boy sat down and the tree was glad and smiled, with flowing tears.

"This is a story, perhaps, for every son," Raghav often came to tell himself, "The tree being the parents. When people are young, they love to play with their Mummy and Papa, and when they grow up, they leave them, only to come to them when in need of something or the other, or when they are in trouble because, no matter what, parents are meant to be always there to give anything and everything that they have, to see their children happy. One may think that the boy was cruel to the tree, but that perhaps is how most sons have been or are generally towards their parents."

The young ones at home have no time for them, he rued. They are busy managing their own affairs while growing up. They forget that their parents are also growing old. Then, the old parents come to feel unwanted in their own son's home. They are expected to leave the drawing room as soon as some friend or guest of their son comes in because their presence would be taken as a hindrance, an intrusion and hence unwanted.

Ever since, Raghav wanted to tell his father whom he loved and respected beyond measure that unlike the selfish boy in the tale, he earnestly wanted to serve and be of comfort to his parents, particularly in their old age. He wanted them to come over and live with him and his family. But then he had unfortunately got embroiled in his own problems vis-à-vis his wife. And now the indomitable fate had willed otherwise. Uncontrolled tears rolled down his cheeks as he sobbed endlessly while recreating the images of his dear father.

Indeed, a train of thoughts and memories came instantly just then to his mind, particularly where his dress sense, mannerism and etiquette were concerned. He used to wear shirts that had separate buttoned-up collars and double cuffs on the sleeves, which got tied up by brass/ivory cufflings—a thing that was generally worn by English people, and was mostly unknown or uncommon among natives. There was a sort of rigorous completeness, a drilled precision about his clothes, about his general appearance and gait, including social behavior and professional conduct. He was a meticulous man, in every sense. To stand next to him was to be aware of the sharpness of his shave, the neatness of his clothes, the smoothness of his well-tied turban, the smartness of his well-stitched suit or long-coat or the shine on the shoes that he wore. At the same time, he was equally traditional when it came to following religious rituals. Like his own father, he also used to happily sport the holy mark of *tilak* (vermilion) prominently on his forehead and the two earlobes after performing *puja* (worship) each morning in the designated prayer room. Once when as a kid Raghav asked him as to why he was putting the mark on his earlobes also, he narrated a very interesting story.

It went like this:

There was a Pathan Muslim ruler who at certain point of time ruled over Kashmir Valley. He was deeply communal and was out to persecute non-Muslims. Under his orders a Pandit, with such holy marks put prominently on his forehead, two earlobes *and in the middle of his throat, was arrested and produced before the ruler, who asked him to explain the significance of all that Hindu religiosity. And pat came the answer from that erudite Pandit who said: "The mark on the forehead goes to signify that Allah* (God) *is one; the two marks on earlobes signify the presence of two witnesses to this eternal truth of God being one; and finally the mark on the throat signifies that whosoever does not believe in this gospel truth, he deserves to be beheaded."*

The Muslim ruler was so very pleased and overwhelmed to hear such a scholarly explanation that he at once not only ordered his release but gave general orders to stop the persecution of Pandits on grounds of their religion or faith.

With that impeccable look, right from his well-starched colored turban (*in the skillful tying of which he would spent a lot of time looking in the mirror often to make each crease pointed and* a *V-shape in the middle of his forehead)* as his headgear to the toes of his well-polished shoes, he emitted grace. The turban once tied on the head was meant to last in shape for at least a fortnight or so, and hence it was taken off on return from office and was placed at its designated place in the upper rack of the wooden cupboard, with great care on a cushioned base and a neat piece of muslin cloth spread over it to save it from dust. In cold winter months, he used to wear breeches (*short trousers fastened below the knees*) with long woolen stockings tied with buckles just below the knees and a double-breasted woolen overcoat to keep his body warm. On the feet it was special type of fur liners. Filigreed with woolen embroidery on the borders, worn in rubberized outers to safely wade through watery or muddy streets or lanes of the city that invariably had potholes at many places.

Not only by his attire, but by his total demeanor, he distinctly stood out in any crowd.

He spoke with measure words, and was never interested in gossip. He tended to give out those chits of information rather than have an unnecessary conversation for he believed that most people idly chatter, making superficial talk and said things that meant nothing; and said nothing of wisdom that would make sense. Admittedly, he was a reserved person, and was sparing both in praise and criticism. He liked silence and would speak only when he thought his speech would enhance the silence. He rarely lost temper. Even if he was under stress or had frayed tempers, and his looks would never betray him. Usually, he remained a sort of a sanctuary of calm thought. Occasionally, he would have a musical evening organized at home when he and his close friends would listen to soulful singing of *bhajans* by a musician, who sang the verses with such dexterity, love and devotion that worked into seamless melody. The musical evening provided a psychedelic whiff, transporting the listeners into a world of divinity, who sat with their eyes closed and expressions of complete peace on their faces. He would often encourage his host to absorb, understand and feel the subtle nuances of music and lyrics with their intermingled relationship in the art of vocal rendition, who was often seen lipsyncing to the lyrics of Gandhiji's choicest *bhajans—Raghupati raghav rajaram* or *Vaishnav jan the.*

"My father's taste for music was perfect," Raghav recollected.

He had a great flair for writing and had excellent command over English idioms. His writing was a colorful prose, gentle probing, innovative forms and startling mastery over the language, which worked through image and metaphor. He wrote with a Keatesian sensuousness and beauty and Wordsworth's belief in quietness and strength of nature, which came alive and were perceptibly felt in his writings. He wrote things as he saw them. Realism was his credo. He had to write because it was a compulsion for him to write. He wrote in long hand on paper churning out page after page. Indeed, his writings were a sheer lyrical brilliance, stunning in its visual imagery, fragile yet taut and powerful in its intensity.

As far as Raghav's own training in writing good prose, he came also to recall that when he was away from home for his higher studies or later in connection with his job placements, etc., , his father would religiously write to him every week, telling him all about that was happening worthwhile at home—in the family, in the neighborhood or anywhere that was of interest and relevance by way of information or general knowledge. And his father had coaxed him or rather drilled into him, over a period of time, to adopt this habit of being regular and punctual in writing back to him—telling him all about his studies, college affairs, hostel life or later about his job, colleagues, bosses, family, household matters and things like that. The underlying purpose was to encourage him to write descriptive letters and thus develop his writing skills, particularly the idiom and expression.

"Your letter giving full details should invariably reach me by every alternate weekend," his father had laid the rule for Raghav, and had warned, "In case of default, your monthly remittances for paying college or hostel fees would automatically get withheld till default was corrected." And in case he found any mistakes of grammar, spellings and wrong or improper construction of a sentence, he would correct these with red ink pen and return the letter for taking note of the specific mistakes. "It was a great learning experience," Raghav reminded himself.

Life essentially seeks out balance, he now thought. It is usually in the habit of trading joy against sorrow or the reverse. In that sense, God perhaps is a great leveler. He had only a few months back blessed the family with great joy when Rohan was born, and now he took away the head of the family, his dear father. After toiling very hard his whole life, it should have been the time for him to enjoy the company of his son and the grandchild. What a paradox?

The Innermost Calling!

After performing the last rites of his father, Raghav with his wife and son came back to Bhatinda. Ragini was marking time to get to the truth of the matter that her husband had referred to but was holding back. She was restless.

After a few days, however, she raised the matter. It took Raghav quite a time to speak and in that long stretch, he wondered again whether at all he should come out with the truth?

"I see a peculiar expression on your face which suggests to me that you are withholding something, restraining yourself," Ragini observed, in whose head rogue thoughts had by now begun to swim. She looked into his face and read something implacable there.

Raghav kept struggling for right words. Tried, but fumbled repeatedly.

Their eyes met, stayed locked, and it was as if she was seeing through—photocopying all that was going on in his head.

Clothes could protect him, he realized. They could make him look the part that he was honestly trying to play—but inside he was feeling as naked as a newborn infant and as insecure as a little child left alone at a desolate market place where he didn't know anybody.

"C'mon, What is it?" she urged. "What's the matter? I am getting worried," she said in desperation. "What is it?" she asked again, her mouth forming a hard line, all color leaving her face. The tone of her voice was like a hard slap—a teacher's voice scolding him, Raghav felt.

He turned towards the mirror and she followed his stare so he was unable to look there without seeking her annoyed expression. She kept asking questions but he continued to be quiet. She was getting more and more annoyed.

"What's it? Just tell me," her voice vitriolic. A nerve flickered at her cheek. There was a part of her, a primitive part, that wanted to demand answers to few incisive questions that were teaming, crowding her mind.

"Should I or shouldn't I give out the secret which is as dark as treacle?" This issue was feverishly tossing in his mind, time and again. But he never wanted to clad himself in falsehood, even an impenetrable armor. Such feelings—some of them came, certainly out of fear; a lot of them came out of real confusion; a lot of it was thinking out loud; but an overwhelming lot of it started with his decision to being honest to himself and his wife, and speak out the truth.

From the inner most recesses of his soul, he honestly felt that he must admit his folly and seek forgiveness. And hoping his voice didn't break or squeak or tremble, he nervously started narrating to her all that came to his lips, that were quivering, about the episode, with an apologetic expression on his face, all the while.

As he went about it, he could see Ragini's mood and facial expressions changing with each of the revelations. He saw a change come over her—an awesome metamorphosis from calm serenity to glaring malevolence, and before he had completed, she got furious and shuddered as though at physical pain—there was a gestalt shift in her demeanor, from simplicity to vileness and from passiveness to aggression—she suddenly got into a *meow* moment, berating the woman for being a bitch of a person, a whore. Her eyes closed tight for a few moments, the blood rushed up to her face and two veins stood out on her forehead like bluish steel cords.

Raghav got unnerved noticing her profile growing spiky with contempt. She appeared indifferent, insolent and discontent. Suddenly, she rushed out of the room, banging the door behind her. For the first time she caught a whiff of squalor about her husband, she thought.

He looked bewildered. "Psychologically, most women have a dormant feral instinct that springs to life if someone or something rubs them the wrong way. The most honeyed tones can turn to acid; from worm they turn to cobra," Raghav got reminded of having read it.

He felt her disappointment vibes like arrows. So, he kept cool and only ran after her to implore her to calm down and urged her to understand his predicament.

"There is nothing between me and Rosy," he tried to assure his wife. "But yet I am feeling sorry for causing discomfort to you."

"Sorry, you say! To hell with that sorry. What shall I do with it? Can your saying sorry get back my peace of mind?" she demanded. "I don't need any assurance after what you yourself have confessed to me," she retorted with a sinister, sibilant hiss. "One thing that a woman hates the most is a philandering husband, you must know," she said combatively.

"But let me explain it fully," he offered, pleadingly.

Even that could not deter Ragini to dug in her heels, who now said, "No," shrugging her shoulders and frowned, "I am not interested to listen to all that dirty bullshit."

He sat back and growled, "But you have to."

"No, I don't," she said incisively, accompanied by a withering stare and a snide raise of the eyebrows—the lack of interest was abundantly discernible in her gaze as well as tone.

Knowing his weakness to enjoy being in the company of any beautiful woman, and when he couldn't keep his eyes to himself, he willingly took a long stare at the woman's perfect body, particularly well-honed bosoms; he thought everybody needed a little salt in their shaker from time-to-time to keep the sediments out, and with those sort of thoughts in mind he blurted thoughtlessly, "There is, I believe, in every disposition a tendency to some particular evil, a natural defect, which not even the best education can overcome. Otherwise, why should we have come to hear romantic link-ups like that of Bill Clinton and Monica Lewinsky?" he tried to reason out.

"I never raise that sort of questions, so the answer doesn't interest me or bother me. And in any case, that is a failing, indeed, an adulterous failing," she curtly responded, her voice edged with contempt.

"But, see how maturely Hillary Clinton, who initially wanted to *cringe* her husband's neck, finally handled the issue and salvaged her marriage." He wanted her to take lesson from him.

"Hi! Listen. You are no Bill Clinton and I'm no Hillary," she shrugged dismissively. "I am an ordinary conservative housewife and can't forget that you betrayed my trust. Trust or faith is like a mirror. If it breaks, it can't be placed back. It is now a big question mark over the status of our relationship," she now said scornfully, with her eyes firmly and resolutely fixed on his face, carrying a sort of militant glint in her eyes.

He shook his head, once, twice as if to redirect or recollect his thoughts, then opened his mouth in sheer dismay and closed it soon, as he feared further flare-up, but soon enough realized that she had a point, and could only mutter in a quelling tone, "What do you mean by looking at me with that scornfully piercing gaze."

As if getting refueled, she replied with a hideous crinkling of her eyes, "I am only seeing how sexually perverted you have come out before me—bare and naked even with your clothes on. You have betrayed me, broken my trust and faith, by rekindling your old romance with that woman, in whose arms you tried to find lost solace," and turned her gaze away.

"No, I haven't. That is an unfounded charge. You are unnecessarily suspecting, and making mountain out of a mole. I find it extremely demeaning to constantly explain myself to you. Indeed, it is has increasingly become a craze for any wife to expect her husband to account for the hours spent away from her; why he didn't call her or take her call or the time he was untraceable on her *Whatsapp* radar. It in no sense can be generalized to assume that the hapless husband is unfaithful. Emotional intensity, in an era of intrusive technology, is scary rather than desirable," he asserted and looked at her with an apologetic gaze, as if begging for an acre of understanding, and compassion.

The Blazing Flare-up!

But Ragini had decided to stonewall his desperate pleas. She was past all reasoning. Yes, beyond logic. She stared at him with a querulous look on her face as if he had made a stupid statement.

"Why can't you just leave me alone? Just go off," she now screamed disdainfully at him, as if some red light in her head had gone on like a police beacon.

Although he got the feel that she was in possession of emotional dynamite, and did not want it to explode in his face, yet he persisted and kept trying to explain his case.

But, she broke out with her characteristic heat into a flood of cruel words.

He made no reply; he merely glanced at her sheepishly in the looking glass before which she had sat. In that glance in which their eyes met, it was clear that she was full of hate, and contempt for him.

After going into a deep, deep thought and a massive silence, he wondered, "How have I all of a sudden rendered myself unworthy of any attention?", and seemed to curse himself, while she kept her guns blazing.

"Ragini," he tried again, "Aren't you going to listen to me?" No matter what he said, she would not respond as if her acerbic, pliable tongue for once had gone dead now. She seemed to be ensnared by the train of her own thoughts.

Now he experienced a feeling such as a man might have, returning home and finding his own house locked up.

There was silence and the silence was charged and immense, and within it he felt himself fall and land in the huge dusty pile of his broken spirits. The two were left in a quietness that their room had witnessed never before. In that situation, it became increasingly difficult to fathom who was getting tired of whom? Both were severely frowning with sullen expressions. Their expressions said more than the words, which they perhaps used as a screen to hide their nasty thoughts for each other.

She paused.

She stayed alone in a kind of helplessly amazed state, a stupor.

Perhaps, she sat down.

A longer pause succeeded, and when she spoke again her voice was edged, swallowing the broken glass of tears, she turned to face him resolutely now, her sharp gaze appeared full of questions that wanted answers. And he saw that her mouth was twitching with anger and her eyes were shinning with a startling sharpness of utter depression.

"You have cheated on me. You have betrayed me. You have shaken my trust and faith in you," Ragini kept on reiterating the charge, and then hissed, paused to wet her lips and spat—"*bitch of a woman*!" There was an undertone of jealousy and envy in her. "You know when a woman acts lustful, assertive, makes demands and gets what she wants, she is labeled a bitch."

To Raghav, his wife's such bellicosity became annoying. Raising his voice and speaking gruffly, he just could say, "What?" But then thought it fit to still keep his cool. "Of course, sometimes blame feels so right. You have called her a bitch. You may even call me a jerk, a nag, a thug…fill in your own label. But blame obviously hasn't helped anybody anywhere in any situation to resolve a problem or misunderstanding," Raghav tried to make sense to her, while continuously keeping denying the infidelity charge, and added, "These charges and countercharges are phony, and pettily contrived. It makes me itch. Trust me."

"To hell with that trust. You merrily go and enjoy the sweet company of that bitch of a woman and you expect me to keep trusting you. What nonsense?" She blurted out.

"I don't want to say anything so as not to dignify your nasty question with my answer," he merely could say.

"But, tell me who is she?" she demanded tartly now.

He let the question hang in the air for he felt all the uselessness and idleness of his words since she was in no mood to listen to him patiently, to understand his predicament. For fear of causing any further agony to her, he thought best not to respond to her urgings.

"I asked who she is?" she repeated. "Why don't you just tell me? Why not?" she demanded, grimacing, in a raised voice, her eyes almost boring into his.

"She was my collegemate. You don't know her because you had joined the college after she was gone on account of her father's transfer to some other place.

Another pause, the silence loading like a gun—just explosive.

She was getting consumed from within. She looked hideous, sitting there and making a tearful wreck of herself, while looking at the ceiling, at the fan whirring away and making a click-click in quick succession that kept time to her heartbeat.

While she waited in silence and immoveable gravity, she couldn't restrain her eyes from being fixed at him with a gaze that spoke all the contempt that existed.

The next moment, she found herself weeping loudly Then she broke down and her whole body rocked with sobs, uncontrollably. She was now shaking violently and gasping for air, with heart-wrenching sobs.

It tremendously unnerved Raghav. He could read from her such tense expressions that all sorts of negative thoughts were rushing into her head, clouding her mind and intellect. He felt the sting of his wife's impatience, which made his heart's pounding audible. He couldn't decide what to do. Fear was written large on his face. But he felt that the unstated derision will deteriorate into plain and simple rudeness, if he didn't respond properly forthwith.

Sensing her unusual uneasiness, he realized there was something hysterical in the air which made him feel nervous and in that nervousness he again begged of her to calm down so that he could explain his unbecoming conduct to her, and try and lay her fears at rest.

And, interlocking his fingers, he stretched them and the joints of the fingers cracked—one after the other—making small sound, as if breaking dry twigs.

This trick—a bad habit that his wife often held against him—the cracking of his fingers, always soothed his nerves and perhaps gave precision to his thoughts, which he desperately needed at that point of time.

To answer her sharp retorts, he asked, "What has happened to you, after all? Why don't you try and understand my problem. I confess I made a mistake," and making an effort over himself and restraining the motion of his fingers, urged, "Oh! Ragini, please don't do that to me."

"Mistake? You call it just a mistake." She charged, "It is a sin that you have committed. In any case, mistake is not a utensil so that it is cleaned up every time it gets dirty, stinking. You have always been like that to me, taking undue advantages of my simple, accommodating nature and disposition—always shouting, humiliating me. You have even slapped, and ran after my blood with a knife in your hand. But enough is enough. Not anymore," and suddenly getting infuriated she expended serious lung power to ask, "What problem? You merrily have now another woman to keep sweet company and why not. Go and enjoy her love. It's a story as old as time itself. But enough with me, okay!"

They were quarreling in earnest now, in penetrating taunts, grunts and then loud shouts. And as always Ragini felt out of depth—blind and deaf to the inconsistencies of her husband's reasoning.

"You must understand," he said, "It isn't love. I've been in love with you, and you alone. I really feel sorry for my past conduct. Trust me there isn't any love between Rosy and me. It was not my feeling but a sort of a force outside me that took possession of me, my wild emotions on that nightmarish evening, as if I was intoxicated or drugged. I didn't know what was happening to me."

She reacted curtly, "With an errant husband it is less a matter of impulse than of need."

"When you have prethought the answer in your head, why then do you ask me the question?" he queried. "Is that the way you evaluate me for just one trespass, if I may call it?" he asked, depressingly. "Anyway, I say sorry. You've now no excuse to ruin our happy marriage!"

In answer to his reproachful looks cast at her, she scornfully mocked, "What? Happy marriage!" and directed her slanting gaze towards him, and said, "I have had enough at your and your mother's hands, since I got married to you. Enough, enough! Don't you pretend innocence. I know your habit that has perhaps grown into a necessity—of ogling, going with lecherous gazes after young and beautiful women," she charged him tersely, trying assiduously to give a stern expression to her face, into which he was looking pathetically, and ardently.

As she spoke those words of insult and insinuation, he felt himself diminishing—to become a wispy, insignificant.

The verbal spat continued, which became more like a sport of testy exchanges, flared egos and war of words between the two, each trying hard to snub the other with eloquence in the way harsh words were flung at each other, least bothered about being philistine and disgraceful.

Then suddenly, catching her by her arm, he cried, "You need not be so fastidious as you are, and…" He grappled for words. Then he cut it short, saying, "You calm down and just listen to me, to my honest explanation."

She resisted and didn't yield—peering at him—her eyes aglow like two black charcoals. Now her jaw rippled as if she had clamped down. Her obstinacy further offended him and he used all the force at his command to physically pull her down on the couch, and cautioned, "Don't deflate me. My pride has already taken such a hammering."

She fell, cried and wept, rubbing her palm on the spreading heat. Something snapped within her. The veins in her forehead throbbed with rage. The ache in her head climaxed to a soaring, unbearable pain. She felt as if her head was whirling around, shrieking in a frenzied devilish dance.

They both got on like a house on fire! Two powerhouse spouses making great conflict.

It was something which announced itself; a chill breath that seemed to issue from some vast cavern wherein discords wailed. She tended to blow like a wind, nay gale or burst open like a pent-up volcano, all the time frowning and grinding her teeth, but didn't say a word.

This caused a strange agitation in Raghav. He regretted the words as soon as he had spoken them. An instant before he had been getting awfully angry, now he wanted to go deep within him and weep. He took a deep breath, closed his eyes and tried to quieten his mind. He found himself talking frantically, as if he was recapitulating the nasty events that led him to this insoluble problem. He was in a way putting himself in the position of an observer of his life, and of his thoughts and actions.

"Why the hell did I decide to speak out?" he lamented, cupping his head into his palms.

A woman can say more in a sigh,
than a man can say in a sermon.

Anonymous.

Now she experienced a feeling akin to that of a person while calmly crossing a precipice by a bridge, should suddenly discover that the bridge is broken, and that there is a chasm below. That chasm was life itself, and the bridge that superficial or deceptive life in which she had so far lived. For the first time, the question presented itself to her of the possibility of her husband loving the other woman than her, and the resultant fear haunted her.

Both, however, remained stoically silent, and sat apart speechless—the obnoxious stillness sitting between them like a vast desert or a rough sea. A situation where time does not pass, but pain grows. Though together in the room, it was a venomous loneliness for each of them. True, sometimes the greatest journey is the mental distance between two people, Raghav thought, with haunted fear.

Perhaps both of them had a case.

It was hideously painful, undoubtedly, for both of them.

Perhaps both could hear each other's heartbeats, such was the eerie silence.

Having enveloped herself in an unbearable silence, she desperately wanted something to happen, anything, but didn't exactly know what? She could see her thoughts taking shape in her mind clearly now, as clearly as a pilot, bringing in his craft to land and can see the runway. And then suddenly, she swallowed the inflated lumps of confusion and stopped crying; she got up in a huff, pushed back her chair and walked out of the room, knocking blindly against the table in her haste. As she banged the door shut behind her, she could almost hear the sigh of relief from inside. In the other room, where Raghav followed her like a faithful puppy, she started packing her things, and without thinking so much of what lay ahead, startled him by announcing: "I am just now leaving your house to return to my parents along with Rohan. That is it, final."

Her voice tight as if strangled. Her lips were straight and thin with fury.

The enormity of that threat slid into Raghav clearly, like the sharp edge of a knife.

Depression set in and froze on him like ice on a winter lake. He felt shivers travel down his spine, one after another, and followed her meekly like a whipped mongrel. She took no notice of him. In utter jitteriness, he urged her to forgive him, for one last time. Then acting on an impulse, he almost fell at her feet and implored, "You need to consider first, foremost and above all else, what will happen to our son, Rohan—for a child needs the love and warmth of both, mother and father. One must be mature and not let the past affect the present."

Perhaps, he was thinking also that her leaving would give undue credence to the alleged romantic link-up between Rosy and him. It could be scandalous. It could be the talk of the town. "What would Dinesh think of me? It would be damaging to my reputation in office," he panicked. So he begged of her not to act upon her rash decision.

But she sounded excruciatingly indifferent and rudely brushed his pleas off, showing impetuous determination to abandon his house. "My opinion about you has crumbled like feathers of a thistle blown to the sky. I'm not going to stay with you any longer, no, not at all now. I want to have nothing to do with you in that sense after this. Everything is over between us," she announced bitterly, turning her head away.

"Do you know how much you are hurting me…(he said indistinctly)… Please I am telling you not to treat me like that (his voice raised)… Please stop this now," Raghav urged fervently, while tears kept flooding his eyes.

"You have left me with no option except to walk out because things have gone too far, just rough and unbearable. A marital relationship without trust and love is to no one's advantage," she retorted, her eyes flashing ominously.

He opened his mouth but no words came out and he just stared at her, helplessly.

He had everything to say to her but could say nothing, as if all the words had dissolved like ice-cream on his tongue. He lay in a hush, gazing, as Ragini put her son in her lap and left with just one suitcase.

Raghav's face turned like thunder, and at the spur of that moment, shouted, "If you cross the threshold of my home, I shall never accept you back."

"Who cares? You will get a befitting reply from my advocate now. Just wait," she thundered.

Raghav wept like a small baby.

The Confronter and The Avoider!

If we want to understand why couples keep having the same fight over and over again, we have to start with the way people deal with each other when they get angry and are under mental pressure. The kind of fight one gets into comes from the kind of person he or she is, basically.

Inherently, a husband or a wife anywhere is either a *confronter* or an *avoider* or part here and a part there. It has nothing to do whether a person is a man or a woman; whether he or she is educated or not; whether he or she is a working person or otherwise; whether he or she is a successful person in life or otherwise; whether he or she is a rich person or otherwise, and so on and so forth. What we are just talking about is whether a particular person is by innate nature or temperament a confronter and thus out to *tear* the flesh of his or her victim like a *dog,* or an avoider who wants to *duck* and avoid the offending person. It could also be that given a particular situation, he or she is a *confronter* and in a different set of circumstances could be an *avoider.*

An irrational, egoistic, rogue person can stubbornly act as a *confronter,* whatever the consequences, and only an inherently meek and timid person can all the time be an *avoider.* There, however, can be a rare situation where an innately good, cultured person, wanting to avoid an odd or hostile situation, acts rationally but in the process is labeled an *avoider.*

A person is a *confronter* if three or more of the following statements apply to him or her:

1. If one hates to keep things that are going bad bottled-up within.
2. If one has a short fuse (short-tempered).
3. If one isn't afraid of taking on the other, head-on.
4. If one believes in calling a spade a spade, irrespective of the fact whether or not it will hurt feelings or sentiments, and cause further agony.
5. If one is not bothered about any outrage among family members, relatives or friends as a result of his or her confronting attitude.

A person is an *avoider* if three or more of the following statements apply to him or her:

1. If one hates getting into a confrontation or conflict.
2. If one is reluctant to bring up his or her hurt feelings or sentiments, fearing it might create more problems
3. If one tries to sweep the dirty things under the carpet as a façade to feel *all is well.*
4. If one, for fear of being taken for granted by the other spouse, and getting rubbed like a doormat, acts meekly.
5. If one, for whatever reason, tends to withdraw—sounding silent and, therefore, weak.

I would urge the readers not to take the words *confronter* or *avoider* as either a compliment or an insult. The two terms have been used to describe a person, as he or she is by innate nature or temperament or attitude. A *confronter,* being short-tempered, is like a match stick—always ready to get ignited, to snap at you like a barking *dog* under challenge or threat. By comparison, an *avoider* is meek and timid, who invariably is going to act like a *duck* if it feels threatened or challenged. Like a duck that flies or swims away when perceiving a threat to its safety, an *avoider* simple withdraws from the hostile scene or just keeps silent.

So, perhaps it would be interesting to assume that if one is a confronter by nature, he or she could be called a *dog.* And if one is an avoider by nature, he or she could be called a *duck.* There should be no issues on that because it rightly describes a person's basic or innate nature, temperament or attitude or approach to life's day-to-day problems.

Thus, we could call a confronter a *dog,* and an avoider a *duck.* That, I believe, should cause no offence to anyone. Isn't that right?

And as far as couples are concerned, we could, depending on their individual temperament or behavior, and categorize them into following five slots:

(a) One spouse as *dog* and the other as *duck*; or

(b) Both the spouses being in a *dog–dog* relationship; or

(c) Both being in a duck–duck relationship; or

(d) Both, over a period of time, evolving and maturing from the stage of a *dog* or *duck* into a happy, caring and committed relationship in matrimony.

If we care to analyze the relationship that existed between Raghav and his wife, Ragini, at different stages of their matrimony so far, it should be obvious to understand the dynamics of most of these categorized slots, as listed above.

To start with Raghav acted like a *dog* while Ragini behaved as a *duck*; later both found themselves in a *dog–dog* confrontation; and finally, Ragini, with time assumed the characteristics of a *dog* while changed circumstances forced Raghav to turn into a *duck*.

Now let us try and understand the position in depth:

A couple in a *dog–duck* relationship is bound to have one spouse, be it husband or wife as *dog* and the other as a *duck*—as simple as that.

In Indian scenario, it usually has been seen that to start with, it is the husband who starts dictating and calling the shots. The newlywed wife traditionally remains silent, passive or submissive by and large. But how things would with time shape up, could be anybody's guess. In any case, the fact of the matter remains even to this day that any husband's craving is to gain superiority—the aim being that his writ should run in all familial matters or otherwise. So he aims at it from day one.

Even in this age and space, in traditional societies, particularly in rural areas, a woman walks a few steps behind her husband, and in doing so, she, in a way, exhibits her subservient position in family and society.

There is an interesting story to elucidate the point.

A certain person with a *duck-like personality,* who happened to be a much harassed husband at the hands of his wife, who had a *dog-like personality*, one day went out to meet his old friend after many years of his marriage. His friend and his friend's wife received him very warmly at their home and entertained him sumptuously. He felt happy and enjoyed his friend's company.

On his friend's insistence, he agreed to stay with them for the night.

At dinner time, he was pleasantly surprised to notice his friend's wife humbly obeying all the orders of her husband, who often shouted at her, and she remained at his beck and call.

He felt curious to see his friend's wife dancing to her husband's tunes, silently ducking all the insults and abuses. He felt curious and asked his friend to reveal the great secret of the subjugation of his wife.

His friend replied thus:

"*Dear friend, you know, when for the first time after our marriage, she served me food in the kitchen, hot from the hearth, I noticed that the chapatti* (home-made bread) *was partially burned on one side due to excessive baking and the salt in the vegetable was not to my taste. I felt irritated. A wife who can't cook a good meal for her husband is not worth her salt.*

Just then, a cat happened to walk across to the other side of the kitchen, and at spur of that moment I picked up a burning firewood from out of the hearth and hit the cat with it, to release my pent-up anger. The cat fell dead there and then. I got up and left without eating. That day onwards, I have my final say in each and every matter.

She obeys me up to the hilt.

So, my dear friend, it's a matter of knocking down a cat. As plain as that!"

Having thus learned the secret of subjugating one's wife, he returned to his house, where his wife was preparing food in the kitchen. Feeling hungry, he sat to eat, and when his wife, annoyed at his having stayed out for the night without her permission, angrily pushed a dinner plate towards him, making all the food and vegetables get splashed around. Just then also a cat happened to pass by. True to the lesson he had learned, he stretched his arm to pick up a burning firewood from the hearth to hit the cat, and equally swiftly, his wife caught hold of him by his wrist and scornfully said: "That could have worked only on that 'first' day, not now for you have long missed the bus."

The hapless husband pocketed the insult and quietly ate whatever was thrown at him, in utter humiliation.

Thus, it would be noticed that in the first case it was a *dog–duck* relationship (husband acting as a *dog* and wife as *duck*), while in the second, it was again a case of *dog–duck* relationship (wife acting the *dog* and husband behaving as a *duck*).

That comic interlude should, however, in no way be construed to mean that any husband can be brute, aggressive or inconsiderate and can go about throwing his weight in dictating things, right or wrong, to his wife. No, never. That would be utterly foolish. It would amount to wrecking peace of the household.

"*Woman,*" the Bible tells us, "*was taken out of man; not out of his head to top him; not out of his feet to be trampled under; but out of his side* (to be precise, out of his ribs) *so as to be equal to him—under his arm to be protected, and near his heart to be loved.*"

But, wives also, who over a period of time, tend to turn hostile, for whatever reason, and start nagging their respective husbands, should know and appreciate that such an attitude to their relationship can equally be disastrous.

Husbands who lack basic sense of psychoanalysis and are not ingenious in their relationship dealings with their wives, and instead tend to doggedly be tenacious or grimly persistent in browbeating their wife unending, even publicly—whatever the situation or circumstance—are bound to hasten their doom. Such brute husbands do not understand that a happy and healthy marital relationship essentially depends upon mutual love and a spirit of accommodation and adjustment.

As far as the *dog–dog* relationship between a husband and wife is concerned, it initially starts with small but rigid attitudes or opinions regarding even very mundane issues like, whether that framed scenery is to be hung on the north wall of the drawing room or east?; whether this kind of furniture is to be bought or that?; whether the color of the new car being bought should be white or red?; whether the party be held this week or the next? and so on and so forth. There are arguments and counterarguments, till gradually the tension escalates and then there are bigger and more serious problem facing the couple. The next thing one comes to know is that they both have become firmly opinionated with fossilized mindsets, which makes life hell for both of them, as well as for others around them in the family.

A husband and wife in a *dog–dog* relationship all the time go on blaming, criticizing, shouting and even tending to hit each other—doggedly behavior that seems to come out of nowhere but yet from everywhere. They turn into, shall I say, two battle strips or battleships—all because one spouse, for example, couldn't say *yes* instead of *no* to the other's proposal to go out for dinner or a movie. As petty an issue as that. Overtime, with mental as well as physical exhaustion having set in, the spouses become uncooperative, unaccommodative, unappreciative and they *dry out,* emotionally. They go through a period of emotional draught. They become insensitive to other partner's feelings and emotions. Their impulsiveness then can lead to verbal abuse or even physical violence, which takes place when a spouse is so unhappy and hurt that he or she willfully humiliates and denigrates the other. Thus, the marriage is on the rocks. While in Western cultures there being no inhibition in calling it *quits* and slamming the door shut on other spouse's face, here in India, still most couples, though being in a hopelessly silly and stinking state of affairs of their marriage, somehow or the other, for one reason or the other, traditionally continue in the relationship of husband and wife that is cold, numb and insensitive.

As against this situation, let us see what happens when a *dog* meets *duck*? I mean when a couple is in a *dog–duck* relationship. The *dog* in the husband chases his wife as it were a piece of meat, and the *duck* in his wife runs away, only to avoid an awkward situation. In such a relationship, the *dog* in the confronter tries to engage the *duck* in the avoider, but the latter being afraid or uncomfortable to face the former, both go round and round, reaching nowhere, getting no solution to their day-to-day marital problems. That is how *dog–duck* couples end up chasing each other all around, day in and day out.

It is not uncommon to find over a period of time (*say, in* their *mid-forties*) that most husbands, for whatever reason, get reduced to a mere caricature of their old selves, and are made to assume a position where they just nod mutely in agreement to anything and everything their better-half or (shall I say) *bitter-half* says or does, whether right or wrong (*not to ignore the cases of odd wives here and there*). Over a period of time, instead of behaving like a *duck* and running around to avoid the sight of the confronter, he or she now finds it more convenient to behave like, shall I call, a *friendly dog* with a wagging tail, who just likes and feels happy to quietly hang around, and obediently agrees to do whatever is told. Spouses in such a state of affairs, eventually becomes *fearfully* polite.

But if such unhealthy relationship continues where either the husband or the wife chases the other unending to *tear* apart the other, or obeys whatever is told, the outcome more or less would be a very cold relationship where the two partners live under the same roof but as strangers because, with time, instead of growing up together, they grow away from each other. And then in most cases, over the years, the marriage either ends up in a divorce, or the husband or wife drag on in that sort of listless, soulless relationship.

Now talking of a *duck–duck* relationship, it has been seen that even if one be a result-oriented, an aggressive, an effective person in office, at home he or she still could be a lame *duck.* And when both the partners in marriage act *duck–duck*, there is a cool, calm, polite surface. They never argue or fight. He goes his way, and she goes her way. In fact, in their matrimonial relationship they go nowhere and resolve nothing. Their putting up facades of calmness or politeness can be termed a mere mask. Unfortunately, most people are wearing many masks depending on a situation. They like to remain under mask because they are afraid to show their real *self,* which lives in utter confusion, fear, anger, envy, malice, ego, aloofness and hence loneliness.

Not many couples are as picture-perfect as they appear to be on the surface. They have many creases underneath. Pretense has become second nature to couples who get into such a relationship. All appears to be normal and well since there is silence, but these are uneasy silences. Below the surface, there is turmoil, a sad sense of distance and of frustration over unsaid, untalked, unmet or unmaterialized expectations from each other. Spouses in such a relationship use their energies not to solve their grudges, disagreements or problems but want to avoid one another so as to get out of each other's way and do not talk anything worthwhile to iron out things. They do speak, but nothing intimate and worthwhile is in the relationship. It is like being around each other without really *being* in each other's life. Let it be understood that disagreements and problems are bound to be there in a relationship. And if these are not handled or dealt with patience and maturity, these are bound to grow, which overtime makes the two partners grow incredibly cold and distant. Though living in the same room, their relationship turns more into something like old friends with faded memories than lovers.

The only thing that such a relationship ensures is that in their day-to-day living, they cause little or no damage immediately to their relationship because they tend to push the problem under the carpet, remaining emotionally distant, and hence they continue to live in that uneasy calm, which doesn't bring them to the brink of a sudden break-up. It is something like the peace akin to a graveyard. The love has faded, but the namesake couple, instead of looking for new partners, live a life of compromise—sans the hassles of divorce—choosing to stay in the twilight area between marriage and divorce. Nevertheless, the real issues or problems continue to fester underneath.

All said and done, terrible things get said and done in a *dog–dog* or even *dog–duck* relationships, which leaves permanent scars. In each case, the spouse on the receiving end takes a long time to recover, if at all. So there is a period of extreme coldness that follows. And as more time passes, the walls of isolation get thicker, and then it becomes equally harder to breakthrough because meantime the ego-barrier reinforcements also get into place. It then is a disastrous situation to get into.

Against the Tide!

Can a dog–*dog* or *dog–duck* or *duck–duck* relationship be healthy for any one of the partners there?

No, never.

Because in any of these situations, the relations get sour, and *holy wedlock* turns into *unholy deadlock.*

Better-half turns *bitter-half,* with time.

No wonder, then even the timing of the stork's visit becomes an issue.

Indeed, there are many issues to fight on. In a way, they fight about nothing and everything.

A working couple in a New York city said, "*We have fights every night about where to get dinner from, which restaurant, since there is no time to cook at home.*"

So when the time comes to place the order, they fight about who should do it.

Often, they end up ordering from two different places.

That again becomes a new issue to fight on.

New Yorkers are apparently not very squeamish about doing it in public—they fight in elevators, on the sidewalks, in the middle of the kitchen, in Central Park, at the dinner table, and in the subway.

Thank God, Indian couples mostly do it in private, in the bedrooms.

But perhaps that was in not too distant a past.

Today, most couples increasingly fight even in courtrooms.

I substantially wish to subscribe to the fact that ever since one becomes aware of the term *better-half,* one invariably finds one's self intrigued by it.

Because while anything can be divided quantitatively into two halves, cleaving *qualities* appears inconceivable—they are *good* or *bad,* and therefore one could possibly know of the concept of *better-half* as the perception defect of others, but which undoubtedly projects that which is supposed to be *better* as *bitter.* And then Gradually, over a period of time or even sooner than later, the *wedlock* turns into a *deadlock.*

Unfortunately, in the present jet age of racy lifestyles, *instant* marital happiness is the goal. Couples today are not willing to understand each other or to learn what it means to adjust. They set limits for their tolerance and are unable to accept misfits or misfires in the marriage. Thus, it is alarmingly evident that, first, divorce has become as commonplace as the flu, and second, that couples do the strangest of things apart from fighting for cash and custody of the child. Even among childless couples, often dog fights break out. The juicy bones of contentions are many and varied that cause turbulence in relationship between couples.

Let us take it that everyone in any relationship is imperfect. It is not husband's or wife's imperfections that create this volatile dynamics. It is either spouse's, or worst still, of both at the same time, readiness to take on the other with all the ferociousness to confront the other, on each and everything happening in their day-to-day lives.

The grave risk of being either in a *dog–dog* or *dog–duck* or *duck–duck* relationship is that it not only creates a hell-like situation between the two, but encourages either spouse or both to seek sympathies and love outside the sphere of their wedlock. This possibility gains credence when either or both partners have careers and start coming home invariably late because of one pretext or the other, and/or spend time out even on holidays. And when most young working men and women come to spend their most waking hours in office, they naturally get close to their opposite-sex colleagues, which over a period of time leads many of them into relationships of convenience. It is also that when career-oriented couples find themselves working in different cities for a higher position, an affair develops with a colleague. Thus, office has become more of a real threat to a committed partner in a relationship.

And, indeed, social networking has of late become the biggest threat to marital relationships because it is believed to generally encourage people to cheat—desire for sexual alternative. There is, however, no definitive single answer as to why people cheat. Psychologist Philippa Perry wrote in the *Guardian* (after a research study estimated that between twenty to twenty-five per cent of married men and ten to fifteen of married women have engaged in extramarital relationships) that an affair is often an enactment of some deep, pushed-away resentment, and that this situation may be heightened if one or the other partner is financially reliant on the other.

Thus, there has come up the scenario of, what is called, the *other*—outside the relationship of marriage—be it a *woman* or *man*. Perhaps, it was there earlier also, but rare and discreet. It was kept under wraps, like taking liquor with cola so that world wouldn't know it. The arrangement could allow partners to discreetly date other people while keeping up an illusion of marriage for children and the community at large. So the *other* used to be kept hidden. Not any more, however. For the *other* is now flaunted even as the *Man No.* 1 or *Wife No.* 1 (as the case may be). According to the experts, two to three decades ago, cases relating to extramarital affairs was about thirty-five per cent in India, whereas it has now gone up to eighty-five per cent.

The situation has got escalated in recent years because of acceptance by various courts being favorably inclined to consider the demand of the *other* for grant of maintenance in case of a break-up. The public is engaged in a heated debate over the ramifications of such a decision. It will actually lead to more litigations. What if a woman who has a one-night stand with someone comes to claim maintenance money?

The liberals though would rather have each case on its merits. It is argued that in a long-term relationship, a woman feels mentally married to a man. In social obligations, she carries on the same duties that a wedded wife would. So why shouldn't she be entitled to money? Indeed, she comes with her share of sacrifices into the relationship. When a long-term relationship ends, for whatever reasons, a person finds himself/herself at square one emotionally or financially. Being adequately compensated so as to help the aggrieved person to start afresh is just the right thing to do, it is argued.

However, in Indian traditional societies, it's usually the wife that gets the sympathy because she is already suffering at the hands of the *other.* Now does she have to share her entitlement too?

But what about the man? He shouldn't have got into this business of the *other* in the first place. And, therefore, nothing should be done to encourage adultery among men. It is reasonably argued that any change in law might encourage a lot of wrongs that could be very damaging to the very institution of marriage.

Otherwise, what a married couple then have is a relationship which is an illusion of marriage, and with time it turns into *split-and-wide-open* marriage. They live in the same house but do not talk to each other, and if at all they talk, they don't talk *to* each other but *at* each other.

With lives dictated by careers, relationships are relegated to the sidelines; there isn't time for each other. Life alternates between hostility and occasional peace, till he and she no longer finds each other stimulating enough. Both hardly feel inclined to have some meaningful company or communication. Life becomes a routine. With slight irritation, both fret and fume, giving out sparks that gradually subside and they patch-up for the time being. It is not wedding but *welding* since sparks fly out off and on. The romance fades away with both living like nose-to-the-grindstone weekend lifemates in the struggle of life; they become like two parallel lines, never to meet—couples staying like two war hawks at home, even after having been in wedlock for many years. Although they continue to live under one roof, they act like total strangers while suspecting each other.

I know of a woman for whom talking to her husband has been like squeezing water out of a rock. Moreover, the old curmudgeon had, over the years, patented such a countenance with a derogatory style of talk that it had made his wife's love and commitment for her husband come off like old plaster on a dilapidated wall. It is futile to tell such couples that they must have failed to recognize the need to understand each other in a better and rational way and to learn to accommodate and adjust. Neither wants to know and understand the other anymore—sleeping in the same bedroom, they turn their backs on each other. They have two of everything—bedrooms, bathrooms, cars, cupboards and all that. But they have no time in their stressful lives to share bonding and space till eventually many of whom start living separately rather than coming to be under one roof devoid of any emotional attachment.

In the present materialistic, immoral and without values world with immense chances for infidelity and promiscuity, marriages require very sustained hard work. Though many marriages may not be made in heaven, but hell, yet some of the couples have worked to make their marriage last! People who stray from their marriage do so out of a sense of boredom and insecurity. That is one prime reason why most marriages fail in present times.

It is a fact that half of American marriages end in divorce, of late. There are many reasons for this sad outcome, but one major reason is *disconnect* between what the two spouses expect from their marriage and what the *reality* of married life presents. Sadly, spouses start with the assumption that their marriage is going to be a bed of roses—tender, fragrant, smooth and consistently charming. The fact of married life, however, is that roses can perhaps be there on the nuptial bed but they are meant to get trampled overnight. The hard realities of a married life then present themselves invariably. It is no longer a roller coaster ride. It is far more unpredictable. But despite this, it's noticed that the attractiveness and the appeal of marriage doesn't seem to have changed very much. People who divorce are not against marriage, but only think and hope it could be better next time. But it never happens. It has thus been seen that numerous people, particularly rich and celebrities, having gone for divorce, marry again—not only once, twice, but many times over. So eighty per cent of divorced persons remarry, and the paradox is that average American now has fewer children than parents!

Slam!

That is the sound that one million American men hear each year as their wives push them out of the doors of their houses and into the divorce courts. Consequently, in three generations, the divorce rate has escalated from fourteen per cent to nearly half of all the marriages. But although this *national epidemic* is widely reported, you rarely hear about the fact that it's *women,* at rates much higher than men, who are the ones telling researchers that they are not happy in their marriages.

Actually, these are the cases who meet, fall in love and have a fairytale wedding. Next thing one hears is that they're getting divorced…and spitting venom against each other. Some marriages are like *dhobi ghats*, considering the amount of dirty laundry that's washed and hung out to dry in public. They spill not just the beans but an entire salad.

Back home, India is catching up. Certainly, in the metropolitan cities the phenomenon is fast catching up. The divorce rate is rapidly growing as revealed by the number of cases pending in the courts. More than 1,36,000 marriages take place in Delhi alone every year while some 8,000 to 9,000 divorce cases are filed each year. In fact, an average of ten cases are filled per day in just one court.

All this because we have been hiding, feeding and harboring the five (*shall I* call) robbers, sitting pretty inside each one of us.

They are:

- kaam (lust),
- krodh (anger),
- maed (pride),
- lobh (greed), and
- moh (attachment).

The real enemies are, therefore, not outside. They are very much inside each one of us. And yet we tend to ignore rather nurse them, in a way. These robbers are quietly and stealthily robbing us day and night of our peace and happiness, and are in fact pulling us down to the depths of degeneration.

Of the deadliest sins, anger is perhaps the one that inflicts most. It makes a person lick his or her wounds, to smack lips over grievances long past; to roll over the tongue at the prospect of bitter confrontation still to come; to savor to the last toothsome morsel both the pain that one has been subjected to as also the pain that he or she has subjected others to.

Anger and passion are in fact short-lived feelings, which come to the fore when reason rides out. To be angry is to invite the faults of others upon one's self. If one allows someone else to make him feel angry, he or she automatically allows the other to conquer him or her. People need to either control their attitude and behavior or else they get controlled. It is easy to get angry, but difficult to be calm and peaceful. One who holds back the chariot of anger, as it gathers momentum or speed, is a real driver while others just hold the reins. By controlling anger of a minute, one may avoid the remorse of a lifetime

In many ways, as somebody said, it is a feast fit for a king. The chief drawback is that what one is wolfing down is *himself* or *herself.* And the skeleton at the feast is none other than *he* or *she.*

When we get overpowered by anger, we do not see that anger is like a cloud surrounding us. We become one with it. We get possessed by it; we get deluded; we go insane; we go mad.

A match stick has a head made from powered chemical. Just stick it against the side of a matchbox and the stick bursts into a flame. Aren't we often times behaving in a similar fashion? Somebody says something not to our liking and we get inflamed. Isn't it?

The problem is that most of us, in the present fast-paced materialistic life and living, have only learned to put one's *self* above everything else. We are utterly selfish and full of desires. Human behavior flows from three main sources: desire, emotion and knowledge. Desire has its seat in the loins—it is bursting reservoir of energy, sexual fundamentally. Emotion has its seat in the heart—in the flow and force of the blood; it is organic reservoir of experience and desire. Knowledge has its seat in the head—it is the eye of desire and can become pilot of the soul. Only knowledge then is power of freedom; and the only permanent happiness in the pursuit of knowledge and the joy of understanding. Unfortunately, of late, we have educated people but not knowledgeable. Indeed, knowledge is much deeper than education because the basic aim is to understand. There are many people who know us, but very few who understand us. Therefore, true understanding, empathy, validation and compassion in one's relationship are attributes that go a long way in achieving marital bliss.

But, it is sad that while most people are engrossed in their desperate attempts to increase their standard of living, nothing is being done to increase their standard of thinking or standard of giving. And for the *I–Me–Myself* generation, it is normal to regard their own needs as primary, and have no consideration, whatsoever, for others. They are not willing to listen and don't try to see the other's point of view also.

Almost every day or every second day, we come across a situation when someone says something to us, which is not very pleasurable, or we choose to perceive it to be so. In either case, we feel insulted and get upset as a result. In most cases, we react and display our hurt feelings, which aggravates the situation and as a direct result it causes depression (decrease) in our happiness index. Why does this happen? It is because we have created, got attached to or identified with an image of ourselves in our mind that does not match with how the others see or perceive us, and as result, we feel we have been insulted and we get upset.

Having the power to tolerate gives us security and trust that we will be able to face it, we will achieve it, and we will move on unhindered. Tolerance is necessary for shared living, to be and allow to be. With the virtue of tolerance, we will be in a much better position to understand the other. We will never feel hurt and never get agitated. We can remain calm and smile. But to smile when someone praises you is not to be tolerant. Instead, when someone turns into an angry enemy and insults you, but you do not have even the slightest sign of anger or dejection on your face, not even in your thoughts, that is to be tolerant. To look, to speak and to enter in contact with feelings of compassion, patience, comprehension, love and respect, with a person that you do not have a good relationship with, is to have tolerance.

To tolerate is to accept, value, understand and appreciate. Indeed, tolerance, acceptance and inclusiveness are the hallmarks of Hinduism.

One can have a different or counterpoint of view, but let him/her say it with dignity. Sadly, mostly people shout back to say, "I disagree," and the tempers suddenly rise leading to a fight.

Of late, the sick phenomenon of Internet trolling, often organized, and the inflammatory remarks by few politicians, intellectuals or other iconic personalities, on both sides of the fence, has created a sense of fear and insecurity. If we can't coexist and listen to each other, we insult and damage our cultural heritage.

How then do we expect the youth to be peaceful, compassionate and tolerant, be it in any walk of their life—before or after marriage?

Money Woes: His money!... Her money!

One of the most serious factors that causes problems between husband and wife is money. In fact, it is believed that an accentuating reason for increase in divorce rate is because more and more women are getting employed and thus gaining financial independence. May be correct or may not be.

But it is also said that a decade or two ago, women were mostly dependent on their husbands for emotional, physical and financial needs. Hence, they used to be more tolerant because they were generally dependent. Those were simple times. And today, because of the streak of independence, they are not ready to be in an unhappy relationship. Increased awareness, financial muscle, changing lifestyles and consumerism have made spouses intolerant. With financial independence has come sexual liberation and women feel that they deserve the best and don't mind going against the societal norms to get it. The cost of living life of one's choice has increased beyond proportion. Thus, the couples now have far higher levels of expectations from each other. In this fast-paced world, relationships are instant, so are material and physical conveniences and pleasures. By and large, money and glamor make the world go round. Everyone appears to be focused on careers and smart looks.

Many women do not marry young, opting to study further or join the job market, resulting in the increase of single women in their twenties or even thirties. Young women even in rural areas are increasingly getting exposed to mass media, such as television, Internet, mobile phones, etc., which has radically shaped their views. Hence, an increasing number of young women are finding themselves jobs, which gets them economic independence and in the process many of them delay getting married or even decide to remain single. It is startling to note that unmarried, divorced, separated or widowed, the single woman now constitutes 21% of India's female population. Her spending power has even caught the attention of businesses. Travel companies customize vacation for her, and online retail services, home deliveries, etc. focus on her safety. Society too has started viewing her in a whole new light.

There was a time when single women were pitted. While women would earlier suffer silently through domestic abuse and violence, but not anymore. And rightly so. The parents too are now more accepting if they walk out of abusive marriages and return to their parental home. Penetration of television and of serials that talk of the perils of sending one's daughter back to an abusive husband have helped.

With regard to modern-day husband–wife relationship, Indians, like Americans, need not give up on wifehood. Instead, they need to strain to create more perfect and harmonious unions on the basis of their women's new status as coearners and their husbands' fledgling status as cohomemakers. Spouses need to be confirmed by their chosen mates and to share a profound understanding, based on mutual love and respect. There is a lot to say about power relations within a marriage, and how each partner should foster conjugal contentment.

Unfortunately, however, there is cry for more—to have more money, achieve more prosperity, more reputation, gather more wealth—more of everything. One then thinks of ways and means, fair or foul, to achieve what he or she wants. For example, a desire to own a car. First there is immense excitement, great thrill and craving. And when the car is there and it stands in the driveway, the excitement is gone because when the desired object is obtained, the craving mind comes temporarily to rest. But it soon gets fed up and wants something else, like a bigger car that the neighbor has, of whom he gets envious. There is comparison, be it car, house, clothing, jewelry, etc. Now when the bigger car or house, the designer clothing or the costly jewelry, is obtained, the emptiness enters again. That is why in spite of all the money, all the property, all the conveniences at one's disposal, people mostly remain beggars, craving and clamoring for more and still more.

Then comes sexual experimentation. Couples these days are impulsive. The *I want it all and I want it now* attitude makes it difficult to work on a problem and easier to find a quick solution outside the marriage.

Perhaps, the present society manufactures neurotics as it does wide-range of consumer items—creating more and more selfish, repressed, atomized individuals than Sigmund Freud visualized.

Money woes have driven wedges into the nuptial knot. From self-doubt to low esteem, tightened purse strings have exposed fault lines and brittle bonds.

Couples are unwilling to give up on frills. The slightest strain, (like wife asking her husband to cut down expenses on smoking or drinking, and he asking her to cut down on her make-up expenses) can mean arguments, counterarguments and conflicts.

Infidelity apart, rampant dishonesty over money matters is the biggest issue between couples today.

At the beginning of their relationship, the two partners may not know what they can realistically expect to earn and save. A husband coming late from office was asked by his wife, "Why do you come home so late?" "What sort of a query is that? You know I bring home over Rupees three lakhs a month. When I get paid that fat a salary, naturally my employer expects me to work harder and longer," he replied. "Oh! You want to tell me you are earning more than me," she retorted contemptuously. "No, I never meant that," he responded. "I know this is not the first time you talked of your that fat salary and why do you do so? Just to tell me I am inferior to you," she now charged. "You are unnecessarily making an issue out of a simple statement I made to you," he said, raising his voice. "That is it! How you get into rage often, and want to snub me," she countered. It triggered a slugfest. And the tirade continued unabated.

If both the spouses are going out to earn, the wife invariably wants to zealously guard her own money and stacks it away—though to the consternation of her husband—while keeping a close eye on her husband's pay cheque. And with time, she wants him to hand it over to her and wants to handle money matters herself, leaving him even cash strapped. Generally, it has been seen that in money matters, it is one's wife who defines it. It is she who calls the shots.

Women generally have a scarcity mentality and act miserly, particularly when it comes to money matters. Husbands generally need her permission to spend, be it anything from buying a new shirt to supporting his aged parents, as a dutiful son. But when it comes to spending on *her* own parents or brothers and sisters, her purse strings are open. Women in general perhaps conveniently overlook a situation where their own sons might tomorrow ignore their parents under the compulsive fear and reprimand at the hands of their wives. As you sow, so shall you reap, is the popular maxim!

In jest someone said, "Before marriage, a man *yearns* for his wife; after marriage, the syllable *y* gets dropped. So, he now only *earns* for his wife."

The fact of the matter is that when problems arise, it is usually because discussions about money are not really about money, they are just as often about *control.* That is how one finds men in market places or shopping malls carrying the bags while their women carry the purse. But, be it as it may, smart and intelligent husbands should, to begin with, talk to the woman about money. What does it actually mean to her? And try and sort it out amicably.

Partners in mature and successful marriages come to understand and believe that when both partners regard their contribution to the relationship and the family as equal, no matter who earns how much, they need to pool their resources without leaving either spouse cash strapped. Such couples come to agree that no matter how much or how little money they have in the pool, they must share the important decisions on earning, spending and saving. Smart and intelligent couples, as a defined rule, talk about money all the time and plan their finances together. And the first and foremost rule about money management is no *surprises* and no *secrets.* But where this rule is not adhered to, the marriage is likely to hit rocks, because basically it is *money* and *sex* that rocks the boat. It has been seen in US and other European countries, marriages have ended in divorce because one spouse secretly defrauded the other as far as their joint bank accounts were concerned. Such spouses are not worth any relationship. Honesty and trust is the hallmark of any successful marriage.

The Institution of Marriage!

"Is the Institution of Marriage cracking up under the stress and strain of present-day hassle of living a married life? Be it love marriage or arranged!"

And if so, why?"

No one has all the answers. But almost everyone has some or the other answer.

Of late, however, elderly, including widowers or spinsters, have to beat their loneliness, and have been increasingly feeling the need for human relationships and sexual intimacy by getting married again as they hold that it has nothing to do with age. Rupert Murdoch, executive chairman of News Corporation, and former supermodel, Jerry Hall's marriages have provoked many kinds of jabs but for a growing number of Indians are embracing *silver-shaadis* and relationships, and such news has resonated with hope. At eighty-four and fifty-nine, Murdoch and Hall, respectively, have become the poster couple for a postmenopausal, post-mid-life crisis, post-happily ever after life, because at that advanced age a couple is much more relaxed, much more calmer and their expectations are not at all romantic (read unreal). They basically are conscious of the fact that they don't have much time on their side and hence they really make an effort to make each moment matter. If more people lived in the moment, relationships would be better, but that doesn't quite happen when people are younger.

But it also is a matter of fact that such a sanity is mostly gained only after one has tied knots one after the other—moving on from one to another in the hope that it could be better next time. Murdoch, for example, married the fourth time. Another example is that of Bollywood actor Kabir Bedi, having been married thrice earlier, he tied the knot once again on his seventieth birthday recently with his long-time partner Parveen Dusanj.

In that context, this satirical piece is interesting:

Two men, one American and an Indian, were sitting in a bar drinking.

The Indian man said to the American, "You know my parents are forcing me to get married to this so-called homely girl from a village in India whom I haven't met or seen even once."

Back home, we call this arranged marriage. I don't want to marry a woman whom I never ever have met, dated and loved... I told them that openly. My parents are furious and now I have a hell lot of family problems." The American said, "Talking about love marriages... I'll tell you my story.

I married a widow, a few years older to me, whom I deeply loved and dated for five long years.

After a couple of years, my father fell in love with my stepdaughter and married her, so my father became my son-in-law and I became my father's father-in-law.

Legally now my that stepdaughter is my stepmother and her mother, that is, my wife, has become my grandmother.

More problems occurred when I had a son. My son is my father's brother-in-law and while he is my uncle also. Situations turned worse when my father had a son from his second marriage.

Now my father's this son, my brother, is at the same time my grandson.

Ultimately, I have become my own grandfather and I am my own grandson.

And here you are telling me that you have family problems because of arranged marriage..."

Before the American could finish...the Indian just fainted.

We need to understand that marriage, be it love or arranged, is that sacred institution where, as the saying goes, two people become one. Yes, post-marriage, two distinct individuals are known as a *couple,* one entity. But in case the couple fails to appreciate and respect the individuality of one another, they may end up trying to dominate the other resulting in one partner ending up as just an extension of the other, which we have seen happening in *dog–duck* relationship.

Losing one's identity and getting reduced to some sort of a doormat is one of the most common post-marital problems faced by most couples.

The problem begins in the honeymoon phase of the relationship when one partner or both in their own time and space feel a strong need to do everything to please the other so as to make a lasting impression. Therefore, each one tries to display all the nice and decent qualities, proper etiquette and mannerisms that each thinks would please the other. Both try to pose as *perfect husband* and *perfect wife.* But this is not their real self but a mask, a facade. Hence, over a period of time, the real self is bound to show up. That gradually then brings in disappointment or dejection. They no more find each other pleasing or charming because what they had seen of each other initially, and which they had expected to last, does not. Sadly, in today's fast-paced world, relationships are instant, so are material and physical pleasures. Nobody has the time and patience to cement the marriage. It is said that the problem is that most men don't want any problems in their married lives. But that in itself is the greatest problem they face. With love comes war, as they say, especially when it is a classic situation of charges and countercharges.

As a jilted lover put it, out of vendetta, raillery or jest (whatever): "Basically in every girl's life there comes a time when she feels she must have someone at her beck and call—to serve as driver, a servant, a bodyguard to escort and one who carries a bunch of credit/debit/ATM cards. Common sense is that most girls can't afford all that. So the best thing they do is to find a boyfriend and if he foots the bill, he graduates to become the husband, better still a good husband. If this works to her satisfaction, fine, otherwise it is quits in most modern-day feminist situations where equality, liberty, individuality and personal freedom are uppermost."

Isn't it then hard to have a lasting relationship in marriage, be it arranged or love. As someone said, *Oh, my God! I don't have time for making love to my wife,* because the bad stuff—the tiffs, the disagreements, the irritability, the misunderstandings, the suspicions, the undue demands and expectations from one another, the anger and tendency to blow it out and what not—seems to take up more time. Naturally it's the good stuff that gets squeezed out.

So here is the question to those who once upon a time loved each other so dearly and took vows to stay together in the relationship of husband and wife: *If you don't have much time for your spouse, how much time do you have for misunderstandings, anger, shouting at each other, and last but not the least—fights?*

Indeed, following marriage, the excitement of a honeymoon is unparalleled—it's time for love, memories, fantasies and togetherness.

A certain researcher in ancient history once explained as to why *honeymoon* is called honeymoon This is what he wrote: The good, old lore has it that when a man married a woman, he would take her to a different place away from other men; where no any other man could get near to her except him, for a period of four weeks or so, coinciding with the cyclic period of menses of his wife, at the end of which, flow of menstrual blood stopped.

And as it became clear that she got pregnant, the husband would be sure that she was carrying his child only and nobody else's.

But that was then.

In most marriages now, the element of suspicion of infidelity perhaps comes in-built. In the present world of illimitable chances of infidelity and promiscuity, relationships invariably come under the scanner. Therefore, a longer and a more expansive honeymoon, than the cyclic period of menses, is perhaps a must for modern-day couples because in increasing number of cases it has been seen that marriage ends where honeymoon ends. A glaring case was recently reported in a daily newspaper where a Lucknow couple flying back from their honeymoon in Goa had such a massive fight onboard, that during a stopover at Patna, the husband just walked off the plane in a huff, leaving behind the deserted, desolate, hapless wife.

Whosoever said relationship in matrimony is easy was perhaps lying. The beginning is, indeed, fun and exciting. First comes marriage, then the honeymoon…then at its heels the divorce. It is real difficult to keep romance alive after the initial rosy days are over. Indeed, as per a recent newspaper report, post honeymoon divorce syndrome has hit Delhi phenomenally. Cases of honeymoon fights resulting in separation has seen a 30% increase during the year 2015, and not just with those in arranged marriages, even those who marry for love. And most of these cases are direct results of upbeat lifestyle, impatience or just mood swings causing unpleasant experiences during honeymoon, such as, "*Heavy drinking by either or both the partners and getting intimate to reveal their past social misadventures; husband going dancing with another woman while wife* is *made to sit in the restaurant; husband's philandering ways and wife's possessiveness; he liking to talk about sports and she wanting to talk about cinema or cooking; wife receiving too many calls from her parents or relations about her welfare and safety, that causes irritation to her husband, etc.* By the time they return home, the relationship seems to have reached its nadir with differences cropping up because of ego issues, leading to rage and fights. With the piling up of domestic irritants, it is then natural to stare into the abyss, and the twosome decide to call it quits.

Husbands mostly do not have the ingenuity to change with changing times. They generally tend to remain what they traditionally have been, by and large—suspicious by nature. They are prone to anger, even violence and aggression, want to dominate, till he is made to fall flat on his face because of obstinate attitude.

Any husband anywhere is fiercely possessive and narrow minded when it comes to one's own wife. His head is full of the *perfect wife,* who massages his ego, looks good herself, is nice to his family and tosses a salad for him when he is back home…someone who fits the tagline *neighbor's' envy, owner's pride.*

But instead of having his eyes adoringly fixed on his wife, he invariably lets them wander and go grazing on other beauties around whom clothing generally has got reduced to an extent that it has come to expose their navels, backs, cleavages and thongs. Men, in general, have something inside them either chemically or instinctively that causes their eyes to rove around. At a recently held LitFest in Delhi, a noted filmmaker was asked about the deification of women and their beauty in his films. He took head on the suggestion of this being sexist. "I'm sexist. I love sex. I love women," he said. "I do feel that beauty of women is the greatest creation of God." He said all this notwithstanding the fact (as per his own public admission) that he was slapped by his former wife when he suggested that her birthday wasn't an event important enough to celebrate.

Nevertheless, ogling has perhaps assumed gigantic proportions and dimensions in these fast-changing sexist times. Most middle-aged and even comparatively old men with wrinkles around are desperately trying to look young and fresh. Or else why should they, like women, be spending lots of time and money at beauty parlors, getting hair dyed, facials and other body treatments done. Whether one is young or old, rich or poor, handsome or otherwise, a saint or a sinner—one does ogle and ogles as much as one can. A college-going youth ogles unabashedly and amorously, which goes to the brink of eve teasing; a young man ogles discreetly in office or market place; an elderly man ogles in a manner as if he is not indulging in any such otherwise syrupy exercise; an old man ogles as if he is appreciating God's creations. A rich man ogles with an evil or immoral eye with a desire to have her in his bed. A poor man ogles with a huge sigh. A modern-day high-profile spiritual *Guru,* too, wants to be surrounded by young beauties as disciples. A sinner, of course, has no shackles or inhibitions to ogling or even attacking her chastity and does it fearlessly, leading to rising cases of onslaughts on career-driven young girls and women, particularly—anywhere in market places, buses or radio-taxis in the late hours. The scene, of late, has gone awfully dirty and dangerous, since juveniles are increasingly getting into this rut while the society at large is busy debating the issue of their legal responsibility.

The fact of the matter, however, is that the role of a modern wife has changed, and changed drastically. Her aspirations are no longer confined to home and hearth. She is mobile. She is seen everywhere. Her expectations are now far more demanding, exacting and vast. Every career path is now open to her and sky is the limit. The most significant victory wrested by the woman of today is the *freedom to choose.* She can be whatever and whoever she wants to be. The modern working woman is faced with a complex life today. She is juggling her career, home, raising kids and looking after other needs of her family. This is no mean task. For any working woman, it, indeed, is very hard to effectively manage one's personal, family and professional life, in spite of a hostile atmosphere inside and outside, mostly. Trying to be a devoted wife, a loving mother, caring daughter-in-law and what not is certainly a daunting job. The situation, undoubtedly, creates stress, and on top of it, is her almost desperate bid to forge ahead particularly when it comes to career growth with an eye on earning more money.

It must be admitted that the relationship between man and woman is essentially an artificial one. Researchers have found that men regularly seek a loving partner who is physically attractive and healthy, while women tend to opt for a partner with status and resources as well as someone who is educated, suitably employed, dependable and intelligent. Since there are no blood ties, no biological bonds, it is essentially two adults, often complete strangers from two different backgrounds—social, cultural, economic, ethnic—committing themselves to a life together in wedlock. It is as good or as bad as a gamble. The process of discovery that then sets in might lead to some pleasantly happy or horrifyingly unhappy conclusions. In worst cases there are too many discussions on trivial issues, such as the distance between Delhi and Mumbai or whether to go there in first class or economy class. Problems could be on trivial matter—he wants to buy a new car, but she insists driving the old one; he wants to have a peg or two of whisky daily, but she puts her foot down; he wants to have a smoke before going to bed, but she objects; she wants to read a book before going to sleep, he puts off the light; she turns her back on him while going to bed together, but he wants her to hug him—the list is endless, really—all ending up in arguments and bitter exchanges, which end up into very bad experiences.

One or both partners in a relationship often say things that they later regret—whether it is placing blame on one or the other for something that isn't an intentional fault or calling a malicious name or abusing each other or their parents in the heat of a tense moment. While it is generally important to speak one's mind and be honest, there are also times when biting one's tongue and taking stock before saying something one doesn't mean actually. Indeed, communication is key to healthy relationship. But some things are best left unsaid when tensions are building up. It is best to avoid universal statements, such as *You always behave nasty* or *You think you only are sane* or *You are mostly busy on your mobile—whom do you keep talking to* or the like, because such bald statements are rarely true and just inflame a situation.

A husband and wife are, indeed, two halves of the whole and, therefore, they need to make their corners rounded, even when these sometimes do not so that gaps through which extraneous issues may fly in like insects in a hot humid evening, are plugged. It shouldn't, however, be construed to mean that they both have to use the same track or path. Each can run alongside the other—helping, caring, supporting, forgiving and above all trying to adjust to each other's failings more than the strengths through mature understanding of each other's typical traits or temperamental volatility. They shall then begin to understand the rudiments of accepting, of loving each other unconditionally and of letting be. So do your relationship a favor and communicate any small grudge or complaint before resentment builds up and one or the other partner starts shouting. A little bedroom reading is alright but don't bring your laptop into bed with you. Don't forget the little things—a simple bouquet surprise off and on, depending on an occasion, or preparing a hot cup of tea/coffee for the other while he/she is still in bed, or preparing a sumptuous breakfast on a holiday, or helping in the kitchen—these can go a long way in sparking passion. No matter how much a couple is in love or for how long have they been in a perfect relationship, it is just never enough. There are times when their love, trust, faith, patience and belief are tested time and beyond. And it is then that a couple has to maintain certain protocols to save their relationship from wear and tear. Relationships are synonymous with warm feelings and contentment. For a healthy relationship, it is essential to have a partner who can stand by his/her partner's side and survive the test of time.

Young couples must know that the time-tested edifice of marriage is mutual understanding, adjustment, trust and compatibility. Compatibility does not mean being like butter in coffee, whereas the combination is bread and butter, coffee and sugar. That goes to show if eatables or things or people are compatible, one can have the taste and flavor, otherwise it is going to be obnoxious. Unfortunately, in the present jet age of racy lifestyles, *instant* marital happiness is the goal. Couples today are not willing to understand each other or to learn what it means to adjust. They set limits for their tolerance and are unable to accept misfires in the marriage.

A happy and peaceful marriage in the present age and time, therefore, seems like a mirage. Most are hitting the rock before it has taken off. Few are healthy, most are sick. The best way to maintain a relationship that is positive and healthy is that each partner should respect each other's individuality; develop and keep mutual trust and understanding in which each partner provides adequate space to the other.

Lebanese poet–philosopher Kalil Gibran in the *The Prophet* has beautiful advice to offer to couples with reference to detachment of relationships:

"Let there be spaces in your togetherness and let the winds of the heavens dance between you. Love one another but make not a bond of love. Let it rather be a moving sea between the shores of your soul. Sing and dance together but let each one be alone. Stand together yet not too near together, for the pillars of a temple stand apart and the oak tree and cypress grow not in each other's shadow."

Certainly, the commitment of the older generation, who were determined to nourish and sustain their marriage, come what may, is utterly lacking in the present generation. A marriage was for keeps—for better or for worse. People had conditioned themselves to adjust and compromise. The attitude was to make the marriage work, in any way. Our parents and their parents were more adaptable to adjustment since mostly they got married at much younger and impressionable age. They had immense levels of commitment, which could nurture the conjugal relationship.

Currently, marriages take place when a person is already in their thirties or even forties, by which time the spirit or willingness to adjust and accommodate has already taken a beating in facing vagaries of today's competitive life and living. Expectations of the two partners in husband–wife relationship have become so huge and unrealistic that even if you were to marry God himself, he would only fail you. A typical thought pattern of couples today is *Why should I compromise? I too want a life of my own choice. It's my way or the highway.*

What has changed is couple's attitude and the level of tolerance? They have come to believe *If I'm not getting what I desire from the relationship, why should I be in it?* Their relationships have become like *fast foods*—short, crisp, seemingly tasty, but unhealthy. Today, couples are more open about the difficulties they face in their relationships and also about their sexuality. They have become more experimental. Living in a compromised marriage is not acceptable any more to them, even though the situation leads to higher levels of stress.

Such couples do not wish to understand that the fundamental aspect in their relationship is that each one of them has needs, which require to get fulfilled. The needs may be physical, economic, social, emotional or whatever, and if these needs don't get satisfied, the relationship is bound to get soured. Then a distinct sense of incompleteness arises. Basically, one needs a relationship because he or she wants to be happy. Or it could be said that each is trying to use the other as a source of happiness.

If one enters into a relationship, trying to squeeze happiness out of somebody, and the other partner also aims at doing the same, it would be getting into a some sort of business-like arrangement. That sort of a relationship could be very painful, because essentially each partner would be acting shallow and selfish—without any commitment. Hence, the recourse is *live-in relationships.*

Living-in, Older than Marriage

As a phenomenon, *live-in relationships* between men and women are older than the institution of marriage, which came much later in the evolution of human civilization.

However, once marriage got wider social and legal sanction, society started viewing *live-in relationships* with disapproval.

In fact, centuries ago when men and women were attracted to each other, society didn't permit them to have sex indiscriminately, or publicly. It, however, did in a given situation, but social order frowned on sex out of marriage. In fact, the only precondition was to marry. Unfortunately, in the present time and age, due to a variety of socioeconomic reasons, all kinds of relationships are considered permissible, particularly in American society. Or has it spread out everywhere in the globe among educated and economically independent men and women?

So, in today's modern jet age, even in our own country, a peculiar notion is gaining ground among most sections of the upwardly mobile boys and girls, perhaps out of their strange sense of vanity that they verily hope will lead them to their quest for identity and independence, to want to hang on to a few girls or boys at a time and, like in the West, even want to have the liberty to live together under one roof—*live-in relationship.* Deciding to move in with one's lover is an important decision. Often people find that after dating someone for a while and before taking the big plunge of marriage, they would like to spend some time under the same roof to see how well they get along.

However, in recent years, there is a growing concern that online dating has reduced the ability of users to devote themselves to one partner due to the shopping-like experience it creates. When you buy something, it's novel, and when you're done with it, you dispose it off. Hence, commitment in such relationships is a far cry.

Ostensibly, it is said, the intention is to be able to understand and know each other better before consenting to get married formally, or just part ways, otherwise. The first few months or so of sharing the same space can be great fun. One would love to be able to come home to one's partner. But, slowly either one or both will also discover the negative traits of the other. They may like to put up with each other's annoying habits or messy ways, but soon enough the cool is lost. Lots of people then choose never to marry, and they maintain a life partner outside wedlock. So why should they feel the need to marry? But those who do marry each other after a live-in relationship, subsequently come to grieve when they compare their sex lives before and after marriage. And most eventually then drift in opposite directions.

A deal that makes sense to such type of people, whose number is growing, is to *date* instead of getting into a matrimonial bond. They, sadly though, believe it is better to be *single* and *fulfilled* rather than *committed* and *incomplete.*

I love you, they say to each other.

Actually, they only love good, free life, without any sort of commitment, with an eye on each other's money.

It's like meaning: "*If your money was to go away, so would I. After all, I can't live on love and fresh air," or, if when your beauty fades, I need an out. All, I need is stimulation.*"

The fact of the matter is that when a relationship shifts into the *living together* phase, it gradually becomes difficult to maintain the excitement spark that existed in the initial stages of courtship. There then is tendency to treat each other as roommate instead of romantic partners, and the flirty, sexy vibes go cool. What then takes place is to charge and counter charge: you don't close cabinets; you don't clean the bathroom; you leave the kitchen in a total mess; you don't make the bed; why did you not buy the groceries when returning from office and *when* exactly are the dishes going to be done? Nothing screams *unsexy* like nagging each other over housework.

Against such a backdrop, it is unfortunate, in the name of so-called, right to freedom, the courts have found nothing wrong with young boys and girls living together under one roof as would a husband–wife do.

They enjoy the live-in company of each other in all respects (*whatever that conveys*) and yet do not have to undertake any responsibility, whatsoever, of each other, since in the eyes of law they can't be treated in the relationship of *husband–wife*. This gives them space, minus the commitment, which is like having their cake and eating it also. Singlehood is now accepted as a choice one makes, and the advantages they look at in being a *loner*, for the time being, are:

Flirt with as many friends from the opposite sex, without having to be defensive or answerable.

- Need not bother about one's partner's mood swings.
- Need not worry about a suspicious husband or a jealous boyfriend while partying in pubs.

Today's boys and girls mostly have reduced match-making and selection process to a sort of regimented drill—seeing, meeting and dating one after the other, at a times over a period of months or even years before settling for someone. Thus, we have of late come to see socially unconventional man–woman relationships.

However, the *marriage* was and shall continue to be a pivotal institution.

But yes, in earlier times, marriage happened to families. It was an institution with set traditions, conventions and rules, which families followed and conformed and the *boy* and *girl* were immature and not fully realized individuals but fragments of the family tree, twigs lacking any independent existence and, therefore, did everything that they were told to do by their elders. They were asked to get married and then to expect love to happen to them. Now in this present-day, new-age marriage follows dating, love making or even live-in relationship. In improved modern Indian wedding, everybody, not just the bride and groom, perhaps get married. Or so it seems, because the scale at which the event is pitched has gone haywire where families still come together not so much in tradition and memory as in celebration in a world of mass consumption that enacts fantasies of grandiloquence. Indian's love for drama and spectacle has led to a unique phenomenon. It is not only enough for the groom and bride to be seen but also they must be packaged as romantically dramatic and entertainment content. The most striking change is the introduction of choreography in which the lead pair, the *groom* and *bride*, take the center stage without any trace of shyness and plan and organize every bit of the wedding celebrations themselves.

The latest fad of new-breed crazy couples is to act out of a scripted romance, record every moment, including capturing passionate love, emotions and drama of their wedding by professional photographers, like never before. They say marriages are made in heaven—perhaps the view from the sky is better too. That may explain the new trend of nuptial proceedings being recorded by drones, buzzing over the heads of guests. "A wedding is a time to spend," as cash-rich parents believe while solemnizing the wedding of their wards. And naturally, the newlyweds clamor for exotic shots. They want to shoot while enjoying the ecstatically erotic moments in repetitive montages of their love making and even sex during honeymoon—live. Such newlywed couples, apparently compatible, basically want a cinematic feel and hence agree on capturing everything in the bedroom. The wedding today is a public screening of private fantasy with every element amplified. In its craving for specialness, the imagination is cinematic—and Bollywood is everywhere. The value of a photo shoot lies in special, intimate moments, which the couple cannot themselves record. A memory is the most beautiful thing one spouse can give to the other; they hold and hence engage professional photographers who can capture that perfectly. It is like *mnemonics* aimed to aid the couple *reminisce* over a moment from the past. It is like a time machine with which the couple can travel back to those special moments.

And yet, what is witnessed is ever-increasing number of failed, broken marriages, leading to ever-increasing cases of divorce. After all a perfect marriage should have commitment with depth and substance, not just shallow glaze, showbiz and glitter.

No wonder the old moralists and purists are made to behave with servility, who cringe while the new-generation lads and lasses have it all and laugh it away.

The Fortress called Wife!

However, the fact of the matter is that every situation has so many aspects that one person's truth is bound to be another's lie. There actually is no one reality. And unless you have a vision that enables you to view the total reality, you are bound to be like the blind men who touched different parts of an elephant and called it a tree trunk, snake, rock or root, depending on whether they touched the elephant's leg, tail, trunk or body.

They say that nobody can understand the reality of a marriage except the husband and wife themselves. Let me go a step further and say that even the couple doesn't understand the reality, because there is no one reality! The husband will have his perception of the way things are between him and his wife. While his wife may have a completely different perception of the same. Then when they actually get talking, they are taken aback at the allegations being flung at them and things keep getting progressively worse.

Cynics, perhaps are right in saying that marriage is a *one-up-man-ship game*. It begins with a struggle between husband and wife as to who will rule the roost. Initially, a husband, here and there, may score a point, but ultimately the woman wins. My own hunch is that after reaching a certain stage in life, and after having goofed up quite a few, shall I say, opportunities, because of being foolishly egoistic, husbands, by and large, start surrendering gradually in a bid to buy peace at home.

Someone said men who marry usually do so because of an overwhelming desire to be domesticated. They want to be happily ensconced in an exclusive relationship with the woman they chose as lovable, graceful, charming and hence special and amorously look into her eyes because eye contact synchronizes brains when people fall in love.

During courtship, the feelings and sentiments of one's wife are most important. The husband is inclined to be much more romantic, considerate and extremely nice and courteous. He is out to do anything to please his ladylove. During honeymoon, he becomes extraordinarily indulgent in all respects.

That is why most wives want their marriage to be like their honeymoon. But when this doesn't happen, and she is taken for granted, she generally feels cheated and starts browbeating. Then the man gradually gets outwitted, unnerved, subdued and loses strength.

There is a story told about a cat and her strong friends.

Once there lived a cat.

The cat thought, *The lion is the strongest of all animals. It is good to have strong friends. I shall go to the lion and make friendship with him.*

She did so and the lion and cat were friends for many, many days.

Once they went for a walk together and met an elephant.

The lion began to fight with the elephant and the elephant killed him.

The cat felt very sorry. What shall I do now? she began thinking and came to feel that since the elephant was stronger than the lion, she should go to the elephant and make friends with him. The cat did so and both were friends for many, many days.

Once they went for a walk and met a hunter.

The hunter shot at the elephant and killed him.

The cat again felt sorry, but she thought, The man is stronger than the elephant. So she went to the hunter and asked, May I go with you?

Alright, let you accompany me to my home and you can stay in my house.

They both reached the man's home, and his wife met at the gate, took the gun away from her husband and shouted at him for being away so long.

The cat saw that and thought: Oh! The woman is the strongest of all! She has the guts to take the hunter's gun away from him, shout at him and the man does not even say a word, what to talk of refusing to give his gun!

The cat kept thinking and wondering at the guts the woman had shown.

The man sat down quietly. The woman went to the kitchen. The cat went to the kitchen, too.

She decided to stay with the woman forever, thinking she is strongest of all those in her experience.

That is why we mostly see a cat in the kitchen, who is out to purr.

Cats are known to domesticate humans—using the softest as well as hardest qualities at their disposal—soft furry body, grace, beauty, facial emotions and expressions that unexpectedly change to flash their claws. The reason is rather simple, cats are spontaneous, opinionated, malicious or spiteful and deliberate, always going that extra mile to be on the look out to jump at and catch their prey.

She must have what she wants, just like a woman.

Perhaps women have acquired some of the feline instincts, being together in the kitchen.

And the hapless man, even after a tough day out, can't complain but has to just adore his wife while thinking to himself: The life isn't all that bad, after all.

Thus with time, what has generally been witnessed is that the woman comes on top. She wins. The husband then settles down to a working arrangement, which is bereft of true love or respect. He dutifully hands over his pay packet to his fortress called *wife* at the end of the month.

And for most to get the pocket money, one is expected to stretch out his palm before her, periodically—usually, second instalment gets paid after the first one has been duly accounted for to her satisfaction. No matter even while in bathroom, he expects his wife to tell him where his towel, handkerchief or socks are; what he has to wear; whether to go or not go to a party; whether to talk or keep quiet in a social gathering; whether to smoke and drink or not, and so on and so forth.

The robbed that smiles, steals something from the thief.

William Shakespeare.

I am tempted to recall a story of an ingeniously crafty husband who in order to impress his male friends about his projected manliness told them that he had decided to take a decision on all big and important matters himself only where his wife would have no say. And that he had left it to his wife to take decisions on all small and petty matters. When asked to elaborate on the details with regard to big or small decisions, he explained thus:

For example, decisions such as (i) *India's military might should be ordered to stop Chinese intrusions in our northeastern borders;*

(ii) *whether, in view of the large-scale bungling of funds in the organization of Commonwealth games, India should or shouldn't bid for Olympic games next, etc.* (iii) *whether, in view of the cross-border terrorism, India should hold bilateral talks with Pakistan or not?*

And the small and petty ones are, like for example, (i) *whether to buy a new car since the old one is rattling;* (ii) *whether I could be permitted to invite my old collegemates to dinner at my place;* (iii) *whether I could ask my old parents to come and stay at my place for a few months etc., are all such matters where my wife has the final word. I've no say there.*

The message, though comic, is perhaps this that when over a period of time the wife firms up her feet through various ways of ingenuity in her armory, the hapless husband comes to find that he is left with no guts to stand up to his wife's domineering stances, right or wrong, and thus willingly assumes a subservient role (*rather no role, except that of bread earner*) in the running of domestic affairs and goes by his wife's dictates to buy peace at home. Marriage for man is, at best, a means, a safety valve; for woman, it is an existential equation. And where there's a clash between the absolute and the expedient, there could be no doubt about the outcome. The husband in his ego may win all the battles but the war, you may be sure, will be won, in all innocence and mirth, by the wife because she is holding all the aces in the game of marriage, and the husband has been dealt a poor hand, which neither art nor artifice can really improve. In short, a date with your wife is a date with destiny! Even a person of the *will* and stature of Mahatma Gandhi fumbled. It is widely known that he kept experimenting with celibacy (*brahmacharya*) and his wife Kasturba said he kept failing.

But this is disposing of the matter at the metaphysical level where the wife remains the everlasting bride. In actual practice, things do not exactly work out to plan. There's oft a slip betwixt the spousal cup and the bridal lip. But even here, though she often takes more blows than she gives, she is seldom the worse for it. Her shock absorbers are so cast as to take in any amount of strain. What she cannot subdue outright she'll conquer through a war of attrition.

In the last resort, she goes hungry, enters the fast of silence, and no broadsides that her husband may fire will help push the siege. The *holy wedlock* then begins to look like an *unholy deadlock.* And to break the deadlock, he does everything that is told. So, either way, she wins.

It's the paradox of marriage that the, so-called, lamb overcomes the, so-called, lion.

What does a Woman want?

What men have said from times immemorial is that women are difficult to read, and their ways are mysterious. What they think, feel, act, walk, smell (like onions) and breathe is difficult to fathom.

"All said and done, what does a woman really want?" asked a harassed husband to an expert on marriage counseling.

"I have a story to tell, that I came to read many years ago. It is hugely interesting and revealing about what a woman wants," the expert replied, "Would you like to hear that?"

"Yes," shouted all the other hapless husbands who had come to him for consultations.

The Expert said: "The story is about a good husband who then also wants to know the answer to Sigmund Freud's famous question: *What does a woman want*?

It goes like this:

A man was walking along a California beach and stumbled across an old lamp.

He picked it up, and rubbed it, and out popped a blithe *genie*, released from the lamp.

The *genie* said, "Okay, okay, my master! I do admit that you released me from the lamp.

Many others in the past centuries have done that before you.

You have not done something exceptional. Don't be posturing in that fashion.

Got it. Indeed, I'm getting a bit sick of having to fulfil people's wishes. I am not in a proper mood now. I was tired and was having a quiet rest and you stumbled upon me. You disturbed me. So you can forget about having three of your wishes fulfilled, as usual. You get just only one. Is that clear? Now what is your one wish?" The man excitedly then said, "Oh! *Mr Genie,* that is great. Thank you, so much.

I've always wanted to go to Hawaii, but I'm afraid to fly and traveling in a ship I get very seasick. Hence, I have not been able to go there till date either by air or ship.

How about building me my own bridge to Hawaii? So I can drive over in my car there whenever I would like to.

The *genie* laughed uproariously with his loud, thick and coarse throat and said, "Oh! my dear master, you seem to be very simple hearted and innocent fellow or have you gone crazy?"

You also sound funny for you don't seem to have given any thought to what you just said. There is the good, old saying, 'Think before you speak.' You don't seem to have heard that.

Have you?

How do you expect me to build a bridge like that? Just think of how long and big that would be. And the enormous problems of building that…its foundation, like how would the support pillars reach the bottom of the Pacific? How high would it have to be to let all the huge ships out there pass under it?

Do you have any idea of the quantity of steel, ingots, cement and concrete it would take?

You're just kidding, I should say. I could have straight away refused to obey you for your command is out of this world.

I could have just vanished into thin air. But, I would like to give you another chance to make your wish.

Mind you, this time you need to think carefully before making your that one wish, here and now."

The man felt embarrassed and said, "Okay, I've got it! I've thought it!"

"Okay, okay, please come on quickly," the *genie* called out.

The man hurried and said, "I've been married and divorced five times. My wives always said that I didn't care about them, caress them, make love to them, take them out for holidaying, on cruise, etc. They called me cold and insensitive. They even called me brute of a man. I have been at the receiving end all the time. I have ever been despairing as to how to make my wives happy. I tried to please them, but I miserably failed because I have come to realize that the mind of a woman is always closed. I haven't been able to understand how to have her pleased? How to keep her happy? It is a nightmare for me. In fact, I could never know what exactly she wants. Whatever I say or do to please her backfires and she stares me like a wild cat with nailed claws. So, dear *genie*, kindly help me. I want to understand a woman! My wish is that I could know how she feels inside at a given point of time for she changes her stance, her moods minute to minute. I wish to understand what her thoughts are like, know why she often goes off mood, gets angry almost at the drop of a hat, know why she starts crying at the slightest pretext, why she loves money so much that she leaves the husband cash strapped, why she wants to have her man at her mercy, nags him and suspects him almost always? In short my wish is to know what a woman really wants? I want to know how to make a woman happy, and..." (the *genie*, having gotten nervously baffled by all those details of the wish) interrupted him, and said..." Wait, wait, hello! just hold on there, there only! What did you wish earlier on? Yes, you said you want that bridge to Hawaii. Now tell me do you want it two-lane or four-lane?"

"What does a woman want?"

The best of erudite experts have said, "That is, indeed, a very tricky issue, anybody's guess! It baffled the *genie* as well."

But *abi picture bakey hai,* said the expert, and the story continues.

Here's the answer, as contained in a legend from King Arthur's time—the legend of Dame Ragnell.

Once upon a time, King Arthur goes out in a forest, hunting a deer. Ordering his attendants to stay behind, he goes alone deeper into the dense forest. Suddenly a Knight, Sir Gromer—hefty, strong and of great might in black armor, with an old grievance against the King accosts King Arthur and threatens to kill him unless he finds an answer to the Knight's riddle.

The knight's riddle was: *What does a woman want most*?

He gives King Arthur one year to come up with the answer. King Arthur returns to his court at Carlisle and tells the noble Knight of his own court, Sir Gawain, of his encounter with the dark Knight.

They then set out both in their kingdom to meet people—to ask them the question: *What does a woman want*? They meet and ask many people, young and old, literate and illiterate, rich and poor, city dwellers and villagers. The answers they gave were many and varied, like: "A woman wants mush, love, passion, money, romance. Feminism has made them want more. Hence, a woman is greedy. No compromises. A woman wants to find true love. She wants the same thing—she wants fairytales. She wants to feel like Cinderella. One thing that each woman wants the most is a person who loves her unconditionally, who tells her that she looks fabulously terrific, always and ever, who doesn't ogle at other women passing by by shooting sidelong glances, who has eyes fixed only on his woman and wants to see her blossom and shine as she glows with the confidence of having someone who loves and desires her. A woman wants to be a tigress at work. She chooses her career hands down, whatever happens to her home. A woman wants a good marriage. She still is traditional. You got it right. She wants to be wooed, and then finally wants to get married happily. She wants to turn a *house* into a *home.* A woman all needs is a shoulder to cry on. She wants her man to listen to her problems in her life—at her office, with her in-laws, with her maid, etc. and wants her man to act like *he cares.* All she wants from her husband is that he pay close attention—i.e. switch of the television, stop reading the newspaper or a book, get off Internet or Twitter, turn down the volume of music system or iPod—when demanded so as to acknowledge in no uncertain measure that his wife has a genuine problem at hand, and that he feels concerned about it. A woman wants her man to help her in the kitchen, to change the diapers, to help kids do the home work, to drive her to the mall where she buys grocery and to lift the bags while she herself makes the payment. A woman loves to receive gifts—birthday/anniversary presents—from her man. The gift must be personal, something so luxurious that she would feel guilty about buying it for herself, and frivolous enough to suggest that her man still sees her as a fun person rather than a staid mother of two. She would be happy receiving a text message from the man in her life to tell her in the middle of the day how much she is being remembered and loved.

A woman wants to be like some high-maintenance gal. Show her the money, honey! Yes, that is what she loves to sing. Gucci bags, Chanel glasses, Solitaires, high heels, Armani clothes and a penthouse.

Aaah!

Now that's what a woman most dreams of. A woman wants good sex. A woman wants a soft peck on her cheeks from her man off and on rather than a frown with wrinkles on the forehead to show off the tiredness on arrival back home from a hard day's work." Finally, someone said, "A woman wants to be an intellectual. She wants to evolve, grow and show the way to living life blissfully!"

But none of these answers fully satisfied King Arthur and Sir Gowain, and they felt what they heard was just run of the mill. They still had not got the right answer—short, crisp and all-encompassing—that was satisfying.

As the deadline approached, King Arthur rode into the forest one last time. There he met a hideously ugly looking woman, Dame Ragnell—the ugly old hag was with warts and her face red and splotchy with bulging bleary eyes. Her yellow teeth protruded out of her lips, nose snorted wither, ears thick and big, her hair snarled and clotted—an utterly frightful face to look at. She greeted the King and offered to give the correct answer to the dark Knight's question, but that she would reveal it to him on one condition, *That he should promise to give her the hand of noble Sir Gawain in marriage*! Otherwise he will have to die at the hands of the dark Knight.

King Arthur then tells Dame Ragnell, "I must first seek Gawain's consent, and know whether he would be willing to marry you." She agrees. And the King rides back to Carlesle and explains the situation to Gawain. He immediately agrees. "I'll wed her at what time you will set, Oh King!" He says. "For love of you I'll not hesitate."

The King soon thereafter rides back into the forest and tells Dame Ragnell of Gowain's consent. She feels pleased and then gives King Arthur the answer: *Some people say that women most desire to be beautiful, or to have lust in bed with many men, or to be always fresh and young, be after money and riches, but the truth is what a woman most wants is sovereignty—the power to choose for herself—the right to have her own way, unfretted.*

King Arthur thanks her, rides off to meet Sir Gromer, the hefty knight and gives him the answer: "What a woman wants most is the power to choose for herself," says Arthur. "*Sovereignty* is what she wants!" Sir Gromer instantly moves his head being in full agreement, concedes defeat and rides away speedily, while saying, "I've nothing against you now, Oh King!"

King Arthur then rides back to Court with Dame Ragnell, and she and Sir Gawain get married while Queen Guinevere and the other women of the Court stand there weeping at the pass of such strange and unfortunate circumstances leading to Sir Gawain's pitiful plight of having to marry such an ugly and obnoxiously repulsive woman. After the wedding, Sir Gawain takes Dame Ragnell to the bridal chamber, and the first thing she asks for is a kiss from him. Without least hesitation, Sir Gawain raises her chin with the touch of his forefinger, she arches her head to receive his kiss. His open mouth touches her lips, tenderly and softly—so perfect, so warm, so yielding. And lo and behold! As soon as their lips meet, Dame Ragnell gets miraculously transformed from an ugly old hag to a stunningly beautiful, voluptuous young woman—the fairest creature that he ever had seen, without measure.

"I had been under a curse," she explained "Transformed by necromancy into a hunchbacked old crone until courteously gracious Knight like you married me and kissed me."

She almost knelt before him and said, "Thank you, my benevolent lord, my dear husband, my love," simultaneously making nonverbal expressions of affection also, like winks and squeezes in close embrace.

Sir Gawain, of course, felt delighted; indeed, delighted beyond measure.

In the morning Dame Ragnell thanked Sir Gowain, her dear husband, profusely for lifting the curse on her.

"But it's not fully lifted," she informs him, "Because of you, I'm now free to be my true (beautiful) self...but only for half the day! My beauty will not hold."

Sir Gawain looks at her bewildered.

So she asked him, "Oh! my dear love, my husband, which do you choose? I mean, would you like to have me beautiful by the day and ugly in the night or beautiful by night and ugly during the day? Choose, choose—I leave the choice to you, my dear love," she urges.

"Alas," said Gawain, "The choice is hard."

"If I choose you to be beautiful at night, I will have to look at your ugly face all day long, and if I choose to have you as beautiful during the day, I will have the ugly hag in my nuptial bed all through the night. That would be obnoxious," he summed up.

"Therefore, I don't know what to do," he continues. "So, I leave this to you, my honey, my buttercup, my pudding," he said while at the same time making nonverbal expressions of affection as well, like winks and squeezes, in return.

"You choose what you think is the best, dear young lady. Do as you want. Do as it pleases you," Gawain said.

"Thank you, so very much, my very dear husband, my love, my pride," said jubilant Dame Ragnell.

"Now I feel on top of the world. You know why? You have lifted the whole curse, because you gave me the choice. You left it to me, my judgment, my decision. You didn't impose your will on me. You recognized my *sovereignty.* That is fine, just wonderful," she exclaimed.

And she declared, "Now you shall have me beautiful both by the day as well as night, always and ever—charming and loving."

Knight Gawain, her beaming husband, felt hugely glad, hugged her and held her in tight embrace.

"Oh, dear! You've freed me to be my beautiful self hereafter, always and ever. You are the wisest husband because you gave me the power and authority to choose what *I* want instead of *you* deciding it for me," she jubilantly said.

"For heaven's sake, kiss me again," Dame Ragnell implored.

And her husband kissed her again, most softly, tenderly and passionately like the famous *kiss* in the world as represented by Rodin's famous sculpture—*The Kiss*—in which two lovers, sitting on the rocky ledge embrace tenderly with radiant energy, and kiss forever—her left hand wrapped around his neck, she seems almost to be swooning or to be singing into his mouth, as he rests his open right hand on her thigh and seems to be ready to play her leg as if it were a musical instrument; his calves and knees are beautiful, her anklets are strong and firmly feminine, and her buttocks, waist and breasts are all heavily fleshed and curvy; ecstasy pours off every inch of them; touching only a few places, they seem to be touching in every cell…it is as if they have fallen down the well of each other; they are not only self-absorbed, but actually absorbing one another. Truly romantic.

"I have been craving for how long, I really don't know, for such a soft, tender and passionate kiss," she revealed, as she looked into his eyes. Her eyes met his, as if to thank him, soulfully.

"Did you say something?" he asked.

"No, nothing really," she said unmindfully, and mulled whether the couple in deep love need to employ any language to communicate. What matters is whether or not they feel comfortable with each other in love. They don't need to talk, it's all a question of vibes. Normally when two people meet they need to exchange words, sentences, idioms, phrases, couplets, notes of exclamation or have queries and questions to which they want explanations and answers. But for the lover and his beloved, whenever they meet, their eyes speak, their facial expressions reveal their emotions, and their body language communicates.

And thus Dame Ragnell, the condemned old hag, had finally got liberated!

And the couple lived happily ever after.

And the moral is that the hapless man, even after a tough day/night out, can't complain but has to just adore his wife while thinking to himself, *Life isn't all that bad, after all.*

"So, what does a woman want?"

"She wants what she wants. She wants her say. She wants the choice. She wants to be powerful. She wants to decide. She wants sovereignty."

The answer perhaps is straight and simple. But, unfortunately, the man continues to want to curb her, impose his say on her, dictate to her. Treat her as his fiefdom. And by the time he realizes his folly and comes to understand

What a woman wants, it's too late—he is old and fatigued. There is no life left in the relationship. It is on the rocks.

The message that this story, told symbolically, seems to convey is that no man is a hero to his own wife. Even men of steel are known to have gone soft in the bedroom. No wonder, then, The Roman philosopher, Cato wailed, *We the men rule the world, but our women rule us*!

No husband, I guess, will ever learn to stand up to his wife till he has learned to sit down at her feet.

One gender pitted against the other!

It shouldn't be viewed that way.

No, never.

It is a little grey or black on both sides and time should not be spent on this otherwise sensitive issue. There is a whole world that makes all the good and bad that is happening. So, it is misleading to blame either sex. We can have the wife we have always dreamed of as soon as we become the husband she has always dreamed of is what the famous writer/thinker Robert Mark Alter has said.

There is another beautiful quotation of Leo Buscaglia, who has written, *Don't smother each other* (*in a relationship*). *No one can grow in shade.* Let no couple suffocate or stifle their relationship in matrimony.

And, unfortunately, the negativity that has of late surrounded the institution of marriage in our cultures, particularly in the European and North American societies, is getting overbearing by the day. Even in Eastern cultures it is losing ground. It is sad. It is unfortunate. People may, however, joke about them, but nagging wives and bossy husbands are in for real. And that undoubtedly is real bad news for a happy and harmonious relationship in any marriage.

Be humble; be harmless; have no pretentions; be upright, forbearing...tranquil, steadfast, master of ego. Standing apart from the things of the senses, free from self; aware of the weaknesses in mortal nature.

Bhagwat Gita.

Why do Men hear Yes when Women mean No

Ever wondered why do things go wrong even during amorous and passionate bedroom trysts? Many men claim that men are not so great at reading body language.

Well a new study has given the answer, by finding that men usually misread signals from women.

When your wife, instead of looking into your eyes and calling you *honey,* turns her sight away from you and merely tells you *suno* (listen), take it that your honeymoon is over. And when in reply to your earnest pleadings, she disdainfully answers, to simply say *nothing,* know it that you are in deep trouble. Small actions or words have large meanings and consequences.

Thc fact of the matter is that wives generally like to use indirect messages perhaps out of concern that husbands might be offended or angered by direct messages, but most men actually accept direct resistance messages easily and without negative reactions.

Why can't men be like women?

In her own self-effacing, almost unobtrusive way, the Indian woman, especially the urban Indian woman, has given her answer to Rex Harrison's peevish query in *My Fair Lady*—Why can't men be more like women? The pursuit of economic freedom is a real social change. Men, who had their spaces intact anyway now have to deal with the contemporary woman's need for her space too. Well, a woman is now in the sense she does what the man does, and sometimes more. Moving through the sands of time, years of male dominance as it were, the question has come to stand on its head—why can't a man be more like a woman?

Remarkably, the Indian male has picked up a gauntlet, and much like a wide-eyed child is surprised to find he is now quite adept to the challenge. Yes, the new-age Indian male—the pot-bellied *babu*, the ritzy business executive, the file-pushing bureaucrat, the absentminded professor—has been making bed-tea, chopping vegetables in the kitchen, changing soiled diapers, going to the grocer's shop, baby-sitting for the newborn at home while on paternity leave, and much, much more, with merry abandon. Indeed, of late, there is subtle role reversal under way–a gender neutralization, if you like it.

The good news is that in most urban Indian homes, the new-generation husband has given up his insular position voluntarily and no longer chooses to distance himself from the hurly–burly of the household chores. Surely, the change did not come overnight. Indeed, the first sparks were provided by breakdown of the joint family system, the growth of nucleus units, the high cost of living and higher literacy among women, which brought in its wake their economic independence—all these factors resulting in migration of couples to cities and even foreign shores to take up jobs.

Nevertheless, in the current newer egalitarian model of marriages, the expectation is that while not every chore could be split halfway, family responsibilities should be divided fairly and decision-making powers shared. Both are expected to respect each other's work and share in the family life, never trying to dominate because of financial muscle or gender. It is best to start off as you mean to go on—to understand each other's need to nurture and protect his or her space and identity.

A married couple who try and assimilate the essence of being in such a state of mind, will never be either in a relationship of *dog–dog* or *dog–duck* or *duck–duck*. They would graduate from that stage and shall get into a higher class of relationship, which would be mature and respectful to each other, as a couple.

There're two ways of meeting difficulties.
You alter the difficulties,
or you alter yourself to meet them.

Phyllis Bottome.

When Judge saved the Marriage!

Soon, Ragini filed her papers in a court for divorce.

Raghav was terribly unnerved to get the court notice.

On the date of first hearing, the husband and wife came face-to-face in hostile circumstances.

Presiding over the court, the Judge, to start with, lamented that while earlier getting a divorce was considered the last resort by warring couples, now they consider it their first and foremost option. That is utterly the wrong attitude. Such couples do not want to invest in the relationship that their marriage demands. Their priority seems to be in present times, sex, money and more money. Patience, adjustment or commitment to their marriage, it appears, has no relevance in their scheme of things. Instant marital happiness is the goal. This would lead them nowhere, and they would cause irreparable damage to the institution of marriage. Hence, as part of the society, Judges, by and large, have now stood up to save the sanctity of marriage.

Taking a look at Raghav and Ragini, the Judge said, "I, therefore, want you to give your marriage a second chance to blossom," and then turning to Ragini he asked, "Who is that in your lap?"

"Sir, that is my son," she replied.

"Why did you have to bring him along?" he now wanted to know.

There was no reply.

And the Judge continued, "In any dispute between husband and wife, the child is the worst sufferer. The child becomes a hapless victim of the feud between his or her father and mother. Whosoever of the two may win, it is the child who invariably stands to lose in either case. Because of the reason that both the parents generally try to use their child as a, shall I say, pawn to prove their individual case in a partisan manner, the emotional pulls and pressures on the child become most devastating. Unknown fears and guilt feelings are born and get themselves manifested in the form of bed-wetting, stammering and stuttering, emotional outbursts, depression and even aggression on self and others. And naturally then such kids are bound to have an unbalanced personality development and, therefore, can be susceptible to vices, including smoking, gambling, alcohol and drugs." As the Judge halted, there was hushed silence in the court room. And he continued, "Therefore, I wish to urge both of you, as mother and father of this little child, to ponder seriously what I have just now told you, and try and give another chance to your wedded life. I give you three months' time to try and iron out your difference. It is never too late to mend your ways and work out a compromise to stay together, particularly when the future of your this little son is at grave stake."

The Judge then asked the estranged couple to meet him in his office chamber after the court had briefly adjourned for lunch break.

Both waited and later met him.

The Judge started by welcoming them and said, "You know, as a socially responsible human being first and a Judge later, it pains me to deal with cases of young couples who do not give some reasonable time to themselves to adjust in their marital relationship, but rush to the court for divorce at the slightest pretext—thinking theirs was a wrong marriage and that next time it would be better. They marry again and with a negative state of mind that they continue to have, things between them never get *better* but only *bitter*, all the more.

So here is my question to both of you, who once upon a time, I believe, loved each other so dearly and took vows to stay together in the relationship of husband and wife: *If you don't have much time to love and live with each other, how much time do you have for hate, misunderstandings, anger, shouting at each other, and breaking-up like glass*?"

The judge continued to say, "The problem is basically aggravated because of the tendency of each of the spouses to find fault with the other, and expect him or her to change. They do not care to understand that if one wants to see a change in behavior or attitude in the other, he or she must first of all see that change in himself or herself. The fact of the matter is that no one can effect any change in the other. What is in his or her power is to change himself or herself, first of all. This could most likely have a spiral effect on the other, and chances are that it could elicit a positive response in return."

"But, sir, I feel I can sort out my differences with my husband. The issues between us get aggravated, compounded because of the undue interference of my mother-in-law, who hates me from the core of her heart. Sometimes I get so tense that I want to either kill myself or hit her on her head," stated Ragini.

Trying to make light of what Ragini had just told him, he referred to a quote: "*God said, I can't be everywhere all the time, so I created Mother.* The Devil replied, *Even I can't be expected to be everywhere, so I created mother-in-law.*" It is a question whether you see God or Devil; whether you want to see good or evil; whether you want to be joyful or sorrowful—one's state of mind! The Judge then elaborately responded by narrating to her this Chinese story: "A daughter-in-law, having suffered insults and repeated humiliations at the hands of her abusive mother-in-law, seriously tossed with the thought of poisoning her. She had an uncle dealing in pharmaceutical products. She went to his shop and asked for a bottle of poison.

The uncle wanted to know the reason for obtaining the poison, and having learned about it, he felt startled. He thought over the plans that his niece had in her mind, and decided to deal with the matter maturely and with psychoanalytical approach. He made her realize that in case she decides to poison her mother-in-law and she dies all of a sudden, everybody around, including her husband would suspect her, which could land her in bigger trouble. She could be charged of murder.

Her uncle's words made salutary effect on her state of mind. But insisted to know what else she could do to get rid of her.

The uncle then told her that he would instead give her some chemical powder, the small doses of which she would have to mix with the food that her mother-in-law ate daily.

This would act in her body as slow poison, and with a year or so, it would have its full impact on her system and she would come to die. In this way no one would have any reason to suspect her involvement and she would be able to get rid of her intrusive mother-in-law.

She felt reasonably relieved.

While delivering the packet to her, her uncle cautioned her that to ensure that neither her husband nor anybody else ate the food mixed with small doses of that lethal substance except her mother-in-law, she would have to cook the woman's food with her own hands and serve her. Moreover, she was advised to put up with any sort of harsh treatment that her mother-in-law might subject her to, and show love and respect to her, though even by way of a mere facade, otherwise she might not accept food from her hands.

She agreed to do exactly as advised.

Her husband felt surprised at such a change in the attitude of his wife towards his mother. Within a few months, the mother-in-law too started having soft and nice feelings towards her daughter-in-law.

Both the hitherto warring women started responding to each other positively, but the small doses of poisoning continued unabated.

The mother-in-law, however, feeling happy that her daughter-in-law was herself cooking and serving hot meals to her and showing love and respect to her, now decided to celebrated her daughter-in-law's birthday and gifted her a beautiful diamond necklace. The gesture was immensely appreciated.

By the end of about six months, the daughter-in-law started feeling very bad about her act of stealthily poisoning her mother-in-law. She felt like cursing herself now.

She then decided to go back to her uncle to tell him about her change of mind, and to seek advice as how to negate the effect of small doses of poison that she had already used.

Her uncle got pleased to learn about the positive developments in the relationship of the two women.

Sensing that his niece was feeling remorseful and guilty for having poisoned her mother-in-law for the past six months, he now revealed to her that what he had originally given to her in the name of so-called slow poison was actually some herbal mixture meant only to boost a person's metabolism. It was no poison.

Her niece felt aghast but certainly relived.

Her uncle then made her realize that the poison was not in the herbal powder, but inside her, in her own mind—the poison of hate, anger, envy, spite and all that and much, much more. And once all that negativity got released, the space got filled with unconditional love. It even started overflowing. And then it got due response in adequate measure from her mother-in-law. Both now found genuine love and respect for each other."

The moral of the story is that love begets love! The Judge concluded the story, but added, since no one is ready to see one's own shortcomings or defects first of all, but gets consumed by a fierce desire fanned by an inflated ego sense, only to change the other, the matters get bad to worse, which makes one go wild with rage. The problem is that when it is a question of finding fault with the other, mostly everyone assumes the role of a judge and goes on passing judgments—he is good, no he is bad; he is guilty, no he is innocent; he is jealous, no he is broadminded and so on and so forth. But, when it is a question of his or her own fault, one immediately puts on the robes of a defense lawyer and starts justifying his or her conduct in defense. This doesn't lead anybody anywhere. Then bitterness spreads like a vine creeping on a wall. It engulfs both of them. They lose all sense of decent conduct and propriety, and go on accusing, shouting, abusing and hitting each other, till they land up in court. I urge you to try and understand the essence of what I have told you just now, and give your relationship another chance to take roots and eventually get firm. You need to reconcile your differences. If for nothing, but for the sake of future of your child, whom, I am sure, you both love so much. I am deeply pained to have recently learned from a TV news bulletin that in Delhi a thirteen–year-old boy, studying in ninth standard had committed suicide because his mother and father had been living separately for the past nine years, and in spite of his best efforts, they did not patch-up their difference—mother was doing a job in Dubai and father working as a photographer in Delhi.

A child needs quality time of both parents. This needs to be examined from a child's point of view. Now is the quality time for your little son: when he tries to take his first step to walk, but falls down, hurts himself, needs a Band-Aid, needs to be fed and put to sleep comfortably. Psychologically speaking, the minimum requirement is that one of the two parents should be at home or constantly available to the child until he crosses the initial formative years of his age. And considering the fact that one-half of a child's knowledge is thought to be attained in the first four years of life, it seems of the greatest value and importance that he be maximally cared for, guided and loved during these formative and impressionable years of his life. Parents only are best equipped to perceive the strengths and weaknesses of their child and fulfil his needs, both emotionally as well as intellectually. The best way to make your son loving, caring, patient and sincere is that both of you have to be that way first of all. A happy childhood is one of the best gifts that parents have in their power to bestow on their child. Instead of costly gifts, what your child needs is hugs and kisses of both of you.

Lastly, let me say this also that these utterances carry my silent conviction that the parents should realize the fact that when they have brought the innocent kid into this world, it is their moral duty and responsibility to care for and raise the child as a well-bred, mature, sensible and balanced human being. If you both as parents to your son, are not, for whatever reasons, able to discharge your this bounden duty towards him, then his future is at great peril. When a child watches his or her father and mother shouting and fighting, following which the mother, as a first reaction, invariable goes into weeping and wailing, it emotionally disturbs the child beyond measure. It is traumatizing. Try and understand that with a calm mind.

This subtle message is enshrined in the beautiful story of a little boy who is sad and tries to find out *Why his Mom weeps and cries*? The little boy asks his mother," Mom, why do you cry whenever Dad shouts at you?"

"Because I am a woman," she answered.

The boy said, "I don't understand that. What do you mean?"

His mother hugs him and says, "And you never will. You are too young."

Later the little boy asked his father, "Why does Mom cry whenever you lose your temper on her?"

"All women cry for no reason," was all that his father could answer him.

When he became an adult, he asked God, "God, why do women cry so easily?"

And God answered, "When I created woman, she needed to be special. So I gave her strong shoulders to bear the weight of the world...and soft enough to be comfortable doing that. I gave her the strength to give and create life. I gave her the patience and tolerance also—the kind that accepts rejection that often comes her way either from her husband, children, in-laws or society.

I gave her the forbearance to allow her to go on even when everyone else gives up—the kind that takes care of her family, despite illness and fatigue.

I gave her the sensitivity to love her husband or children unconditionally, even when they might have hurt her deeply.

I gave her the strength to endure her husband in his faults. And even to stand by his side often without any grudge.

And finally I gave her tears to be shed whenever the situation became unbearable.

You see, my son, the beauty of a woman is not in her physical looks, nor in the clothes she wears or in the way she does her hair or make-up.

The beauty of a woman resides in her eyes.

It is the door to her heart, and the door where her love resides.

And it is often through her tears that you see her heart go by," concluded God.

Men anywhere, therefore, must make it a point not to do anything that compels a woman to shed tears.

Concluding, I wish to urge you Ragini to go back today to your own home and allow your little son to live and grow in the loving company of his both parents. I have devoted a lot of my court time today to deal with your marital problems, not from a judicial point of view but from a humanistic angle. I hate to see young married couples get divorced without putting proper efforts to sort out the difference cordially and patch-up. So, I have decided to keep your case in suspended animation for three months. Give your relation an honest try. If you still come to find that it doesn't work, come back to the court and I shall decide your case. And remember God has bestowed human beings with intellect. Intellect is like a filter, which has the function of discriminating, of judging the thoughts and deciding which ones to put into practice and which ones to weed out—basically filtering them. Unfortunately, in the current times, the filter of the intellect has become weakened, confused and unsure; it has become blocked by many incorrect beliefs, misunderstandings, etc., due to which this filtration does not take place properly—as a result many wrong thoughts get converted into actions. A lot of times during the day, thoughts become actions so fast that the filter of the intellect does not even come to play i.e., thoughts become actions bypassing the filter. So you both need to be watchful that the filter of your intellect doesn't get chocked.

You can now go. Raghav, do take care of your wife and child. Remember, every girl may not be a queen to her husband but she definitely is a princess to her father. And also this that there are two things to remember in life, one, "take care of your *thoughts* when you are alone," and two, "Take care of your *words* when you are talking."

The tongue has no bones, but it is strong enough to break a heart. So both of you should be careful with your words. And finally, Raghav, it is for you, particularly. Let me tell you also a small story but with a deep meaning, which a young American boy had shared with me some time back in USA. He said, "As a kid, I remember that my working Mom also used to cook dinner for all of us in the family. I do remember a particular night, when she cooked dinner after a long, hard day's work in office. She was tired. The breads she prepared got burned partially. I remember waiting to see how Dad reacted! My Dad reached for a bread, smiled at my Mom, and asked me how my day was at school? I don't remember what I told him in reply, but I do remember watching him smear butter and jelly on the burned portions of the bread and eat every bite of it. When I got up from the table that evening, I remember hearing my Mom apologize to my Dad for her carelessness. I will never forget what he said to her: *Honey, it's alright. You know I love to eat burned bread.*

Later that night, I went to kiss Dad goodnight and asked if he really liked those burned bread loaves? He wrapped me in his arms and said, *Your Mom has put in a hard day's work in office today and she must have been really tired. Besides a little burned bread never hurts one's stomach*!

The above incident could be extended to any matter or situation that threatens to mar a relationship. In fact, compassion is the base of any relationship, be it a husband–wife or a parent–child or brother–sister or a friendship. God bless you," concluding thus, and the Judge sent them out.

Apparently, both Raghav and Ragini were feeling much relieved and relaxed. Raghav looked into her eyes while taking his son into his arms, and with puppy eyes invited Ragini to his car to go home. She hesitatingly followed.

Don't cry because it's all over, smile because it happened.

Anonymous.

An Awareness Bath!

At home, there wasn't much talk between the two. Ragini cooked, and after taking dinner, while Raghav kept fondling and cajoling Rohan, his darling son, she went to bed.

That night, Ragini shifted restlessly in sleep, having dug her face into the pillow. Then drifted into a dream and traveled upwards, in cool and quiet mists, hills of deep, lush green foliage that rolled to forever, and...

"She came to a plateau nestled beneath some ancient oak just below a steep drop-off. The place sat upon the tip of a long finger of steeply rising land, a ridge of hills, which extended out of a towering knuckle of peaks in the far distant. Fleecy white clouds loitered around and floated lazily on which little angles danced giggly and played musical instruments. She was drawn to the twinkle and glitter of the star patterns above. They seem to beacon to her to reach out beyond her temporal existence and its desires, and search for something more meaningful, more soulful. The setting was idyllic—an aura imbued with the invigorating freshness of nature.

As she climbed around one of the massive stones, the fog that had suddenly appeared, now disappeared to hazily reveal a thin hut, which was curtained by the opaque parade of trees around it. It sat smugly on the edge of the slope.

In front of the hut, Buddhist prayer flags fluttered atop bamboo poles. There was something holy about the place, she experienced.

Ragini approached it and tapped lightly on the door. To her utter surprise, a resonant voice rang out in quick response, with unexpected warmth and tenderness, as if she were a long-awaited guest. "Do come in traveler, come in, seeker?" that soulfully pure and sublime voice resonated. "Come in. You are welcome." It was a voice like rose petals—soft, sweet and fragrant.

And so wandering off the beaten path of her life, she opened the door slowly and found a pair of large hazel-colored eyes on a round face of smooth olive skin, with a thick, bold round mark of vermilion powder on her forehead. She took a gaze at her—a gaze that sliced clear through her like a razor meeting the supple flesh. There was a celestial aura around her—a glorious light emanating from her. A strange sensation tickled the pit of Ragini's stomach. The deity like being exuded serenity, bathed in purity. She sat quietly—smilingly. She seemed to belong to a wholly different species of being—more perfect than any human form could possibly be.

She sat like a feline grace, erect yet relaxed, balanced upon a cushion of leaves lavishly sprinkled with flower petals of various hues, on the earthen floor.

There was glint in her eyes, a tad more sparkling than the fire.

The verandah outside seemed plastered with cow dung freshly as the smell it emitted was raw to the nostrils. The air inside was laden with incense that was still burning. The surroundings around her wore pious, neat and orderly look.

She infused a bracing warmth and freshness to the surroundings. She was draped in snow-white flowing robes that had a blaze of crimson silken border on the sleeves. Her serenity and peace made her appear angelic in nature, enlightened in substance. Truly celestial!

Ragini's eyes welled up with awe. In that suspended moment, her choked voice said, "But, who are you?" eagerly imploring with purity of emotions.

The celestial body didn't say anything for a moment, only looked at her and appeared to consider her query, and then said, "A reflection in a quiet pond; a ray of moonlight on a dark night, as young as the morning dew and as old as the Earth. My love affair with Divine is something *karmic.* All things are in me, and I am in all things."

For enough reasons, Ragini could discern, goose bumps appeared in her armpits.

"But, how shall I address you?" Ragini now asked.

"You can call me *Mother,*" she responded.

"Fine. I shall call you holy mother," Ragini decided.

A cool smile flickered on holy mother's luminous face, and as she spun around, and saw something on Ragini's face, that laugh died on her lips. She stopped and gave her a long, considered look and talked in whispers to say: "There is something stirring in your head."

Ragini began to feel oddly disoriented. She lost her bearings in time as well as age. Nevertheless, she felt happy to be in the beauty and splendor of that tiny slice of heaven-like place. She savored those moments.

"Well, well, I have something of value to tell you, to share with you," the holy Mother spoke.

Ragini felt relieved. Soon her composure dissolved and she began to laugh a gentle laugh that softened the harsh lines on her face, and felt sorely tempted to hear her say more to her. She decided to shed the shackles of reason and placed her trust in her intuition. With a baited breath, she then waited for an elaboration—her eyebrows getting a bit hiked with curiosity, with interest.

There were many questions in her mind, but there was a long silence during which Ragini tried hard to think of an arresting opening line that would lead the holy mother to converse in a way that could quieten her mind.

"Okay, fine. Are you now ready to listen to what I have to say?" the holy mother now asked, and asked her to follow her to the garden outside.

Stung by the note of urgency in her voice, Ragini responded by saying, "That sounds hugely interesting. Yes, I am ready," and followed her to the garden.

The chirping of birds on the tree tops around and the cascading fall of water into the pond from the small stream made such a sound that was just music to the ears.

Pointing to a tall tree—with a straight, light grey trunk, rising over twenty feet before stretching out its arms on either side, covered with large, elongated leaves, then resuming its skyward climb throwing more tiny branches and leaves in its full splendor—the holy mother said, "This tree is host to a large variety of birds, particularly those that like to hide behind thick foliage: *koels*, *barbets* and *woodpeckers*; others like *mynas*, *doves*, *pigeons* and *babblers* seek shelter in it from half a dozen stray cats that have made my home theirs or maybe even a stray jackal.

When I want to break from the routine of praying, meditating, introspecting, reading and writing, so as to prepare for my lecturing/discoursing sessions, I come here and look at this tree for hours together, watching this majestic tree and it's avian guests flying in and out. You don't listen to the words. Listen to the silence and poetry, the rhythm, the song of these birds and water fall. Listening to such a unique celebration is inarguably among the best stress busters. The more we develop the art of focused, conscious listening—to our own internal self, to people, to music, to nature—the more we can hear and appreciate their subtle messages to us. Listening is learning, because when you listen silently the whole existence starts speaking to you. When you are absolutely silent, that is the greatest moment to learn. Life reveals its secret when you are silent. One needs silence in the heart. When you learn to be silent you learn to laugh as well at the fake living that most people live. Allow your laughter to be total. I call it jogging of the mind. A total laughter is a rare phenomenon. When each cell of your body laughs, when each fiber of your being pulsates with joy, then it brings a great relaxation. Your decision is your destiny.

Okay, that was by way of preparing you mentally and physically to be attentive and listen to what I now intend to tell you *the secrets of alchemy*—like turning base elements into gold," she held out the promise.

"Turning me into gold. Wonderful!" Ragini exclaimed.

"The alchemy of which I speak can transmute the baser elements of your life—the fears, the hatred, the anger, the confusion, the enviousness, the ego, the spite and so many other vices that humans of this day and age are afflicted with into gold of peace, freedom, clarity, serenity, joy and ecstasy," she renewed the assurance.

Ragini thought the matter over in her mind, and suddenly raised her hand, as though a thought had just struck her from nowhere, and gave out, "I've lost my peace of mind. I've lost my sleep. I'm prone to anger. Naturally, my married life has got affected badly. I need solutions to my problems."

"Yes, yes, I' m aware," she replied, and mumbled something that Ragini couldn't make out. While she was mumbling, Ragini stole a curious glance at her, but meantime she had pursed her lips and was shaking her head in utter disappointment. And then, she instantly went silent, as if wrapped in some serious thought. As she finished speaking to herself internally, she cleared her throat, and hesitated. Later keeping her voice casual, she said with business-like briskness, "You have unnecessarily created a terrible mess of an otherwise simple issue at hand, with your husband."

Ragini nodded silently. It left her dumbstruck, feeling alienated from herself.

She kept wondering, till the holy mother, on a serious note, now said," The mind in its own place and in itself can create heaven of a hell; a hell of a heaven! There are two people living within you at all times: *one*, is the ego, which is demanding, which is garrulous and is insane because it will have you convince yourself that you are something that you're not—which is what insanity is; *two*, then there is hidden higher self, who is rarely heard or attended to. That is the piece of you that allows you to observe and think objectively and positively. That is your sacred self. All that the sacred part wants for you is that you be at peace with yourself. You need to meet the little voice inside you! The question is, 'Does whatever is going on in your life promote peace in you, or not?' If it doesn't, it's your ego; if it does, it's your higher self. You need to listen to this higher self more and more and keep the ego under check." "I am not quite sure if I am following what all you have said," Ragini told her, "Can you please say it simply, clearly, plainly?"

"Well, let me tell you this: your body is like a television set. It displays visuals all the time. So when you find negative things being displayed, you need to change the channel. Whatever we think or do is to make life comfortable, beautiful, peaceful and entertaining. Relationships sour due to rash actions born out of ego. Use your ego. But do not allow your ego to use you. It is to be used only as a tool. If you have learned how to use it, it will build you and give you many wonderful things.

"But how do I deal with my husband since I know he has deceived me, shattered my trust and faith in him. He could harm me or my child?" Ragini was impatient to know

"Okay, okay! Just a minute. Do you think you can change the situation by breaking off the relationship with him. If yes, go and change him by marrying someone else. What will happen to your son? Or can you persuade yourself to try and understand your husband as to why, in which circumstances he did what he did. In this you could be helped by the fact that after having committed that folly, he summoned the guts to come clean before you. He could have kept it under wraps and you wouldn't have come to know of it. He could have acted double-faced. Don't you appreciate his honesty of purpose, for whatever reason?" explained the holy mother.

"But, how do you…" Ragini wanted to say something.

"Don't interrupt me. Let me first complete in one go what I want to tell you," she instructed.

"And, you know, the fact that shadows exist in the world and in ourselves, should not blind us to the light. Tension occurs in the absence of right knowledge. The fact is that you get overwhelmed by your emotions. It's not by facts, but only by sheer imagination, that you get filled with fearful stress. There is a primordial form of fear that keeps one always on the edge. It is *existential angst*. The following story is illustrative:

'There was once a little mouse that lived in constant fear of the cat. The anxiety of running into the cat made it live a life of misery. God, overcame with sympathy, decided to turned the mouse into a cat so as to ally it's fears. No sooner did this happen than the cat began to get nightmares about the dog. Wanting to appease the tortured soul, God turned the cat into a dog. The dog now began to get fearful thoughts about being chased by a wolf. God then turned the dog into wolf. But again the wolf started getting fearful thoughts about being chased by tiger. Becoming a tiger should have been the end of all his woes, but no, the tiger now felt the creeps at the thought of an armed hunter spotting him and then…at that point, God turned the tiger back into a mouse.'

The moral of the story is that no physical form will ever rid you of your fears because the fear is not of one's form. It is of *imagination*. The fear tends to magnify only the negative outcomes because the imagination conjures all sorts of potential *worse than* scenarios. A positive attitude in such a situation leans on *better than* scenarios. Both schools of thought don't change reality. They only modulate the mindset by making it either bearable or unbearable.

And shall I now say that you are perhaps suffering from a disease called *shak* (suspicion). If someone praises you, you think you deserve it, but if someone praises your husband, you nurse suspicion; if some other male appreciates your beauty, you like it, but if your husband appreciates the beauty of some other woman, you get into suspicion. The fundamental conflicts are deeply embedded in psychology. You can narrate the *Mahabharata* all your life because you are likely to meet the characters in *Mahabharata* in your day-to-day life. Indeed, this epic is about life itself. If one strips it bear, it is a universal story that plays out every day—fratricide, greed, jealousy, revenge, lust and treachery. I don't mean doom or disaster. I hardly mean anything sizeable at all, only the living texture of each moment and each gesture. I feel the life under my fingers—sometimes rough, sometimes impossibly fine, and I can read it like Braille."

"I have difficulty in assimilating the essence of your such thoughts," Ragini expressed her doubts.

"Okay, let me explain it thus," she clarified, "For example, if someone says something unkind or offending to you, your ego will immediately rush in and perceive this as an attack against, which it must defend itself. It will naturally then fill you up with anger, hostility and fear. It can prompt you to attack that person verbally or physically. But if you could have understood your ego or false vanity and the frightened defensive mechanism born out of it, things would have been different for the simple reason that you would have then looked at the problem, with which you were faced with, from a mature understanding or positive perspective. Remember that you are *responsible* and can choose your response to a particular *stimulus* appropriately. Stop making life a contest between your husband and yourself. Obstacles can't stop you. Problems can't stop you. Most of all, people can't stop you. The only one who can stop you is you, *Yourself*. To find yourself is to find God, and to find God is to find yourself. The fact of the matter is that since *You* matter to yourself, you need to take care of *Yourself*. It's important to make someone happy; and it's important to start with yourself. Be what you are, and do what you ought to do the way you should do it. You have got to discover your real self. But, mind you, it is not as easy as it is said. You have to work with yourself whole time and introspect till you really find your true self. It is said of a great Sufi mystic, Bayazid.

One day, some people came to Sheikh Bayazid's door and knocked.

He opened his upstairs window and looked out enquiring, *Who is there*? *What do you want*?

Oh! they said. *We are looking for Bayazid.*

He replied, *Well, I've been looking for Bayazid for many, many years now, and I have not found him yet*! and closed the window.

This is what introspection is all about: trying to find one's true self. When you know yourself, you come to know that *you are not*! And all struggle ceases. When self-realization dawns, all questions cease. If you would like to know yourself, you should know that you are created by two things—one is your body and your outer appearance, which you can see with your eyes, the other is your inner forces. This is the part you cannot see, but you can know it with your insight. The reality of your existence is in your inwardness. Everything is a servant of your inward heart. Anyone who has probed the inner life to a certain extent, who has sat in silence long enough to experience the stillness of mind behind its apparent noise, is faced with a mystery.

You have got to finally stop running away from yourself. After all, who else is there better to be with? You have to be comfortable in your skin. So, enjoy life! There is no rehearsal. We have it only once. Don't take it too seriously. No one gets out alive! Running water does not flow back. So is life—make it flow smoothly, happily and enjoy!"

"But is it going to be so simple, as you have made it to appear?" Ragini wanted to know.

Mother continued, "To evolve and gain that sort of wisdom or perspective in living life, it means asking yourself: *Am I willing to change*? Or *Am I completely set in my own ways with my fossilized mindset*?

Change is the essence of moving ahead—of maturing, of growing. Nothing in the world that is alive remains unchanged. All nature changes day-to-day, from minute to minute—only the dead stop growing and are quiescent. Fresh water runs on, and if you stop it, it becomes stagnant. So also is with the life of a person or life of a nation. Whether we want to or not, we grow old. Babies become little girls, little girls big girls and then grown-up young women and then old women. And, finally, let me tell you that marriage is not a *finished product* but a *struggle*—a continuing struggle. You have to live with it and work it out. You can accept or reject the way you are treated, but until you heal the wound of your past, you will continue to bleed. It doesn't matter where are you coming from. All that matters is *where are you going*? And finally, let me tell you this also that true prayer as about thanking God for all that has come to you. Actually, since childhood we have been told to *tell God what you need*. But this suggestion is incomplete. It is only half the prayer. We rarely use the other half—*thank God for all he has done*. And that is the reason the prayer continues to remain on the surface, due to the baggage of desires embedded within it. There is no spirit of surrender to God. Surrender comes only when you drop that baggage and pray unconditionally."

Concluding thus, the holy Mother suddenly vanished.

While Ragini was sleeping, Raghav had kept sitting by her bedside as if to keep a watch over her, as though he wanted to take her under his wings, under his protection, never to leave her. "I perhaps have a gift for intense feelings for looming over the pain like my father," he thought internally, and as he looped his pale eyes were staring away like that of a listless or tired pilgrim.

He hadn't himself been able to sleep, feeling stressed under the apprehension as to whether or not Ragini will withdraw her divorce application; whether she would forgive and forget. He rolled over and propped his head on his hand and continued to watch her sleep, as she breathed in and out rather unevenly, at times going into some hard and long breathing. From his wife's occasional moaning, it appeared to him that she probably was sleeping a languorous sleep, interwoven with dreams—as if in oppressive stillness while occasionally he noticed her lips moving involuntarily, as if whispering something to someone. For him it was excruciating to lay there in wait.

He felt the urge to hold her hands to assure himself that he would make her withdraw the application. But he resisted, for he wasn't sure and thought that if she got woken up, she might again create a ruckus, at the dead of night. He shuddered at the thought: "What if she doesn't forgive me, and leaves?"

He gradually brought himself round to think that if someone is dealing with an unresolved conflict, it's best to open up for it is going to be therapeutic. It's best to accept it—preferably pen down the feelings—make an honest confession and try to resolve it. "Words are easier to write than to say, and when the tempers are frayed, writing is the best way to *speak* one's heart out," he thought.

And he instantly drew out a sheet of paper and uncapped his pen. But for a long moment he kept on eyeing the sheet blankly for numerous conflicting thoughts raced his mind, at the end of which he sat down to write:

Dear Ragini,

Err...darling, I'm sorry! What I am going to tell you is in the nature of my written confession. I feel the pen is the most honest way to communicate. I know I caused you agonizing time.

Please forgive me.

I love you. An intimate feeling like this does not bear much telling. But I know you shall not trust me anymore. Nevertheless, I want you to know that I passionately love you. I cannot imagine my life without you and our newly born son, Rohan. No matter what happens, my heart will always want you both in my life. I am aware that most marriages today go wrong for temporary pleasure and lust. But, trust me, my marriage with you is for keeps. A little faith will bring your soul to heaven. But a lot of faith will bring heaven to your soul. I lay awake for I cannot sleep. I have lost it. I have never felt so horribly miserable before and can understand now how in utter desperation a man jumps off a balcony or slits his throat to put an end to his troubles. But I am not going to do any of these mad acts for I know my love for you shall bring you round. I know this bad phase in our lives will pass over.

I can assure you that I intend to stay married to you for the rest of my life—which is a very long time to expect any two people to be in total agreement on everything. So I know we're going to disagree, even fight. But, when we're arguing, I try to remind myself that since we're in this for the long run, we're obviously going to make-up eventually. That makes it easier for me to make up sooner rather than later.

Everything of the world that is nice and beautiful to me is bound up in you. Is that wrong to tell you? I close my eyes to see you even now. You are such an inseparable part of my life. And this bond has further been strengthened by the arrival of Rohan. He is a gift to both of us from the divine. You are his mother and I consider a mother next only to God. A mother is a form of God. So you are divine to me.

I write these words not knowing if you will care to read them. I am in your room, just before you on your bed, while you lay in sleep. I can do nothing except remembering you in these words—remembering the sacred vows we had long back taken together to take care of each other, in bliss and in pain; in happy times and bad in times.

Getting to see your point of view only is good, but even better for a peaceful household is letting yourself see your spouse's point of view also. I'm sure you realize that if there was only one point of view or one way or one side only to a problem, to view a situation, you wouldn't be having an argument or fight at all. Recognizing the possibility that both of us have a good reason for seeking it the way you do, is a solid move towards having better argument.

This is life's greatest truth and its hardest lesson. It is a great truth because it reminds us of our power—not power over others but on ourselves so as to live the life we have imagined. It is a hard lesson, because it causes us to realize that we have chosen the life we are living right now.

What will you see when you look at your life ten or fifteen years from now?

What will you choose?

Life is full of choices!

You have chosen to marry me; you have chosen to live with me and raise the progeny. Or let me put it this way: you choose the food you eat; the clothes you wear; the thoughts you think.

You choose to be calm or restless; you choose to feel appreciative or ungrateful.

Love is a choice!

Anger is a choice!

Understanding is a choice!

Each one of us has the power to choose.

Sometimes we choose the best version of ourselves, but often times we choose the worst.

Everything is a choice.

Perhaps one day we can come to the realization that we have a free hand and can choose the right way only.

I hope that beautiful day for two of us could just be *today*.

Let us accept this day with the wonderful realization that we have the ultimate power to choose between being happy or unhappy; peaceful or agitated; forgiving or resentful. We have power over our mind—not outside events. If we can realize this, we will find strength. Very little is needed to make a happy life; it is all within us, in our way of thinking.

There is a saying, *Life is ten percent what we make it, and ninety percent how we take it*; *how we react to any person or situation*!

Please forgive me, one last time.

I write these words to feel your eyes reading them, resting on them to feel my anguish, my sentiments, my emotions.

I am feeling suffocated. I can hardly breathe.

Have I written that already? I don't even know what I have written—what I wished to say to you, have I said that all?

But yes, I know, I want to definitely say this: Please, for heaven's sake, try and understand how dearly I want you and Rohan in my life. I love you both…

Raghav perhaps wanted to go on writing but saw Ragini slowly moving her limbs. It was dawn. He quickly wrote the following foot-note…

(The pen with which I have written this letter was given to me by my *Papaji* as a gift way back on the day I had graduated. In that he had symbolically perhaps told me that I could write the destiny of my life with it, some day. I didn't understand his sentiments and the value of the gift then, but today when I could somehow retrieve this pen from the cupboard, I thought I could attempt to write the destiny of our marital relationship afresh—burying the past. I mean it. Trust me. And finally, may I wish that you may gain the awareness to trust me…)

...and folded the letter to keep it in her purse, lying there by her bedside.

Ragini gradually woke up, feeling uplifted, more uplifted than she ever had been. Truly, blissful. She felt decorated and beamed, as if she was an X'mas tree. Raghav noticed it and felt immensely pleased.

Getting Empowered!

Ragini woke up, perhaps not knowing where she was—a wee bit disoriented, initially. She slowly awoke to the changed thoughts and appeared meditative, in silence. She appeared to be sitting on an immense stillness and quietness, with recovered spirits and sanguine looks. Her mind circled for a moment, like a bird looking for a place to perch. The chirping of a bird resting on the open window of her bedroom, caught her attention. She fixed her gaze on the bird for a while.

From an intensely expressive emotion slowly developing on her face, it became evident to Raghav that she perhaps was feeling uplifted due to the musical note in that bird's chirp. Her eyes were still partially closed. She rubbed the eyelids, and opened her eyes. There was shine in them. Perhaps, she was feeling uplifted, more uplifted than she ever had been. In a subtle way—blissful. She felt decorated and beamed, as if she was a Christmas tree. Raghav noticed it and felt immensely gladdened. It was a salubrious feel—akin to a sudden drop in air pollution around due to rain. He could now breathe clean and free.

However, not a syllable passed aloud between the two, and they waited in silence. She softly smiled. Her eyes seemed to take on a knowingly playful look.

The first light of dawn was filtering through. The sun was just breaking through the morning mist, as she woke up. Without any thought, Raghav felt that there was infinitely more to that morning's sunrays than was apparent; there was more oxygen in the air. "That soft luminosity filtering through the window was life giving, not life ebbing for him," he thought. Somehow, he was led to feel hopeful for he had seen light at the end of that obnoxiously dark tunnel-like night. He felt inclined to do everything possible to help him draw Ragini out of her dreary past. She sat up weary-eyed. When he darted up to her, he noticed her face was no longer stern or scornful; her eyes were moving with a glimmer and, he felt, as if these were telling him, *it would be alright hereafter*. He saw a flash of something in her eyes though they looked weary, and although that flash died away at once, Raghav was happy for that moment.

He felt a sudden lightness in his chest that he couldn't name immediately, but couldn't deny either. He couldn't as yet recover from the surprise of what had brought about that massive change in Ragini's disposition.

"Of whom, of what are you thinking?" he asked her, whose countenance he had been watching for quite some time with great puzzlement, arrested by the absorbed expression on her face which seemed to have seized and fixed every feature into a kind of statuesque repose.

"Nothing, actually," returned Ragini, lowering her voice to a whisper and looking at him with peaceful eyes. The blaze of her pain had all gone, vanished. She looked more beautiful than ever there at home, Raghav got the feel. But her new and unexpected mood was completely baffling, bewildering to him. Nevertheless, he felt curious while feeling his eyes getting moist, not because of any sadness, but because Ragini's changed attitude was unbelievably uplifting, inspirational and even heart-rendering.

Now, he saw a deliberate composure on her face, though he felt depressed for being unable to understand this sudden change in her disposition. Although in a way it invited easy confidence, yet he felt to persuade himself to hope that perhaps worst was over.

Ragini wondered whether he was thinking what she thought he was thinking, and then she heard the edge to his voice, "Are you still angry?... I mean..." She heard him in silence.

Not exactly sure of what he meant, she interrupted him to say, "What I want to do, (pause), having just thought of it, is to meet her...what's her name?...you said!" Her words sounded measured and well considered.

Raghav heard it abruptly, least expecting it, and felt nonplused for he couldn't follow that rather curly question. He strained his ears hoping he heard her right. "What did you say?" he asked, putting his right hand to his ear, unable to trust what he had just heard.

"I want to meet her; yes I got it now. Rosy, your friend," she repeated.

"And...then what?" uncharacteristically he asked hesitatingly, an odd note stealing into his voice, as he appeared desperate to know the purpose. He could not understand the purpose.

Her soft and small voice, almost languid demeanor and understated style appeared deceptive to him because only sometime back, with her mouth curved in derision, she had shown unwavering hot temper, decisive attitude, assertiveness with stentorian rebukes to uphold her cause against her husband, whom she had labeled as unfaithful and adulterous. And now here she was calm, unruffled, dignified—ready to accommodate and sounded business-like.

"What had happened during the few hours that she had fallen asleep," Raghav wondered, perplexed. He became nervous, and didn't know how to respond to his wife's strange demand. He remained speechless for a long moment.

"I said something to you, just now," she reminded him.

In fact, her softness and economy with words made him still more restless. He wanted her to reveal the reason for this sudden change of her heart, but couldn't ask.

"When do you want to?" She cut him short to say, "Invite them both at tea, this afternoon."

That totally unnerved him. He stood still like a stone. His eyes looked as big, conspicuous and startled as two boiled eggs on a black plate, and he looked ardently into her face.

She looked back at him.

They paused, motionless, watching each other, for a moment she was precisely what she appeared to be, in a relaxed frame of mind.

"She had raged and stormed and called her all sorts of names—a bitch, a whore—and now she wants to invite her for tea," Raghav looked perplexed, completely at a loss. "What a terrible scene she had created, which is still as fresh and green in my mind as vegetables in my refrigerator. And now this scene of reconciliation," he kept scratching his head and racked his brains to unravel the mystery, "How can a person change so suddenly. It's hell–heaven!" He remembered having been told: *When life is sweet, say thank you and celebrate. When life is bitter, still say thank you, and hope for the best to grow.*

They settled into another silence, one that was neither intimate nor particularly uncomfortable. But since he could feel a leeway in the tone of her voice, he conjectured, "She is back to her normal self," and naturally started feeling easy for it gave him reason enough to feel that there was more in the air than oxygen.

It seemed to be a change of season, a warmer tide seemed to have washed over her, the sense of which made Raghav feel ecstatic. Getting reasonably assured that his wife was now behaving normally, he said to himself, "And so my duty is clearly defined by the change of circumstances." Picking up the telephone he dialed Dinesh's number to say, "My wife Ragini and I have come back from Srinagar with our newborn son. She wants to meet you and your wife, both. Could you please come over to our residence this afternoon to meet over a cup of tea."

"I think it's just fine with me, but just a minute, let me check up with Rosy and I will come back," he responded enthusiastically.

Soon the bell rang and Raghav picked up the receiver to hear, "Yes, we are coming. See you at 4 o'clock."

He felt stunned, in a way. He had expected Rosy wouldn't agree. But realized that as a result of her emotional maturity and literate exchanges with her husband, leading to effective dialogue, understanding and commitment in relationship. "They have found deeper respect for each other and thus have been able to overcome that rough terrain, to move ahead in life," he thought.

"They are coming," he informed Ragini. "Do you want me to get anything from the market or do you want me to stay back to help you in setting up things for the meet?" he asked.

"No, don't you worry. I will manage," she assured.

"That is fine. I am going to office then," he responded.

To Ragini her husband, who was known to be impatient with the other's point of view, that day appeared contemplative, almost philosophical, rather calm. She found him in a strange reflective mood, but happy at the turn of events.

After Raghav left for office, Ragini wore a blue apron and sang to old film song track playing soulfully—*Tumhe Apna Banane Ki Kasam*—while dusting and scrubbing the drawing room clean and putting things in place, for an hour or so. She then thought of a shower and instantly remembered her friend having told her once, "Shower doesn't just rid me of grime. It also helps me kick-start the day on a fresh note. And more than that, a good warm-water bath in the tub mixed with soothing music leaves me feeling invigorated because it is the most efficient mood elevators and tension tamers." Ragini mused. She certainly wanted to feel rejuvenated and kick-start her day on a fresh note, devoid of any stress.

So she switched off the radio, played some soothing instrumental music on the tape instead and just slipped into the tub, sipping her favorite drink and forgot the world. She felt herself completely in the moment, and hummed the tunes under her breath. Relaxed, she later came out dripping till she wrapped herself in a towel and then stepped into a new sleeveless sexy white muslin gown with thigh-high slits and slashed low at the neck, and stood in front of a huge mirror to comb her long black hair.

She felt her brassiere strap a bit loose on one end. So she took off the gown to pull the straps up and adjusted these onto her shoulders, that brought out the right shape of her plump, round fulsome breasts. She gazed in the mirror in a manner as if she had started noticing herself in it with a signature look, and then hesitatingly took her right hand forefingers to touch her bosoms softly, tenderly as if to feel their tautness and found them firm yet yielding. She put the gown on again which clung so tight to the contours of her body as if to hug, and the exuberance made her feel prolific, in a subtle way. Paying a close attention to herself, she bathed in a glow of slow-pulsed joy that seemed to rise mysteriously out of the music heard from within.

"Do I look beautiful?" purring she uttered, after putting on make-up, looking into her eyes in the mirror and turning from left pose to right and then left again. She felt sizzling and smoldering in her gown. "Pampering one's self—body, spirit and mind—gives a woman her most intense feminine experiences," she thought to herself. Then she wore big size sparking diamonds on each of her earlobes, a small one on left nostril and flower-shaped ring on her middle finger. She, indeed, wanted to pamper herself with something luxurious. She kept staring into the mirror to adored her svelte and glam figure and then with eyes widened and tongue stuck out, she felt amazed at her own prolific figure, as if she was Narkissos—the youth in Greek myth who fell in love with own reflection. A case of narcissism, perhaps, when one's excessive or erotic interest in oneself makes it hard to recognize one's self.

There perhaps was a reason to feel so for she after all had found her way out of the depression she had gone into. Her heart, which had been thudding against her rib cage, had gone back gratefully to its normal rhythm. And she heaved a sigh of relief and gave a shout of joy. A great calm seemed to settle upon her now.

She later ordered, on phone, to have sweets and some snacks delivered at home. "I must receive and entertain the couple well," she told herself with a light chuckle, while going about organizing everything around.

Then when she opened her purse to keep the money handy for paying the bill, she found Raghav's letter kept there, and opened it. She read every word—intently, patiently. Finding the letter extremely sentimental and sniveling in tone, and feeling emollient she felt like scolding herself silently for the mental torture, she thought, she had caused to her husband on an otherwise simple issue. She read the whole letter again, and it reinforced her love for him. Tears kept coming to her eyes while reading the letter and unconsciously she took her lower lip in between her teeth and kept chewing, until it was raw and bloody red as meat.

It was the innocence and purity of passion of Raghav that had struck her like a spear, she now felt. The feeling endeared him to her, rather again. She quelled her misgivings. "It's just fine now," she told herself firmly, and breathed a big, genuine sigh of relief. A peculiarly soft feeling washed over her—a feeling that was unfamiliar but very delicious, very entertaining. So overwhelming! Tears kept streaming down from her eyes with sudden foreknowledge.

After all the turmoil, a radiant peace had now settled upon her. Having decided to forgive and forget, she heard her mind telling the self, "I'm now feeling better, together, sane and healed. I kind of went into a shell for a while. Got closed. But then I could venture out and see light after the noble-hearted Judge had brought me to senses, following which that dreamy interaction with that celestial body—holy mother took place." She visualized all that again and knelt to say, "Thank you, Oh God!" There was new sense of elation in her gait and her body swayed like a flower-bedecked branch.

Now she felt exulting, and it helped her soak in her own positivity and then she could see things for what they appeared—good, healthy and peaceful. Although she felt the pang of remorse that she had unduly made mountain of a mole and caused extreme pain to Raghav, yet now she was feeling the gnawing desire to be with him, wanting him back home soon. She felt emotionally recharged.

Raghav came home early with a face that was like stone—cold and motionless. There was lurking suspicion, obviously concerned about the outcome of the meeting of the two, so to say, warring women. "Would it lead to fireworks between the two?" this apprehension agonized him mentally. Questions were shooting through his mind like arrows. His heart drummed with fear. For a moment, he was shivering with the thought: "What if Ragini caused any ruckus?" And he wished ardently that both may refuse to bite the bait.

Ragini looked at him and could see the lurking pain in his eyes. "You may like to have a bath to get ready," she told him. Her voice was unusually cool and soft—one that an early spring breeze possesses.

"Yes, I would," he replied, unsuspectingly.

"What is that? You wore a T-shirt with a picture of Gandhiji printed on it," she observed, bit unsure.

"Yes, I need peace. Definitely. And *ahimsa* (nonviolence) certainly," he responded, with a chuckle or was he perhaps really seeking permanent truce, symbolically. Then on a serious note, he told his wife, "Hereafter I want to experience nothing but peace, joy, love, bliss, purity and wisdom by giving attention to the self and checking and changing the self."

Ragini on her part, having read his loving letter, was experiencing regret at the turn of events. She had heard the sincere dignity in his words, and now had something of a valid reason to forgive her husband. And in that single moment her heart turned over and she knew that she still loved him dearly.

To Raghav she now looked equipoised—that precise moment in the ocean when a wave neither rises nor falls—as if she had reached an equilibrium after counter-balancing things or events; her eyes as soothing as a smooth green lake into which he wanted to dive in and lose himself for the moment. He felt his fears and sorrows passing away and giving place to a comforting peace and contentment.

The couple seemed to have mentally traveled quite a vast distance towards each other through the night, and subsequently. By now, a kind of equilibrium, though unsure but safe, had hung between them. Ragini, to him, now appeared hugely changed—less vulnerable, more understanding, less distant, more reachable—than the previous night. Both changed—less vulnerable, more understanding, less distant, more reachable. Both now seemed pulling together by tender feelings and emotions that in a subtle way encircled their necks with its fine soft threads.

Relief flooded through Raghav. He felt pleasantly surprised when he noticed all the preparations that his wife had made for the ensuing meet. It was a moment he wanted to be certain, and to feel assured that he wasn't dreaming, he pinched his right thigh. "Thank God," he said in a whisper to himself, "It's really true! It indeed is! It's wonderful!"

But there was very little talk between the two. He wanted to but was not quite sure how she would respond. He thought best to bid time. "I need to focus not on what is wrong but on what is right. What I need to do is to say a quiet prayer," he thought mentally. And this is what he did and kept on reciting *Gayatri Mantra* addressed to the immanent and the transcendent Divine, in a determined bid to usher in light, the inner light.

This, he believed, to be one of the most sacred universal practices that invokes the creative principle of the Sun in the form named *Savitr*:

Aum

Bhur bhuvah svaha

Tat savitr verenyam

Bhargo devasya deemahe

Dhiyo yo nah prachodaya

In essence, it means, *Oh, Creator of the Universe*!

I meditate upon thy Supreme splendour.

May thy radiant power illuminate my intellect,

Destroy my sins and guide me in the right direction.

And then he felt he had seen enough in his wife's face to impel her to take her hand and clasp it for a while as he said, "Thank you so very much, Ragini."

He kissed her soft palm that pressed upon his lips.

She responded with a warm smile.

There were sparks between them

He gave her a squeeze, tenderly.

She welcomed it.

Both then hugged each other, tightly…just then the doorbell rang.

The Meeting of Hearts and Minds!

"I think they have come. It is 4 o'clock" Raghav said, looking at his watch.

And both hurried to cool down and compose themselves—Ragini arranging her disoriented looks fixed her braid with the adornments and settled her sari folds in place.

The bell rang once again, followed by a quick knock, as if the visitors at the door had police on their heels.

Raghav and Ragini rushed to the front door.

Dinesh and Rosy were there. They were warmly greeted—Ragini leading her husband.

After presenting Rosy a bunch of colorful tulips, which she accepted with a veneer of sophistication—looking straight into the expectation of her eyes—Ragini said a hearty welcome, though coolly for she perhaps waited to swallow her shyness. Rosy hugged her enthusiastically with apparent warmth, as if they were old friends, catching up with each other after ages.

Ragini then shed that look of waiting on her face because she now thought to herself, "She's different. She's special. She isn't what I had thought of her."

"How are you, sir," Raghav asked Dinesh, who laughed benignly.

"It's nice you have come," Raggii told Rosy, enthralled by her graceful charm—petite and ethereal—there was something that produced a physical effect of a radiant figure.

"*Lijiye hum aa gaye,*" Rosy said genially. "I would have in any case shown up even if it meant canceling an audience with the Pope," she said with felicity, followed by a buck-toothed smile that came out like the early morning sun. She spoke those words in a way that brought out her friendly disposition and her unquestionable honesty, Ragini felt.

She wasn't prepared mentally to respond with such instant warmth, and remained a bit shy, if not cold. She couldn't match Rosy's extravert bent of mind, whose personality she found gorgeous, with ebony cascading locks spun and combed for confining pin to restrain, skin the color of cream, two lips that were pointed and were as red as ripened cherries, with big blue expressive eyes that were soft, serene and truthful—so clear that one could swim in them, with curves and boobs, her jeans following the curves of her butt like a second skin and a sweater-dress that showed off her assets. The lines of her body were long, clear, distinct and symmetrical—just perfect.

Ragini gave her one long speculative look, her gaze searching over her like a spotlight, and found her refreshingly graceful in every step she took, pose that she gave and gesture that she made. She couldn't keep her eyes to herself; they just helped themselves to a long stare at her perfect body because her personality was as engaging as her looks—the liquid pool of her fawn-like eyes, her sylph-like grace and her heart-stopping smile.

"The graceful severity of poise and movement made Rosy different from the crowd," Ragini mused with eyes full of drool. To her she appeared an extremely bubbly person, just exuberant—sharp, trendy, elegant, sophisticated. So she now responded gracefully by softly holding her hand to usher her into the drawing room, where she followed her with her eyes wherever she went.

Dinesh and Raghav kept talking in the corridor, for a while.

"Ragini, it's nice meeting you," Rosy said with the childishness of expression and smiled, a glacial smile, out of the crease of her mouth while her big blue eyes freewheeled around the room, like a flying kite, staying nowhere, moving quickly from one direction to another and on again, and on yet again. She circled the whole room without moving from her seat. And then, she did a touch up of gloss on her lips in a way as if she was loving every inch of her body.

Ragini smiled, a tad coyly.

Rosy had come dressed in comfy casuals, dressed rightly to suit her shape. Ragini noticed that she appeared to be feeling good in her own skin with blonde hair and an effortless smile, but it was her chubby tummy and fuller legs that specially invited her attention. She looked beautiful with a super strong presence to carry off her bold look. She wore her beauty and charm lightly on her lithe body. She drew a strand of her hair down on her face and it flew loosely in front of her face. She blew it to the side and blinking or arching her bleached, tweezed eyebrows, she said, "Ragini, dear Ragini," as if testing her name like an old key, and trying to see if she could enter her heart and make her forget the dirty episode, involving her husband, so that she could feel comfortable in her company, "You know how I wished to meet you. I feel nice, I came here," and laughed a small laugh as if trying to wipe clean any smug look left on her face.

Now Ragini felt no labor to like Rosy. Indeed, she felt drawn to her like a magnet—to become intimate with her—as she found her to be an exceptionally simple and graceful lady, whose warmth bowled her over. Though coveted for her bearing, her breeding, her looks and her beauty, she exhibited no vanity, threw no tantrums. Her whole demeanor, vivacious and effervescent, made bold and elegant, yet unspoken statements. In her presence, Ragini gradually felt festive, light and important. Radiance spread over her face. Therefore, she now enjoyed fraternizing with her because she gradually came to find *substance* over *style* in her. Indeed, a great camaraderie was instantly born out of genuine love and respect for her. Nothing fake.

As Dinesh entered the drawing room, it seemed to get filled with his graceful presence and air of humor when, making himself comfortable on a cushy sofa, he said: "Ragini, you know what? Don't you look surprised! Let me tell you I have been in love with this beautiful woman (turning to his wife) since we got married. I know she could be an irresistible attraction to any Romeo who would wish to cling to her like a plank during a shipwreck. (*laughs*). That makes me feel proud, and I often feel like singing a song in her praise!"

Rosy immediately moved closer to him and reaching out, planted a peck on his cheek. Next, Dinesh returned the warm gesture, and even bowed to kiss her hands! "My pleasure, Madam," he said romantically.

Rosy blushed a little and beamed. Then turning to Ragini, she said, "I admire him because besides being a good loving husband that a woman aspires for, he is above all a wonderful human being—very understanding, compassionate and considerate." With a twinkle in her eyes she further added, "He is so chivalrous. Be it getting into an elevator or a car, or sitting down for lunch, it's always women first for him. He loves buying me gifts, so do I. But we don't need to give things to one another to prove our love and admiration for each other. It's there in any case.

Dinesh then turned to Raghav and said, "You know, what? After a few years of marriage, a husband tries to find her girlfriend in his wife. Mostly he loses both because of his stupidity. I'm lucky, I've found my wife as well as girlfriend in Rosy. I am a very successful man in all what I do, and she is surprised at my lucky-go-way-of-life. In fact, I'm fun loving and she's a person loving fun. And you know what? There is a good, old saying: *Behind every successful man there is a woman*. But I hold: 'Every successful man has a *surprised wife* besides him.'

No question of being in front or behind. And for a long and happy married life, the husband should be *successful* (but not egoist) and the wife *beautiful* (but not insipid)."

"On that I've a take," Raghav responded in a rather self-conscious manner, "A certain wife asked her husband: *After marriage, how much you've changed?*. *One has to change*, he replied and added, *This shirt I'm wearing if I don't change it for a week or so, it will stink. So it is high time you also change from a jealous girlfriend to my trusting wife*."

"No surprises, there! Only realism," Dinesh responded, and went on to add, "A spouse, particularly, the wife gets upset when the other partner does anything without his or her knowledge and will question, argue, get suspicious and often times then will stalk him or her when one comes to believe something is cooking up behind his or her back. They then keep a watch on each other on the sly. If one is found talking on mobile beyond the reach of the other, or sending an SMS, the alarm in the belly start ringing. This situation comes up when any of the two become obsessive. It is like behaving in an animalistic way.

Obsessive people get upset by the partner's interest in anything other than him or her. The fact of the matter is that one may possess the whole world and remain free of *my-ness* and *mine-ness*. Or one may have very little but be hopelessly dependent, possessive and miserable! The turning point is to look within and become aware. Awareness is a function of the intellect. I need to look *within*! Am I jealous, vicious and negative towards people? Or am I compassionate, loving and affectionate? Am I small minded and obsessed with myself or am I inspired with a broader and higher vision? In this context, I may refer to what I recently came to read. President Pranab Mukherjee's wife Suvra had said that she and her husband had never fought even once during the fifty-five years they were married. Indeed, every night, no matter how busy he was or how late his day ended, when he got home, Pranab Mukherjee spent time with his ailing wife. This was the routine for the last six to seven years that his wife was unwell. He spoke to her, comforted and soothed her. This was the moment she waited for every day—her time with her loving husband of long fifty-five years."

"There is a great insight, I must say," Raghav commented.

"But, you know, what?" Dinesh continued, "The only way to stop emotional infidelity is to build emotional *intimacy* in the relationship of husband and wife between the two partners. Any couple needs to be honest to each other even when having trespassed somewhere or the other, and act with maturity to reconstruct their marriage. Healthy relations focus on solving problems of mistrust, not on who wins or loses. Apologize and seek forgiveness. After all this is the person you have vowed to love and spend life with!"...and he continued further, "And you know what?" but then paused to say... "Am I using that typical prefix, that throwaway line—I mean *You know, what*? too often? I'm sorry...it just doesn't go off my tongue, I picked it up while in USA. I feel I can't communicate without using it."

While the conversation got light and sparkling, there was lot of laughter and banter. From titters and giggles to guffaws, chukles and cackles—laughter became contemptuous as well as fun. The moments glided on, and a feeling of good fellowship passed around the circle like a mystic chord, now holding and binding the two couples together with jest and laughter.

Watching everyone laughing and enjoying the fun-filled company, Dinesh said, "A thought has flitted through my mind. What if the entire world's laughter was to be canned. Would it stay? Would a whiff of it make one happy? Doesn't the sight of someone laughing helplessly set you off as well? A genuine guffaw is contagious."

"That is very thoughtful of you," all said in chorus.

Indeed, the ambient atmosphere had brought the two women, Rosy and Ragini, close to each other, for not only Rosy moved from her seat and sat next to Ragini but complimented her for her nicely done-up home. "Very aptly, decently furnished!" she told her, and followed it up by adding, "But to borrow Dinesh's *takiya-kalaam* (leitmotif), *you know what* (in fact he says it in such a catchy monotone that I feel tempted to use it myself)...the fact also remains that whether I like my room or not doesn't depend on how the furniture is arranged...it's how I arrange my mind."

"What a wonderful thought, dear! It's, indeed, pregnant with whole lot of meaning," her husband said with satisfaction, bowing to her ineluctable charm and grace. "And you know, what...an open, orderly, intelligent, erudite mind is what ultimately makes or mars our lives. The fact of the matter is that in everyone's life there are uncertainties. We all go through inner conflicts. It would be a mistake to think that all things are under our control. In times of frustration, dejection, worry, grief etc., in life, it will be foolish to abandon hope altogether. It would be wise and prudent to go to someone you can trust and unburden your innermost feelings and emotions, rather than getting closed like a lock and invite untold miseries for self and others around. Just as physical body can get infected with disease, the mind also suffers as a consequence of what we say or do. While medical remedy, at whatever the monetary expense, can be made available to an ailing body, but when the mind suffers an aberration owing to one or the other traumatic events, the consequences can be hugely damaging, irreparable. Sometimes, if things are not handled with swiftness and maturity, it could lead to a point of no return," Dinesh elaborated.

"Obviously, you appear to have the innate sense to explicitly explain the matter the way you have done. I like it, want to taste it, record it," Raghav said humbly. Ragini kept listening attentively, all the while, as if drawing lessons.

"And you know what...?" Dinesh said, but...before Dinesh could proceed any further, his wife felt impatient and interrupted him to ask, "What is the matter with you today? I suppose you are more *chirpy* than ever before, even going hoggish, monopolizing all the attention; reveling in the spotlight."

"Now, isn't that being envious?" her husband quizzed, "It is not done. A good, devoted wife will not cut short her hubby. Isn't it?"

"Now listen, the traditional wife who used to submerge her identity into that of her husband no longer represents a viable model for most modern-day women," his wife responded.

"Yes, I appreciate that. But one has to have values to be honest in any relationship. And finally, caring is the rock that has to be there before love is possible. Caring is the feeling of what the other person is feeling. Some people call it empathy, I mean you develop the capacity to exactly feel the way your spouse feels—good or bad and seeing things from each other's point of view. It would be foolish not to love your spouse for what he or she is basically, and instead base it on the condition that what one wants him or her to be. You just want to turn him or her into someone to fill your needs. That would be absurd. Genuine caring about people usually leads to success and, therefore, happiness. And as a couple grows in relationship their understanding of each other; their influence over each other is subtle. And let me say that when I follow my heart, I don't forget my head."

As if to take over from her husband, Rosy now added, "A husband and wife must learn to accept each other with love, pride and dignity. Each spouse must be honest to the other, even though occasional mistakes, misunderstanding occur. There will be disagreements, arguments and small fights. Perfect communication is when both partners are able to open up, be honest and actually tell how they feel about each other and thereby help each other sort out differences in a mature way. Therefore, as soon as the clouds generated by occasional tiffs, float away, intelligent couples must be able to see the azure sky beneath. They need to be in love, whatever the situation. I must explain to you, dear Ragini, the kind of equation I share with my husband. It is so good to have him there in my life because it feels like someone is standing behind you, whatever the situation. I feel protected. Having that sense of support makes me deal with my problems, if any, in a much better way."

Raghav felt like responding, and said, "Perhaps love needs to be expressed in hundreds of small little ways. Just saying, *I love you* is not enough. A certain wife asked her husband: *Do you love me*? *You can read it in my eyes*, replied the husband. *But dear, you know I am illiterate,* countered the wife" (laughs).

"Apart from being literate or illiterate, you know what...beyond love and attraction, there has to be a genuine concern, mutual respect and real friendship on a day-to-day basis—learn to laugh, agree to spouse's point of view, change the topic or just keep quiet; talk about subjects which interest the other, not just yourself, even if those subjects are truly boring. Remember, being flexible in approach, being able to see and understand other's point of view, stopping to make hasty judgments is the essence of moving forward in life. To be stiff, obstinate is not going to help. Stiffness is the sign of a dead body; being humble and susceptible to change is the sign of life. But, if a wife senses that her husband is trying to change her, she will resist to change. Instead of criticizing, the husband must say to her: *Honey, all these years I've been trying to change you, but now I realize that it's me who needs to change first.* It means he now focuses the change on himself, on his own attitude or mindset about the way he has been, about the way he has been treating her," elaborated Dinesh, and continued to add, "Never ever turn your face away from your spouse. I attended a Christian marriage held in the neighborhood church. After the rituals when the man and the woman were blessed and greeted as husband–wife, the erudite priest gave the couple one-line lesson in happy matrimony:

Never say shut up to each other!

This means to *listen to what the other spouse has to say, even if it is trash,*" he explained.

And he continued, "There can be difference of opinions; there can be disagreements because points of view differ, but the rule should be to patiently hear out the other. What is needed is to raise the level of reasoned words but not the level of voice. A lot of effort and patience are required to make a marriage work. It's important to be open to growing together and when the going gets tough, the two partners need to jointly work to smoothen the rough edges by being open to hear the other's point of view. It's said don't change your partner, change your expectations. Good and intelligent couples never take a fight to bed. They may not have any black-and-white rules, but what makes their marriage work is a basic frame that they don't cross. In decisions, they think about the other's feelings."

Ragini's eyes got teary as if she was reliving her own life experiences, but with a flutter of her eyelashes she concealed her emotions to say, "That is an erudite disposition. Enlightening, indeed. It's inspirational, it moves, motivates and forces you to think. Indeed, I get a nice feeling that what all you have said is scripted for me. There are terrible skills in you to connect with people instantly for you talk of relevant concepts and big ideas. Why don't you write a book on the subject? I am sure you can breathe humor and life into your writing," responded Ragini.

Raising his hand as if seeking permission to interrupt her, Dinesh said, "You seem to be overlooking that we need some tea and snacks now."

"Geeta, will you serve the cold drinks and make tea also, please? Thank you," Ragini called out to her maid, and to Dinesh she said, effusively, "Sorry, *Bhai Sahib* (brother), I got totally engrossed in your words of wisdom, all this while. It has been wonderful listening, indeed, thought provoking."

Rosy couldn't help wondering if the politeness in speaking to her maid was due to the fact that Ragini was playing it nice and beautiful in the presence of her guests or was it her natural disposition? And as she looked towards Ragini, she, as if to answer her guest's unasked question, gave her such a genuine smile which perhaps meant to convey to her, "I've always tried to be polite with everybody, including my domestic help, but, yes, temporarily I had lost my balance of mind to create the ruckus with my husband, but the ambience of today's meeting did change my perception totally."

"Oh! what a nice spread! It's just fabulous tea, mouth-watering snacks, exactly. I particularly like those delectable, piping hot *samosas*—the quintessential Indian snack. I call it *tasty triangle.* Some say that it came to India from Persia. Abul Fazal scholar-statesman, one of the nine legendary gems of Mughal Emperor, Akbar Baadshaha's court as well as Ibn Batuta, the Moroccan traveler who visited India in the fourteenth century, have chronicled that this delectable snack invariably found a place on the guest's plates. It has been a dish fit to be served to Emperors. So, I feel like being treated as a king right now. And you know what...?, I am literally sold out on *samosas,* and picking up one to savor it which filled his mouth, he paused with a thoughtful expression on his face, as if he had some subtle or profound message to give, and he elaborated:

The *samosa* is the archetypal Indian snack. You can have hot *samosa* with green mint or *imli* chutney or just ketchup alongside your tea or you can have it cold, several hours after they have been made. You can have your *samosa* filled with spicy keema (minced meat) or you can have totally vegetarian version filled with smashed potatoes, paneer, peas and other fillings. You can enjoy the hefty Punjabi version or you can have the thinner, more delicate Bohra version from Mumbai. You can eat your *samosa* on the railway platform anywhere in our country or you can buy it even in supermarkets in UK, USA or Canada. It has gone international. And there is more as to its chronical…"

"Now, now, hold on! just a minute," called out his wife, "Are we here to listen to the familial history of your this, what you called, *tasty triangle*?"

"Rosy, my dear! You know what?…sarcasm just precedes anger as one of the most common stress inducers," Dinesh reacted, and continued, "Talking of sarcasm, I'm reminded of an episode. A woman had once invited the famous movie director, Sir Alfred Hitchcock, home for dinner. She had put in a lot of effort into planning the menu but somehow Hitchcock was upset that the portions being served were rather small and he was left hungry. As the evening ended, the woman bid him farewell. *I hope you'll dine with us again soon*, the woman said.

By all means, let's start right now, replied Hitchcock, dripping sarcasm. That stunned his hostess, and left her deeply embarrassed, even hurt. The right approach, I suppose, for Hitchcock would have been to appreciate the taste of the food and to ask for more helpings rather than having remained half-fed, with a grouse. That is what you seem to be doing to me." (laughs).

"Oh, no dear!" urged Rosy, "Ignore my words, but sift the substance. I mean let you eat to your heart's fill. Shall I serve you more *portions*? (laughs again).

"That is fine," replied he, "Actually, one need not respond to whatever is thrown at him or her. Sarcasm is a weapon that hurts only if one picks it up and decides to stab oneself. I don't do that. I can simply walk away. And so let me have another *samosa.*"

Raghav now said to Dinesh, "But, that is hugely interesting to listen to. Indeed, your oratory infused with apt sense of humor is ineffable—too great for description in words, I must say."

"Oh, come on, don't you sound like a sycophant," snapped Rosy.

"Alright, let me change the subject. Listen to a good joke on sycophancy…" Dinesh now said.

"Oh, no. Enough! I know everything you do is a grand gesture, never small or mediocre. But more next time," Rosy reacted, incisively.

"Just a minute, please. I haven't finished yet," her husband said, and then paused, contemplatively, for a few seconds, as if weighing whether to continue or not. "It's bad manners to cut and finish somebody's sentence. The way we fail to listen is symbolic of the way we live. We often treat communication as if it were a race," he elaborated, "But that apart, what I meant to stress was that a thoughtful spouse should learn to follow the adage: *What I cannot love, I overlook.* Strange, as it may seem, by accepting ourselves and our partners as we are—even embracing one another's peculiarities with affection and humor—we open the way to mutual adjustment, growth and transformation. Thus, what most people call falling in love is really falling in pattern. But allow me to say this also that nearly all women are less satisfied with the companionship of their respective husbands after a few years of marriage than they formerly were, because *most men use their partners as sleeping* pills. And with the advent of children, many husbands are prone to feel the necessity to work harder and longer which means remaining out on work for long hours and that in turn makes many wives complain of loss of spousal intimacy. Sometimes, in an odd situation, the allegation flung at each other is that he or she comes late from office because there is the *other-woman* or the *other-man* in the frame. Both then start drifting. It's sad, unfortunate. But it needs to be understood that marriage provides a constant demand to grow up or get out. Some of us choose the latter option, trading one partner's irritating traits for someone with a new set of offending habits. And we end up repeating the same bad experiences until we finally commit to a relationship for better or worse, or decide to stay single. But at what a colossal loss and suffering?"

"How truly perspicacious!" said Ragini, who was all along listening intently, patiently—assimilating the essence of what all Dinesh was saying. She felt impressed by his incredible sense of humor, his erudite knowledge and power of oratory, the musical cadences of his delivery and the poetry of his expressions, which came from his heart more than the head—not a word was out of place, not a joke humorless, not a thought thoughtless, not a sentiment out of sync. She looked at him with eyes full of appreciation, stood up and clapped thrice and said, "Three cheers. You are truly amazing, full of wisdom, interesting and humorous. I had been feeling low on spirits and energy. Your words have worked on me like a booster and stabilizer, truly uplifting. All this while, I have been marveling at your verbal dexterity. Truly, you allow words to breathe through you."

Dinesh then responded to say, “OMG, Thank you, thank you so much! You know what? I like to dress my words in humor. Someone said if you want to make a point, make them laugh. Humor and laughter are a reflection of one's internal state. One need not wear anything if one can wear a smile on one's face. If you can bear with me for a little while more, I want to recall an episode from the days of my hostel life.

There was a hosteller named Kothari, nicknamed *Munna.* One day there was a knock on my room door, which became louder and desperate—bang… bang!

‘Who is that?’ I called out.

‘Me, Kothari… I mean *Munna,*’ your buddy, hostelmate.

‘But what do you want at this unearthly hour? It's past midnight,’ I now asked.

‘But why don't you open the door first?’ he inquired, ’It's something urgent.’

‘Wait a minute, just opening,’ and the door opened. What is it?’ I shouted at him rubbing my eyelids.

‘I desperately need to go to the washroom. It's pressing. I can't hold it any longer,’ he said.

‘But what to me? Damn it!’ I asked with startled eyes.

‘Why the hell do you look at me with those two pairs of protruding eyes that are almost ready to come out of their sockets? After all I haven't asked for your kidneys,’ and he laughed his usual uproarious laugh that left me perplexed.

‘*Yaar*, it's all dark out there…a fused bulb, I think,’ Munna continued. ’Can't you escort me there? I want your company, please!’ he mockingly said and ran away to his room, leaving me fretting and fuming. For a little distance, I ran after him, mouthing abuses.

Munna liked playing pranks. He was known for his gut-busting humor. Indeed, he was a great punster.

‘So, how did you get the knack of it?’ many mates would ask him, perhaps wanting to be like him.

'Since childhood I have gone through tough situations. You could either run away or fight or makes jokes. I decided to make jokes to laugh away a dirty situation. Humor is a sure way to handle life better,' he would say. Never in temper, he would disarm his opponents with his wit and jokes, sometimes even risque ones. He had a puckish, whacky sense of humor—a mix of comedy and double entendre, which was as unmatched as it was irrepressible, howsoever serious the occasion might have been (and that, as in the case of Laurel and Hardy), invariably landed him in a mess. But, in any case, it was laughter all the way. Humor, the daughter of reason, left him never. And let me also tell you that anger is the easiest emotion to portray for anybody. But to make people laugh, isn't."

"Enough, enough of that stuff," cautioned Rosy, "It's time to leave."

"Dear, were we to put hand on heart, it would not be difficult to say who among us would not like to self-express with abandon every once in a while. I got a huge chance today. But sorry, I mean yes, you are right. We must now leave," responded Dinesh, "Let us go."

Ragini feeling charmed with the open and frank talk of Dinesh, said what came to her lips, "I suppose it has been a wonderful meeting, as if choreographed for an event—aptly and deftly. I have immensely enjoyed it. The flow of your words has been simple and natural. In fact, Rosy and you have both showered all manner of delicate attention upon us and you touched upon the issues as if to help me in a subtle way, to dispel all my misgivings by gaining new perspective on marital relationship. Indeed, as I said earlier, I feel you should write a book on, shall I say, *How to live a happy married life*?" That could be a big sell.

"Hopefully, let me see, but I'm happy with what I'm doing," Dinesh responded.

Raghav endorsed what his wife had said, "Exactly! It has been thoroughly enjoyable to meet you both," and then Ragini spoke in a manner that was half an idea and half a plea: "If I suggest, you stay for dinner, you may please accept? I mean whatever I can arrange, we can have it together."

"By all means. Shall we start right now?" purred Dinesh in the tone of Alfred Hitchcock. (hearty laughs). "Please. It's not that we don't want to spend more time with you. Actually, we would not like to move out of this moment. But, next time. I'm sure we shall meet more often," Rosy responded.

"We have dinner with you sometime next," Dinesh now added.

"But next time why don't you visit us," proposed Rosy. "Yeah, surely," endorsed Dinesh, "That would be fine. Okay, we shall organize it."

At the door, Rosy turned back for a moment.

"I'm hoping," she said, "That you'll..." Then an idea seemed to have occurred to her and she appeared mulling the issue over in her mind, and finally whispered, "It's alright. When we meet next, we shall talk."

And then, Ragini, with all the civility at her command, twisted her head into a bow that seemed to assure Rosy and her husband as plainly as words could have done that it was wonderful meeting both of them.

And they left.

You come to love not by finding the perfect person, but by seeking an imperfect person perfectly.

Sam Keen.

Yours, Once Again!

After seeing them off, Ragini, said, "Indeed, they are an amazingly loving couple." Raghav cast an obliging glance towards her, who then impulsively preened, "I may not have looked as fabulous as Rosy but I believe I certainly conducted myself well. The meeting went off so very well, didn't it?"

"Yes, surely. You managed it so very well. Indeed, you upped your glamor quotient and confidence to come into your own. Congratulations and surely we need some celebration," Raghav responded. His voice was genuine and sincere.

"Really, I am struck by the lack of striving of the couple, their humility for they never tried to impress or convince. There was simply no personality. Rosy did not put up any overbearing display of style or attitude. All their utterances that had subtle meaning, came from nowhere, no one, and yet their gentle openness was obvious, apparent as if directed towards both of us and yet certainly unhurtful. The graceful couple conducted themselves like a team, like a dream. Indeed, I must say that meeting them, I feel in love. Well, just before you may get me wrong. It's not in the way the men in the world do, but I love the human being they both are, particularly Dinesh who is a genuinely thinking person, and is extremely simple, clear, emotional and sensitive!" she opined.

That night, while Ragini lay in bed, she mentally kept visiting the satisfying thoughts that Dinesh had aptly crafted like a good screenplay or a dance well-choreographed, perhaps keeping her recent mental turmoil in focus. The thought... *What I cannot love, I overlook*...still kept spiraling inside her and she kept rehearsing it almost a hundred times until it had become as familiar as a bosom friend

And after that evening's meeting, it became obvious to her that the visit of the couple had been uplifting, rejuvenating in every sense. There appeared a little smile on her face, as if she was searching for an answer to the question: *what else could I enjoy doing to make living life easy and peaceful.*

Raghav raised his head instinctively to look at her wife's face and definitely saw her returning to normalcy. She now appeared to him shedding light—luminous, phosphorescent. Her large eyes held her face under their sway. It took him quite a while to come to terms with how fast events in his life have changed and realized that its reality was actually far too sweet to be believed.

Though no word was spoken, both knew what must be done to live a happier, fuller married life hereafter, together. Perhaps they had realized that a couple can improve chances of their matrimonial harmony by learning to communicate freely so as to resolve differences in unthreatening ways. Then their eyes met that got moist, almost instantly.

Raghav decided to take charge of his life since he had over a period of time increasingly come to feel that he was getting hyper and edgy even on small and insignificant issues, be it at home or in office. He would mentally tend to carry his office to home. Being alive to the day-to-day happenings in one's life is a great experience, a great learning experience, he came to realize. Never regret anything bad that has happened in one's life; it cannot be changed, undone or forgotten. So take it as a lesson learned and move on.

"Overtime, I have got convinced that to build a strong relationship, the couple must ignore many of their selfish impulses and focus instead on the other partner, which certainly calls for huge commitment and dedication. It is hard work to be undertaken with patience. But it surely is going to be life enriching, not depleting. Nobody can give the two partners in marriage the meaning of life from outside; it's within us. We both carry it within us like a bud that is going to flower. The blossom vanishes on its own as the fruit grows. So, does one's lower self vanish as the *Divine* self grows. Living life in a meaningful way involves flowering our potential in the best possible way," Ragini recalled having been told.

"I'm sorry, really sorry," Raghav now said again, contritely, in her ears, "We need to leave our acrimonious past behind and move forward in positivity. I have recently read a good self-help book. It urges people to try and develop an *inner friend* that can often whisper to them: *There's more to life than what we've experienced so far.* The *Bhagwad Gita* describes three types of people in the third chapter. It says that the *Sattvic* live with the attitude of service and sacrifice and enjoy the unasked fruits thereof. They have peace of mind and live a blissful life. Their minds learn to discriminate between good and bad. Some, however, assume wrongly that leading a *sattvic* life means to wear ochre robes, carry a rosary in hand, do recitations, sing *bhajans* and lead a retired life; the *rejasic* work for themselves and suffer stress and strain. They are fixed by ambition rather than by a concern for the good and virtuous. Lust, greed, avarice, arrogance, conceit, hate, fear, anger, envy, jealousy and egoism are their attributes; the *tamasic* want everything without giving anything in return. They live a dark life of ignorance. They prefer the gross pleasures of lassitude and inactivity.

When *sattva* functions in the mind, merit is acquired. When *rajas* functions, demerit is produced and when *tamas* functions, neither merit nor demerit is produced, but life goes on in vain. Human nature being constituted by varying combinations of the three substantive forces and the predominance of one of the three *gunas* over the other two determines a person's nature. Hence, it should be the endeavor of every right thinking person to gradually but consistently work to elevate his or her self from *tamas* to *rajas* and finally to *sattva.* So, I am earnestly working to graduate to that final stage as a human being. Sorry, once again."

She looked at him with an expression in her eyes that perhaps meant to convey that to say sorry means not only to express regret for one's bad deeds in the past but also to commit oneself to renouncing similar actions in future. And then said, "When your wife becomes your best friend, marriage is a fun trip all the way. It's not like having couples who have no tiffs or squabbles and fights, but I have now understood that intelligent and matured couples soon leave it behind them and are able to laugh together. I think a successful marriage is all about respecting one another, understanding each other's idiosyncrasies and giving one another space. Couples must try and turn each other's weakness into strengths. It's also about trying to change, mould and bend a bit to accommodate your partner. An unknown recipe for a successful marriage recommends that you don't carry your grudges and differences over from one day to the next. Know how to drop them before going to bed."

Raghav responded, "Silence is golden! To be able to *hear* the other person first of all, one has to learn to be quiet. It means silencing the ever chattering mind, and revel in the quietness of *Self.* Mind means words, and self means silence. True friendship comes when *silence* between the couple is comfortable.

A very helpful way to exercise on this aspect of learning is to try and develop a habit of keeping *silence* for a few minutes every day at a fixed time, to start with. Great stress has been laid on the ancient Hindu tradition or concept of *mauna-vrat* (enforced silence) on certain days or occasions as an ideal trigger for introspection and reflection. Derived from the word *Muni* that refers to an ascetic who practices silence, *mauna* ideally symbolizes a state of oneness with the *Self.* Or even the Christian custom of going on retreats during which one speaks only during the designated periods of the day. Sometimes it is good to keep silent so as to be able to hear our heart beat."

Prayer within breath is silence;
Love within infinity is silence;
Wisdom without words is silence;
Compassion without aim is silence;
Action without doer is silence;
Smiling with all existence is silence.
Mauna is a stage that is beyond thought and speech.

Ramana Maharishi.

And then Raghav held up his hand, palm upwards, "My apologies, once again," he whispered. "Forgive my many faults and the many pains that I have caused to you, so long. How thoughtless and foolish I have been many a times towards you? And, trust me, I sincerely wish to wash out with my tears every little scar upon your happiness," and his eyes got moist, and he let a few drops fall one by one—tears of sorrow, of release and of hope.

Ragini took the corner of her sari's *pallu* to wipe out his sadness and with a lightened expression said, "Everything is now fine between us. What more can I ask for. But yes, we have now to get your mother, *nay,* our dear mother here to live with us. I hope she will forgive me for being rash with her in the past." and she turned contemplative.

Now to Raghav life appeared enjoyable, interesting—as enjoyable as the planting of a kiss by a lover on the cheek of her beloved, whom he loves, wants.

She felt emotions bubbling, and then her own eyes got teary. On her part, she kept on musing on the perspective that the celestial body, the holy Mother, had given to her—that one about *marriage is not a finished product but a struggle*. Ever since she had understood that the statement, it conveyed lots of meaning, and the essence of it had seeped into her mind as tea from a tea bag or water into a flowerbed from a hosepipe.

"But promise me one thing, will you? All I ask is never ever allow nasty past thoughts to assail your mind. Don't you ever think of leaving me," Raghav now said while lifting her tear stained face and kissed her tenderly and then with rising passions, she returned her kiss equally tenderly.

"I feel so light and sort of floating," Raghav said at last, looking at her face with caressing eyes, hungry eyes.

She winked gleefully, to rest his doubts, and drew him to her with her eyes. He put his face against hers, placing her lips against his, which he felt as if these were like a freshly cut two pieces of ripe fig—reddish pink, juicy and sweet. She laid her head against his chest and let him hold her. She closed her eyes to feel his chest rise and fall rapidly beneath her cheek. He wreathed her by his arms. It was blissful.

Lifting her chin a few centimeters, her lustrous black hair twitching slightly, he whispered to say, "Oh, dear! I can't imagine my life without you."

Love is not measured by how you feel,
but how you make the other person feel.

Julie Andrews.

After all the mental turmoil and agony that both had gone through in recent days, it was now for them like listening to some great and ecstatic *Sufi* music, which transported them to an enhanced world where they felt as if floating in misty clouds full of fragrance for it took them outside the banality of earthly existence, to a place where their existence now lay in harmony, in tune, in melody in soulful music, and outside all that which language aspires to but never achieves; where each spouse in the relationship speaks through baited breaths and eyes full of expressive love and warmth for the other. And both went to bed in a huddle as if going into a secret conference, where they merged into each other to became *one*.

Lord, help me to keep my thoughts pure, my words true, and my deeds kind: that alone or with others, I shall be one with thee. God, be in my mouth and in my speaking. God, be in my heart and in my thinking.

Sarum Primer,

Speak in such a way that others love to listen to you. Listen in such a way that others love to speak to you.

A proverb.

Soon, Ragini was carrying again. Raghav this time made it a point to be by her bedside when she got admitted in the Nursing Home for delivery.

Dressed in a snow-white Anarkali *shilwar-kameez* that showed her cute baby bump, Ragini looked like a schoolgirl with clipped-up hair, pink cheeks and rosy lips.

After a few hours her labor pain started and she turned pale and disoriented. That whole night Raghav watched her in great pain. The body with which she had borne the aggravated state of her pregnancy flowered into shooting slabs of pain. Almost as though her body was being churned up…she lay prostrate on her bed. The labor pains now gripped her. The woman doctor attending on her was perhaps trying out if there could be a chance of vaginal birth of the expectant infant although at that point of time women who had already given birth to earlier child by caesarean section, like in Ragini's first delivery, were never allowed to have their next child naturally because of the possibility of a likely rupture of the earlier incision.

And she tore the ceiling with her shrieks. Her mother came to hold her hand, and stroked the back of her head. She smoothened her straying hair, which was slick, slightly coarse, like an Otter's pelt. Her face, stabled now, had sweaty shine. Her sweater was unbuttoned and she exuded a complex essence made up of sweat, prickly-heat power and the ineffable profoundly familiar smell of her flesh, Raghav smelt.

It was scary, intensely scary for him to watch his wife withering in labor pain, gasping for breath, thrusting herself inside out, and before long it came to the point where he felt she wasn't alone who was birthing the child but the two of them for the reason that he literally felt and experienced the intensity of his wife's pain—his own breathing hastening or going shallow, as the shrieks heightened or subsided. His heart was beating like a drum that is beaten to scare away wild animals—fast and hard. He felt as if no blood but fear flowing through his veins—fear of the unknown which had even driven away for a moment his otherwise unshakeable faith in God.

But as he found the anxiety of impending fatherhood increasing, he somehow managed to pray for a few brief moments while her shrieks were nerve wrenching. She kept twisting or pulling violently round or sideways. With a pregnant woman's ferocious instinct for survival of self and the infant stored in her womb, she bore the intensity of that pain while giving out a maddening groan that struck around like a repeated lightening and perhaps shook everyone and everything in its passage. Her growls contested with her screams. Her face got full with beads of sweat. Her mother, wiping the sweat, kept caressing her hand over her face and forehead, and then an instinct perhaps older than time pushed a balmy melody out of her, and that—a slow, sweet, consoling lullaby soothed her daughter's nerves and certainly, surely helped her to receive some little relief from pain, it became apparent, to Raghav.

Whole night passed that way for the woman doctor wanted to wait and watch if normal delivery could be effected. Finally, in the morning she decided to operate, and Ragini gave birth to a girl and the shrill cries of the little one tore the quiet of the hospital corridor.

As Ragini held her newborn in the warmth of her lap and kissed her softly, gently on the forehead, her eyes, her cheeks, her chin, her little fingers, on her tiny hands, a strange tremor of emotions swept her whole body, cell by cell.

"I was able to feel safe, blessed. I was allowing my mind and body to let go and be free to experience the changes taking place within in preparation for giving birth to a new life, while surrounded by love and care of my near and dear ones," she later told her mother.

We are a Family!

Returning home from the Nursing Home, the first thing Ragini wanted her husband Raghav to do was to go to get his mother to live with them. Thus, Raghav almost rushed to bring her estranged mother home. Ragini welcomed her with open embrace and then fell at her feet seeking to be excused for her past bad conduct towards her. Raghav's mother hugged her and blessed her. Indeed, love, kindness and bounty in personal relationships energize, both Ragini and her *saas* now came to realize. A deep feeling of relaxation and satisfaction overcame and helped them to sit back and gain the insight and direction for future interactions. "From now onwards, I shall henceforth treat you just like my mother," Ragini made a forthright statement to her who, in quick response, took out the heavy gold chain that she was wearing on her person and placed in Ragini's neck, and hugged her. Raghav, for one, beamed to witness this endearing spectacle and felt obliged to his wife to now show such love and warmth towards his mother. His heart swelled with emotions and the chest welled up, literally. When husband–wife become proactive in their day-to-day interactions they like being in each other's company. They live and laugh together in matrimony. They create a family, and at that a happy family! They do then find occasions to express love and appreciation in ways that will help the other spouse to feel good. Such expressions could involve simple gestures, like: giving a timely compliment or present, or simply saying *thank* you for offering a hot cup of tea as soon as one returns from work, or cooking a nice meal or helping each other in the kitchen. Small gestures can have large meanings. The whole exercise is to keep each other happy and in good mood, by being able to create humor in life.

A happy person is not a person in a certain set of circumstances, but rather a person with a certain set of attitudes.

Huge Downs.

One evening returning home very late from office, a husband found his wife in a bad mood. He neither asked her the reason, nor gave any explanation for his late coming. Acting smart and intelligent, he instead asked her, "Dear, have you noticed that TV advertisement?"

She didn't respond.

"That, indeed, is a very thoughtful ad!" he now said.

"Which ad?" she asked curtly.

That one where a young boy approaches a young girl waiting for her bus at the bus stand.

She is having a chocolate, and the boy says, "Can you please give me a small bite out of your chocolate?"

The girl feels nonplused for a while and asks, "Do I know you?"

The boy says, "No!"

"How then?" she inquires, making a quizzical face.

The boy now responds, "My mother has taught me to eat something sweet before doing a good deed."

The girl mulls contemplatively for a second, and gives him a bite, and then asks, "By the way what is the good deed that you are going to do?"

"I am thinking of escorting you to your home, it being late evening now.

And both looked at each other with amorous eyes, and laughed heartily.

They became friends!

"By the way what is the good deed you want to do for me?" inquired his wife.

"I am thinking of giving you a body massage to lift your dampened spirits," her husband replied, with a mischievous smile lurking on his face.

It unnerved his wife and sent the couple into paroxysms of laughter.

A bad, gloomy situation was saved because of the husband's ability to create humor

The message is that each husband must make it a point to turn his wife on by making her laugh *with him*, *at herself* and *at himself*. Undoubtedly, in life come many zany situations which make one laugh. These rather than eliciting a sort of canned laughter that comes out of stock situations like making people slip over banana peels, should go scatological or hit and pinch each other insanely. When a person has gained the ability to laugh in any situation, he or she has truly evolved and laughs the best.

A couple in marriage need to capture the humor, anger, joy, loss, hope, frustration and friendship—all—as and when these situations present themselves in one's life. Such a union demands commitment and recommitment, almost on a day-to-day basis. The wisdom is to avoid all thoughts that weakens. Every single thought can be assessed in terms of whether it strengthens or weakens a person. The automatic thoughts can be positive or negative. The positive thinking that typically comes with optimism is a key part of effective stress management. And effective stress management is associated with health benefits. If one tends to be pessimist, there is no need to despair—one can learn positive thinking skills. Positive thinking doesn't mean that one ignores life's less pleasant situations. Positive thinking just means that one approaches unpleasantness in a more positive and productive way. The message is to control bad temper through silencing the mind.

People like and love a life of peace, order and happiness. Yet isn't it strange that the activities of most people cause troubles and chaos for themselves and others in society because they basically seek happiness for their ownselves without bothering for others. The desire to seek happiness for self only, places a person in hell-like situation while the desire to operate out of happiness for all, places him/her in heaven.

There is a story about a Buddhist monk who had a dream in which he asked a wise priest to describe hell and heaven to him. The old priest took him to a dining hall where many people were seated on chairs placed firmly around a huge dining table, on which a lavish banquet was laid out. The chairs were placed so far away from the edge of the table that the people seated couldn't reach the food. They were not supposed to get up and leave their chairs. Obviously there arms were not so long as to reach the food placed on the table. However, there was only one wooden spoon with a handle long enough to reach the delicious dishes placed on the table. As expected of selfish people, everyone was jostling desperately to reach and get hold of that spoon. At the end of such a chaotic scene, one person got hold of the spoon after a hard struggle. He then picked up some food with it and tried to feed himself. But the sheer length of the spoon made it impossible for him to put the food in his mouth, and his repeated attempts to do so made the food fall down on the floor. Soon someone else grabbed the spoon and snatched it away from him after much arm twisting. He too then attempted to feed himself but couldn't. There was utter chaos as each one was desperate to get hold of the spoon. Each one was shouting, yelling, gesticulating in anger at each other. It was hell.

And after a while, the priest took the Monk to another room where also a similar lavish banquet was laid out on another huge table, and the seating arrangement too was on the same pattern, as also was the long wooden spoon to feed with. But the difference was that no one was fighting to grab the spoon. Each one was by turns picking up the spoon to reach out and pick the food to feed the other. Thus, each one was feeding the other, and in turn he himself was being fed. On his turn, each one said to the other: *Please allow me to treat you with as much love and kindness as you treated me with.*

He then knew what was meant by a heaven-like situation. Indeed, it was heaven.

The moral of the story is that heaven and hell are both *within* the self. It is a question of one's own state of mind. Happiness, therefore, happens when one fits into one's life. One is said to find harmony when, without thinking of his/her own self, he/she thinks of the happiness of others.

Being happy does not mean everything is perfect, it means you have decided to look beyond imperfections.

Albert Camus.

If we ask *how* to be happy, we can never be happy. There never is, nor can be any *how* to it. The *how,* in fact, is the core problem. Desire is essentially destructive. It leads to avarice and greed. Despondency follows. Desire and despair is an old rule.

That sort of insight was assimilated by Raghav and Ragini through the course of their interactions with the Divorce Court Judge as well as by the most positive attitudes of Dinesh and his wife Rosy, who made them think afresh to empower themselves so as to give their marriage a second chance in the best interests of their child.

Both then made it a point to share such thoughts with each other, as often as possible.

They both have matured, now.

They don't act cold, any more.

There is warmth as never before—a quiet teasing, a solidarity, a deep care and concern for each other.

They have grown.

But they don't look old.

***"The goal of our life should not be to find joy in marriage,
but to bring more love and truth into the world.
We marry to assist each other in this task."***

Leo Tolstoy.

What is the best compliment a husband can pay to his wife when he is out with her for shopping or attending a party? He could tell her, "Honey, you look like a billion dollars cheque that I'm in possession of." Never ever give your wife an opportunity to ask you, "How do I look?"

And when such gestures of love and affection become an unalloyed reality in day-to-day living of a couple, they would then come to recognize that for the survival of a happy, vibrant and value-based society and for the good up-bringing of its progeny, it is still *a good thing* to have a *wife* and to be a *wife* so as to have a happy *family* and be able to create a new *life*.

The requirements for today's *wife* give added meaning to the biblical proverb:

Whosoever findeth a wife, findeth a good thing.

Because a man only then is able to create a new life—a FAMILY!.

From a child's perspective, *FAMILY* should mean:

(F)ATHER (A)ND (M)OTHER (I)(L)ove (Y)ou.

"The more I have been introspecting, the more I have found that I have less and less to say, until finally, I have learned to be *silent,* and began to *listen*—a moment not for reflection, but just to be, a moment in which I just exist and do nothing else. I just am!" Raghav shared this awareness with his wife, since the day she started complaining about his new-found silence.

Added he further, "My life overtime has taken a 180 degree turn. Ever since my direction turned inwards, my life has become more *Sufi.* And shall I say that the best music of our lives is created *within* with the quiet and calm of our souls. Everything sort of gets aligned itself in the same direction. I am working to learn to be *silent,* and began to *listen* more. Am gradually giving myself the opportunity to hear myself more and more, and as all noise, all distractions recede, I feel the calm enveloping me. In silence lies the nourishment, the nectar that quenches all inner thirst. I feel myself melt into a nothingness that becomes one with nature. Silence is lovely."

"I can describe a person, a book, a day, a memory—*lovely*, but silence…?" she reacted, a bit amazed.

"Isn't it pleasing to have a word like *lovely* up the sleeve of your tongue," he countered. After all, am I lovely to you? Am I not?" asked Raghav, at the spur of that moment. "Just for now," as she spoke there was sort of a small tantalizing smile, which he fancied.

"Just for now, only… Is it?" he asked with slightly abashed glee, and winked naughtily.

She now smiled like a babe and said, "Yesterday night since I was watching my favorite TV show, you 'd gone to your bed earlier than me, and when I got inside my bed later I was pleasantly surprised to find that my bed was warm and cozy as you had kept the electric blanket switched on for me. So thoughtful of you, I mused, and thanked you profusely in my heart of hearts for wearing that niceness on your sleeve." And she laughed.

He heard music in her such warmth-filled utterances, so he grabbed the comforter and wanted to wrap it around himself for all the time to come. He wanted to graft that moment on to time and keep it with him. He experienced feelings as pure and pristine as a child's imagination. "You know, *aisi chhoti chhoti baatein* notice *karteen hai, yaad rakhti hai toh* it really feels good and nice. You have wonderfully well personified the hopes, dreams, aspirations of my life alongside bearing the pain, anguish and ups and downs of daily life. I can never keep that out of my mind," Raghav said with intense emotions in his eyes. "I want to give you something," he now said.

"Please don't give me any more compliments. These embrace me. All else you can give me," Ragini responded, and opined, "When you're doing good to others, you're doing good to yourself, I sincerely believe."

"Oh! that's a wonderful perspective," he said with a gleam on his face, and went on to recall a story he had read in a book called *It's a Meaningful life* by BO Lozoff.

A woman once came to the Maggid of Kozhnitz asking for his blessings for a child since even after a number of years of marriage, she and her husband were still childless.

The Maggid replied, "My parents, too, were childless for many years. Then my mother sewed a coat for the Ba'al Sham Tov (*sixteenth century Jewish mystic*), and after that I was born."

The woman exclaimed, "I'll gladly sew a coat for you, a beautiful coat!"

The Maggid shook his head. "No my dear woman," he said, "That will be of no avail. You see, my mother did not know this story."

The Maggid's mother in the story above probably saw that the Ba'al Sham Tov did not have a suitable coat, and regardless of her own problems, her innate goodness naturally moved her to make one for him. She contributed to life by making a coat for a holy man without expecting anything in return. So life then contributed to her in the form of her pregnancy.

Most of us have experienced this phenomenon at some time or the other time; we let go of self-interest and then discover usually to our surprise that our interests have been taken care of anyway through some divine intervention.

Thus the essence of compassionate service—not how much good we do—but rather doing good all the time—waking and sleeping, eating and breathing, working and playing with an unforced, underlying attitude of goodwill, no time off.

It's alright! Now listen how it works. To do this, I want to tell you about a situation that parallels the human mind.

Suppose a farmer has some land and it is good fertile land. The land gives the farmer a choice—he may plant in that piece of land whatever he chooses. The land just doesn't bother. It is up to the farmer to make the decision. We are comparing the human mind with the land because the mind like the land, doesn't care what you plant in it. It will return what you plant.

Now let us say the farmer has two seeds in his hand—one a seed of corn, the other is nightshade, a deadly poison. He digs two little holes in the land and he plants both seeds—one corn and the other nightshade. He covers up the holes, waters and takes care. What will happen? Invariably, the land will return what was planted. As it is written in the Bible, "As you sow, so shall you reap." Remember the land does not care. It will return poison in just as wonderful abundance as it will corn.

The human mind is far more fertile, far more incredible and mysterious than the land but it works the same way. It doesn't care what we plant…success or failure; a concrete worthwhile goal or confusion; happiness or misery. But what we plant, it must return to us. You see, the human mind is the greatest unexplored continent on earth. It contains riches beyond our wildest dreams. It will return to us anything we want to plant—good or bad.

Therefore, you need to take responsibility for cultivating good thoughts as against bad thoughts. Let you stop focusing on all that is wrong and instead focus on all that is right. Stop cribbing about what you don't have and look instead at what all there is for you with the grace of God."

Ragini heard the story with rapt attention and commented, "Kindness isn't about big charity. Rather it's about being considerate in one's everyday life. It isn't about writing a cheque. It's about doing small things with positivity which make someone else happy. And then why shouldn't I get doing that for my own dear husband?"

"You'll never cease to surprise me, interest me! Your propensity to surprise me is enormous. I just want to say that basically you are a child at heart. You never grew up because that child within you never has disappeared. With you by my side, my life is complete now," he said with joyfulness.

"I'm humbled, rather flattered!" she responded gleefully, and added, "There is, I suppose, too much of sweetness in your those words which could cause diabetes." (laughs)

"There are certain special things that do not bear much telling, my father used to say. And you know, what? (laughs) (oh, I seem to have picked up Dinesh's that slang) In spite of being miffed with me on many occasions; in spite of the many rough patches that we have gone through in our married life so far, the one special gesture on your part, irrespective of the situation—good or bad—towards me has been…you know, what?…*if there were only two apples or oranges on the table, you invariably picked up the smaller one, leaving the bigger one for me*…and every time you have been doing that, it certainly made me feel reassured that you continue to value me, love me, irrespective of my nasty attitude in the past. Isn't that? That feeling has ever made me move on, notwithstanding the many road-bumps that our relationship have had," Raghav told her with a child-like innocence.

"And, let me say this also that after a lot of reflection, self-talk or what is called introspection or, shall I, put it as the awareness to listen to the voice within, which speaks in wordless language of the heart, there has been much more clarity, more awareness, compassion and I am able to give the other the benefit of doubt. It is invigorating to meet the little voice inside one's head! I have gradually been feeling better physically, mentally and spiritually," he said, gazing her with a lepidopterist gaze.

"There is a sweet note, a melody in your those words, which I long to hear and enjoy in the same way a buffalo enjoys the luxury of its bath in some cool pond on a hot day. It is soothing," she said and instantly clung to his wide chest and rubbed her face against his left cheek. He took a hand to stroke her hair, and said, "You are the woman I have grown to understand, respect and love, after all! All your life you have lived with a twenty-four-carat heart in spite of going through rough patches many a times, but you worked not to allow your gold to get contaminated for long with any other inferior metal. I shall continue to celebrate the fact that I am married to you," and then wrapped his arms around her like a layer of bandage around a wound.

Today, Ragini experienced a strange but holy feeling—she found her husband's touch akin to a worshipper who touches flowers meant for the deity…gently, lovingly, reverentially. It was healing, blissful!

"Picking up a red rose from the flower-vase and inhaling its fragrance, Raghav whispered into her ear, "I love you. I don't say it just for the fun of it or to make a conversation. I say it to remind you that you are the *best* thing that ever happened to me. I like your spirit, Ragini—your independence and your honesty of purpose. I love the way you always sound as if you're about to laugh. I love your stillness when you're listening, love your violent mood-swing, and love the manner you soon become meditative, peaceful, forgiving. There is nothing guile about you, no contemptible wile."

"Do you really think so?" asked she, brightening up for a moment.

Raghav replied, "Trust me! hundred per cent."

Love at first sight is easy;
It's when two people have been looking at each other for a lifetime that it becomes a miracle.

Sam Levenson.

Ragini felt happy and smiled that shown on her pretty face.

"Your smile is a signature of God on your face," Raghav responded, "Don't ever allow it to be washed away by your tears or erased by your anger."

They both have matured, now.

They often look into each other's eyes.

They no longer act cold.

There is warmth as never before—a quiet teasing, a solidarity, a deep care and concern for each other.

Their son and daughter have both got married, settled down and made their own nests to take care of their individual families.

Raghav and Ragini, indeed, have grown.

But they don't look old.

Life, indeed, is a great learning experience, if one remains conscious, Raghav and Ragini have now come to realize. Fortunately, it didn't take Raghav much time to become a matured or saner person. He has cultivated the habit of rewinding his life in *past-forward* mode for just two to three minutes each night before going to sleep, and it has really helped him to evolve.

"Why do you do sitting cross-legged with closed eyes just before lying down to sleep?" his wife asked him one day.

Replied he, "I capture the *past* in my *present* every day just before going to sleep. It whispers history, and I draw valuable lessons. I've come to believe that maturity has more to do with what types of experiences you've had, and what you've learned from them, and less to do with how many birthdays you've celebrated."

"Oh! dear Raghav," she said impulsively, "Love you passionately, dear. I am reminded of an unforgettable feeling I have been living with since long and I now want to give words to it:

If you live hundred years, I want to live hundred minus one so that I don't have to live without you.

It has been the prayer on my lips."

O learned person, may we live in your company
for a hundred years.
Let not our bodies decay before that period,
in which old age, our sons become fathers in turn.
Break ye not in the midst our course of fleeting life.

Yajur Veda.

Just then his son Rohan entered the room and said, "I've heard what all you were telling Mummy just now. I have an idea. Let us celebrate your past in the present day—I mean celebrating golden jubilee of your marriage." His sister hugely supported the idea, and both took it upon themselves to organize the event gracefully.

"Longevity of life does not serve any purpose if apart from eating, living, sleeping and earning money, one is doing nothing to be a good, honest human being first of all," Raghav responded and informed his children that some years back a Sage had said to him:

'The fact of the matter is that if life happens, death is a natural process. Being afraid of a natural process is unnatural. So those who are already there and those who will sooner or later get to old age, the wisdom is to enjoy life while you live.

There is no second chance!'

And continued, "Those words about a *second chance* made my cheeks flush. And my heart was slamming hard under my fingers. I could feel it right through my woolen jacket, and I abruptly blurted out, 'I have got it. I mean life has given me a second chance!'

The Sage raising a skeptical eyebrow, looking at me askance. There was an intensely puzzled look on the Sage's face. He met my gaze squarely, his eyes narrowed.

'How? What exactly do you mean?' he questioned me.

I was unnerved, momentarily, for I was not prepared to recall what all I had been through, even if it was something that happened with me only about three years back, as you are aware of. I collected my composure and started narrating the story of my, shall I say, second birth, thus:

"It was in June month of the year 2010 that my elder brother had mooted the idea of going on a pilgrimage to the holy shrines of Kedarnath and Badarinath in the Himalayas.

Many people in his extended family greeted the idea and wanted to join him in this pilgrimage. So a group of thirteen people, which included a doctor in the relation, started off from Delhi on a seven-day trip in June, 2010. The journey was hard and tough, even excruciating or dangerous, at certain stages.

One such stage, particularly for me, was at an altitude of more than 11,500 ft. above sea-level when the group-entourage was nearing the shrine of Kedarnath. We were all going up the mountain ranges on horse backs, to cover a distance of about eighteen kilometers. The horses visually appeared of different breeds, and colors. The color of the horse that I rode was piebald black and white, and seemed to have a musical ear and perhaps fond of devotional songs that the horse-man—a small paunchy man with fleshy bulges all over—was playing on his handheld small cassette player. As my eyes journeyed over the undulated geography of his anatomy, I noticed tremendous movements of the horse's nostrils and the head as if in rhythm with the devotional music being played. Most horses looked buoyant and demonstrated their sense of well-being and sturdiness by playfully jerking their raised ears and moving their tails.

Since each horse, depending upon age, frame and sturdiness, had its own speed and rhythm, besides a fixed track to tread on, naturally some of the members of the group were getting far ahead, some in the middle and rest left behind at some distance.

Time was around 4 p.m. It had started raining suddenly—sometime light, other times heavy and torrential. The climate got windy, damp and cold. The oxygen at that height was low. One could feel difficulty in breathing. I felt myself almost gasping for breath.

The last steep ridge remained to be climbed and negotiated to be able to reach the outskirts of Kedarnath valley. My horse and that of the doctor in the group were far behind the other members.

Amid those tense and difficult moments, I gradually felt giddy because of less oxygen intake and the next thing that I remember was that I was being laid down on the ground near a way-side make-shift tea stall by a few people whom I didn't know.

Later I was told that I had gone unconscious and hence had fallen down from the horse on the rough stony road. My pulse had got snapped for a while and my body was getting numb and cold. Doctor Bagat was instrumental in reviving me in time.

Later, an elderly local gave me a piece of camphor to be kept almost tugged to my nostrils till I remained at that high altitude.

It gave me some little respite, some relief.

I am completely blank as to:

- How did I fall down?
- How my two feet that were squarely placed in the foot-holds dangling on the two sides of the saddle came out so easily leading to my fall on the road (had any of my feet got stuck or entangled in the foot-hold I would have got dragged by the horse, my head hitting the stony surface below)?

How had the attendant walking ahead of my horse and holding it's reins to give it forward pulls somehow looked backwards in time to notice my fall on the road and had raised an alarm to invite other's attention?

How was it that even after falling down on pointedly rough, hard, stony road surface, I didn't get trampled under the hoofs of the horses that were going up or down in numbers on that narrow muddy and slippery path-way—each horse using its full horse-power to jostle and push each other to gain right of way.

- How was it that I didn't get hurt anywhere on my body parts, not even a bruise or scratch?

I believe it was some kind of Divine intervention that restored my heart beat, revived me and miraculously saved my this earthly life.

However, after I regained consciousness, I could not breathe easy and hence had to be carried in a cradle-like basket made of wicker on the back of a porter to the sanctum sanctorum of the holy shrine. My hopes, wishes, gratitude and heartfelt thanks, all got enveloped into my folded hands, to usher in a devotional prayer on my lips. I knelt as tears rolled down my cheeks.

The irony of fate is that my elder brother, who had taken great pains to take care of my mental and physical state then, was himself dead just after a few months only. His life was claimed by cancer in a matter of few weeks, after a few days of excruciating agony and pain."

I closed the narration with teary eyes."

Silence! utter silence filled the atmosphere for quite a few minutes.

"That is the vagary of life. It is a paradox! I think I know it. And I believe, you know it too. It is true! Death is the inevitable destiny of everyone.

Death comes to all who are born. It is in the order of nature. Regardless of what you do or have done in this life, your deepest, most lasting peace and happiness will come from admitting it to be God's plan and submit to it obediently. The one who lives a pious life lives in peace and never dreads the call of death. Death for such a person is in fact a time to meet the Beloved—it is death of death. So when one's time is up, one should die with dignity," the Sage had then said to console Raghav.

Never wish life were easier.
Wish that you were better.

Jim Rohn.

Having listened to that interaction with the Sage, Raghav's children responded to say, "Papa, that is all the more reason for Mummy and you to take your wedding vows afresh in your this second life, as you call it."

It's Yesterday Once More!

Yes, there is a wedding!

A special one, at that.

"Welcome, you are most welcome!" a soft, sweet, honey-dipped voice spoke on the public address system—heartily welcoming the guests.

It's the celebration of golden jubilee marriage anniversary of Raghav and his bride, Ragini. She has been the petite bride to Raghav all through the long period of over fifty years that they have remained married to each other. They are reliving the wedding—again today—with renewed vows, and there are plenty of *wows* as well, as never ending stream of guests drive into the venue. The guest list has the *wow* factor, the designer clothes people are wearing has the *oomph* factor and the celebration itself is oozing class. It is a starry affair.

A traditional *mandap* (stage), in a definite way reminiscent of the old charm and grandeur, has been erected in the center, which is decorated with garlands—red roses, tulips, wild blooms, orchids—and, of course, thin banana tree leafy-trunks on four corners, to complete the auspiciousness of the grand event. The clarity of air and minted dignity of the charming venue is refreshing the senses.

At a distance, around this hugely decorated *mandap,* chairs in the rear and sofa-sets in front rows, have been placed for the guests to be seated comfortably. As the guests, sporting their stylish best, start arriving in swanky cars of various makes and hues, one after the other, the security men, in tidy colorful uniforms, provide security cover. One of them a tall sturdy man with a handle-bar moustache like that of a wrestler, which is neatly combed and curled at its ends with needle like tips, stands in attention and rushes to open the car-doors at the arrival lounge with his white-gloved left hand and almost simultaneously his right hand goes up in a smart salute to honor the guests, who are then presented with a rose-bud each by lined-up young and smart girls to usher them in with due aplomb and dignity. Everything there looks very different, bright and colorful. Indeed, the venue looks no less than a set straight out of a big budget Bollywood movie.

And every time a couple walks in, the ambient air suddenly smells refreshingly soothing because of hefty whiffs of scents and perfumes exuding from their expensive clothes. There are quite a few *crème de creme* couples who being center of attraction, are accosted for soundbytes and pictures. Once inside, most tend to mingle with the high and mighty among them, making shutterbugs go into tizzy. It is a high-spirited affair at the venue.

Entering the venue, most elderly couples seem to feel they've stepped through a time machine and on into the *past* which rekindled the spirit of Retro-era since this fiftieth marriage anniversary celebrations of the seventy-seven-year-old groom and his seventy-four-year-old bride, has a *Retro* theme

The year is 2012, but the feel is that of 1962 when the graceful couple had first got married. They appear reveling as if they are reliving their own olden times, when the living was simple and easy; the relationships warm and cordial; the children loyal and caring. There was enough time to pause, stand and stare; look out for peace, harmony and good things in life, unlike the present times.

As in the past, the two erudite *Gurujis* (priests), one each representing the bride's and groom's side, arrived in the *mandap* and proceeded to lay out their paraphernalia—the *hawan-samigrihe*—the large green banyan leaves, the burning sticks of holy incense and *dhoop,* the colorful strings of *naada-chadi*, the pellets of camphor, the trays of cut-flowers, the garlands, the rose petals in a heap, the vermilion with sacred threads and the half-torn, discolored booklets containing holy *mantras* (holy verses).

And there amid the playing of *Shehnaaye* and blowing of conch shells, that fills the air, the groom, attired in rich embroidered creamy *bundgalla* suit that looks elegant with a flower-bedecked saffron-colored headgear, flanked by his stunningly looking demure bride who looks all poise in a *zaree* wide-bordered crimson red *lehenga* (designer dress) resplendent with sandalwood paste, heavy gold jewelry and bold moon-like vermilion *tilak* on her forehead, walk holding hand-in-hand, slowly but gracefully into the *mandap,* smiling and waving at the gaggle of photographers and video cameras, while the *Gurujis* recite sacred *shlokas* from Scriptures to usher in the Divine blessings.

The couple whose marriage was solemnized more than fifty years ago in accordance with *Manu Smariti*—Religious Constitution of Hindus, which holds that marriage is an institution created by man on earth that formally unites two souls preordained to come to-gather, by the very creator of the Universe, are feeling a surge of emotions on reliving in the *present* their that *past*.

Cameras—still, digital, video, mobiles—all start flashing as the bride agrees, albeit, reluctantly to pose for lensmen, standing by her groom's left side—both of them appeared blushing as a distinctly pinkish tinge grew on their cheeks. Surely, vintage never does lose its flavor, does it? The jibs are gentle, the tenor fond, yet firm. But most importantly, the characters are completely real; feisty and unflawed, and it's going to be real exhilarating and intoxicating for them. There is a mad scramble among the close relatives and friends to get clicked with the couple.

Yet hardly anyone knew that before the couple got there—the heady cocktail of matrimonial success; of being together for more than fifty-long years; they have survived a thousand disagreements, tiffs, heated moments, depressions, rejections, misunderstandings, expectations, ambitions, unbridled me-centrism, desolation of loneliness and finally coming of age and maturing like old scotch, to sustain love, taste and flavor through a determined spirit of adjustment, understanding and accommodation.

Thus for the greying couple, it's *Yesterday Once More*!

The account of their journey through life is going to be interesting.

"*Hai, Tusee Kitnay Sohnay Lagdey Ho*! (Oh dear, how charming you look!) *Nazar Na Lagjaway,*" (God save you from evil eye), said bride's good, old friend Lata, giving her a tight hug and a soft peck on the cheek.

It brought an effervescent laughter among the guests around, and when it finally subsided Ragini, who looked elegantly cool, said soberly, "The wedding is being reenacted traditionally. That is what our children and grandchildren wanted," and turning to them asked, "See that the guests are well looked after," with the gesture of her right hand.

That's when most women noticed, she was wearing blood-red nailpaint! one of whom commented,

"Perfect color-coordination *issey kehte hain*" (that's what is called). "Congrats! May God bless the couple," Lata, her best friend, said loudly.

And the best part of the ceremony came as the good, old, and gorgeous couple yet again exchanged *Var-malla* (wedding-flower necklaces) amid chanting of *mantras* by the priests. With misty eyes they once again come to renew their matrimonial vows before the sacred fire according to Vedic rites. The relatives and friends came to shower rose petals upon them amid chanting of hymns.

Exactly fifty years ago, they had pledged love and commitment to each other, but it now seemed to them like only *yesterday*. The groom had promised to love his bride, to honor her, to love her, to comfort her and to keep her happy and contented. She had, in return, vowed to be loyally committed to him and make their home full of joy, happiness and bliss.

Perhaps, it is time for them to look back and ask themselves how have they, over the years, stood the test of those vows?

"I have been in love with the same woman (amorously gazing at his wife's face) for last fifty years," Raghav said in a flash. "Perhaps, it is time for us to look back and ask ourselves how have we, over the years, stood the test of those vows?" Ragini added—light-hearted smile playing on her lips.

"But that, indeed, needs a quiet reflection, an honest introspection," Raghav responded, and continued, "I wish I could someday tell that familial story." And for now, their children and grandchildren, who all have worked painstakingly to plan and organize this happy event, are there to love and adore them.

As the two priests now started chanting *Vedic Shlokas* which resonated through the cool and crisp forenoon in the flower-bedecked lawns, the blessed couple once again got to listen to the proclamation made by the ancient sages that a human has four duties in life—*Dharma, Artha, Kaama, Moksha*—made possible only through a passage into:

Grihastha-*ashram* (matrimonial life).

So with both their hands placed in a firm yet gentle handshake, the bridegroom and the bride had then taken those vows amid Vedic chants, in the presence of the omnipresent God, and thus the twosome had, fifty-years hence, entered into their new future together—*Kutumbha* (family) with the promise of togetherness till eternity.

And here the ceremony is being reenacted/relived today to do a mock-up in front of their close family members and guests. And the good, old graceful couple are enjoying every moment of it for, they believe, they have together withstood and sustained the vagaries of time-span of more than fifty years and have truly arrived. The presence of their children and grandchildren by their side is perhaps to stand witness to the fact.

Crème de la crème, among the guests, has added elegance to the ambience. A seemingly important guest, sitting in the front row on a cozy sofa, said to the one sitting on his left, "Today, after fifty years of their marriage, the priests have made the couple to take those seven steps afresh as bride and groom, to renew those vows—history repeating itself. That must be hugely uplifting and rejuvenating, for any such couple whose commitment to each other, I am sure, gets defused, deflated, derailed, drained or whatever, over the years."

Just then, the ceremonies over, the flower-bedecked bride and the groom walked around into the guest-enclosure to meet and greet the invitees personally.

"Hello, Raghav! Wonderful to be here with you and your soul mate on this your reenacted marriage. Hi Ragini," (looking towards her), called out a close friend of the couple, from a distance, while walking hungrily towards them and the two almost jumped into each other's lap. Holding their hands dearly, he asked:

"How do you feel having reenacted your marriage?"

"Oh, it's wonderful, I mean the institution of marriage," Raghav responded "Isn't it great to survive the time-frame of more than fifty years with all its ups and downs and stay-put with the woman I married and loved? It has been a wonderful journey together that gave us many lessons!"

"Yes, I can appreciate," the friend consented and said, "Such a phenomenon is mostly unheard of in western world, particularly America where marriages have a very short shelf-life, generally. Recently I was in England and was surprised to know that in Wales thirteen divorces had taken place every hour (a divorce every five minutes) in the year 2012. The standard narrative in such cases was either to do something with uncompatibility because of ego clashes or unfaithfulness called infidelity—calling each other (*mostly against men*) *scumbags* and cheats. It is indeed suffocating to be spied upon and mistrusted by one's partner or spouse."

An elderly guest who seemed to have heard that with rapt attention, added, "What really makes a relationship last long term, isn't that undeniable chemistry, but a deep meaningful friendship. Volumes have been said and shall be written on that basic point. Yes, it is important to be loved. May be a husband or wife, of course, love each other—in a worldly sense of that emotion, but do they like each other like who he or she is (as a person, a partner, a father), too? That is crucial because when each spouse likes and values each other as a *person* it sustains a relationship of being also a friend to each other."

The women sitting by the side simpered self-consciously, while it brought out a laugh in half-suppressed spasms, a giggle on the face of the smartly dressed woman in the front row with her pulchritudinous charm—wearing a dress of waist-length well-cut black coat to bring out her bodyline with a just-below-the-knee burgundy skirt and nylon skin-colored stockings plus obtrusively garnish head-scarf and one bold piece of jewelry like a brooch or necklace that was not loose or hanging—definitely a coveted style statement. She gave out a perfect mod look that was captivating—a sure shot formula to grab eyeballs with her amorous and lecherous looks. Dabbling at her eyes hastily with a handkerchief perfumed with some special cau-de-cologne, whiffs of which were soothing the nostrils around, she turned in a certain style that invited attention and said in a somewhat admonitory tone:

Perhaps, renewing vows infuses life afresh into the relationship—rekindling love and warmth. That is why you celebrate marriage anniversaries or even wedding anniversaries.

"How very true!" Ragini responded, in agreement and added, "Truly, it gives the nice feeling and warmth of traveling in time. Indeed, in a subtle way Raghav and me have enjoyed the actual journey of reaching this day and time. It has been a great learning experience, I must say." Raghav (looking into Ragini's eyes) then said, "*I'm so lucky* to have you in my life." She responded to say, "A husband telling his wife sometimes something as simple as that actually means more than those three words."

Both then gave each other a cute hug that obviously filled them with pure love. Moving around there was laughter, DJ music (spinning up a riot among the youngsters) and good food in an array of choices that emphasized variety and novelty—using the exotic, the vividly colored and variously textured items on the exhaustive menu, unlike the feast on their original wedding day, more than fifty years hence.

And as it appeared the couple, while profusely thanking their children for all the wonderful arrangements, had set themselves off on the tumble of endearments and words of wisdom. Holding his wife Ragini's both hands and looking into her eyes, Raghav said, "My ageless diva, shall I say, you have been the inspiration from a point, and now I find our love for each other has matured like some hefty fixed deposit in a bank. Love is the sweetest word in the language of all cultures. It inspires, impassions, moves and delights. It is also the highest, noblest, most stirring emotion that one can experience."

"Nice, you love me so much; you call me ageless. That for a moment makes me forget I wear my upper-denture," she laughingly said and hugged Raghav, again.

Wc live in an awesome world.

Make your each day an awesome day.

Live simply.

Love generously.

Care deeply.

Speak kindly.

Wish peace to all.

Leave the rest to God.

It is hoped that the story of the two amazing couples—Raghav and Ragini, Dinesh and Rosy could make a positive difference in a reader's life, if at all.

In conclusion, I want to say just two words:

Thank you!

(J.L.DHAR)